THE *new* APARTMENT BOOK

THE *new* APARTMENT BOOK

by the editors of *Apartment Life* magazine

Text by Rick Mitz/Revised text by Cara Greenberg

Harmony Books/New York

ACKNOWLEDGMENTS
This book comes not from one author's vision but from the shared
sensibility of a community; it is really the life work of a magazine
staff and their like-minded friends.
The New Apartment Book is the legacy of *Apartment Life* magazine
published by Meredith Corporation from 1969 to February 1981. In
April 1981 the magazine changed its name to *Metropolitan Home*.
But the same editors who made those magazines made this book.
They are:
Joanna Krotz, Ben Lloyd, Carol Helms, Donna Warner,
Steven Wagner, Marcia Andrews, Bob Furstenau, Pam Hanks Kenyon.
Rick Mitz wrote the first version of *The Apartment Book* in 1979.
Cara Greenberg brought her great style to this updated edition.
Harmony Editor Harriet Bell, Art Director Ken Sansone, and Publisher
Bruce Harris remain, as always, the perfect publishing partners.
Dorothy Kalins, Editor

Published by Harmony Books, a division of Crown Publishers, Inc.,
One Park Avenue, New York, New York, 10016, and simultaneously in
Canada by General Publishing Company Limited

HARMONY is a trademark of Crown Publishers, Inc.

Manufactured in the United States of America

Library of Congress Cataloging in Publication Data

Main entry under title:

The New apartment book.

Rev. ed. of: The apartment book. © 1979.
Includes index.
1. Apartments.   2. Interior decoration.   I. Greenberg, Cara.   II. Apartment life.
NK2195 .A6N48 1983   747'.88314   83-10761
ISBN: 0-517-55045-8
10 9 8 7 6 5 4 3 2 1
First Revised Edition

Contents

Introduction

The Apartment Book is back, with one hundred brand-new pages.

It's still a book about sizing up your needs, solving your space dilemmas and making comfortable choices for the way you live.

We're still here to tell you that you don't have to be dictated to by decorators, and that you don't have to get religious about periods and styles. Functionalism and flexibility—making both furnishings and living space work hard for their keep—are still way up there in our priorities.

So why this new, improved, revised, expanded and updated edition?

Because interior design is fashion for the home and—as on Seventh Avenue—things change fast. They've changed sufficiently in the last few years to warrant a new look—and a new book.

Our eyes have also changed—the collective eye that tells us what looks dated, what looks fresh. Since the first edition, enough new trends have surfaced to gently sway our perceptions of what works visually and what makes sense for this point in time.

For one, the industrial revolution has come home. We've grown quite used to seeing hard-edged, sleek materials from industry in a domestic setting—rubber deck-plate flooring in the kitchen, metal factory lamps dangling above the dining table, wire shelves where once it was all wood.

High-tech hit hard, and then the counterreaction set in. A new softness, with a color palette borrowed from the muted, dusky pastels of the post-modern architects. Revival of interest in classical forms like columns, pediments, architraves—all those wonderful terms we remember from Art History 101. Greater freedom in mixing the periods of the past, without undue concern for historical accuracy or chronology. And a new opulence, achieved not by the spending of money alone but by playing out a recently discovered love of luxury.

There's plenty of both in the pages to follow—the swing to hard and the counterswing to soft. You'll find stimulating proof that the boundaries of what's "permissible" in residential interiors have become more elastic than ever to encompass the two extremes.

Another major development since our first go-round is that new options in living space, beyond the white-box apartment, have continued to open up. Lofts are now mainstream options, having lost some of their pioneer cachet, but gained accessibility and no longer demanding the extensive sweat equity they once did. More people are living in vintage houses and buildings than ever before. Cruising antiques shops and flea markets has become a national pastime.

In this second edition, you'll find greater emphasis on rehabbed spaces, an expanded *Lofts* section, and New Antiques sprinkled liberally throughout. We'll show you how to play off the detail found in old buildings, without feeling you have to match it egg and dart for egg and dart. Or, on the other hand, how you can bring some heritage into a space that's totally devoid of it.

In *The New Apartment Book*, we're giving you thousands of ideas and images from which to draw inspiration. We're also giving you permission to change your thinking about your interior environment. If there's a theme here, it is Trust Yourself. Have fun, loosen up, relax. Forget period, as in Louis XIV. Forget style, as in Early American. Style is you—the furniture you pick out in shop or showroom, the objects you're drawn to at the tag sale, the colors that make you happy, the arrangement of space and furnishings that feels right.

As you look through this book, let the old systems crumble. With these pictures to spark your imagination, take stock of your space. Think of ways to rezone it, make it more efficient, pare down the clutter, revamp the image, update the look.

Money is not the bottom line. Ingenuity is. Check out the How To Do Its, our step-by-step instructions for building many of the items you see in the photos. You'll find that things that at first look complicated and expensive consistently turn out to be merely incredibly clever. And very do-able—we're not jumping off from the assumption that you're all master craftspeople.

We might have called this book *The Best of Apartment Life.* It is, essentially, a twelve-year compilation of the unfailingly inventive approaches the magazine was well-known for taking toward apartment problem-solving.

The photographs represent a unique type of photojournalism, a carry-over from the magazine's characteristic hands-on attitude toward interior design. Each is the result of in-depth analysis of the problems inherent in a space or situation, and tailor-made solutions that are nevertheless adaptable to other sites as well.

Apartment Life moved into a whole generation's new apartments. It was there, among the cartons, ladders, drop cloths and paint cans, with its message of support: that apartments are not way stations on the road to that Permanent Home, but places for here-and-now living.

Over the twelve years of its existence, the magazine gradually evolved, along with its readers, into something much more sophisticated than it started out to be. Much of that new sophistication is reflected in this new edition, which includes material from the last two years of *Apartment Life,* as it metamorphosed into *Metropolitan Home.*

Premiering in April 1981, *Metropolitan Home* addresses itself to the people *Apartment Life* readers have become—design-conscious individuals whose tastes for the Good Life have grown along with their means.

In this book, *Apartment Life*'s special vitality, exuberance and hands-on problem-solving are all assembled—for reference . . . and for posterity.

A MATTER OF STYLE

TONGUE IN CHIC

Yes, there is a way to fight Creeping Chic—those expensive styles and looks that designers generate and magazines regenerate. With imagination, you can find alternate sources and materials—minus the initials—that put it all together. With elan and ingenuity, you can approximate designer creations without paying name-brand prices. There are ways of getting around the magic names by using a little magic of your own. Improvise, don't imitate.

It is not just antisnob appeal. If you admire the aesthetic quality of a look but do not want to make an emotional or financial commitment to something that you might not want to live with for the next decade, you will be glad to know there is an alternative.

Of course, certain objects are expensive because of the hand-crafted workmanship and fine materials. Some things are pricy because they are priceless —old or rare. Others are simply in vogue, thanks to status, initials or the cachet of the source. We show you both ends of the scale—the high and the low— not only to amaze but to illustrate the point. It is our design one-downmanship. A tongue-n-chic approach that is there for the taking: at the Salvation Army, thrift stores, restaurant suppliers, drugstores and the five-and-dime. Looking around lets you have your look, and afford it too.

MUSICAL CHAIRS
Breaking rules is what it is all about. Old Fashion dictated that you must—*simply must*—put a period piece in a period set-ting. Period. For example, that Early American wing chair *must* flank an Early American fireplace. And that streamlined chrome lamp *has to* enlighten a marble-topped table.

Nonsense. Musical chairs mean furnishings that work in all environments. Yes, you can put a camelback sofa in a space-age space. Sure, a chrome and glass table can live amicably next to a golden oak breakfront.

The rules have been broken; it is open season for options.

To unlearn these old habits, see how the same setting can work for two quite different styles of furniture. Stretch rigid standards of what is appropriate and what is "now." Give yourself permission to mix and match, to take some design risks and to trust your instincts. The following pages show you some examples.

TONGUE IN CHIC: Country French

The look is rustic, warm and ingenuous, and the provenance is Provence. Some original French country pieces, dating back to the 1700s—pine cupboards and tables, ironstone china, porcelain ware—bring enormous prices; just the accessories *ordinaire* can break a bank. Can you approximate this fresh, appealing look without a heavy cash outlay? *Mais oui!* Here's how:

TOTAL: $14,024.00

Curtains: Small print cotton by Pierre Deux, $24 a yd.

Baskets: For picnics, bread or just for display, a selection of new and old, $28 to $95 each.

Table: Classic country pine, glowing with ages-old patina, $2,000.

Covered casserole: Part of a unique Folch ironstone set, $550.

Platter: Heavy ceramic, an everyday item in nineteenth-century France, $225.

Oval plate: Nineteenth-century French provincial, with pastoral scene, $95.

Chairs: Louis Philippe fauteuil replicas, with rush seats, $350 each.

Figurines: Ceramic celadon roosters, $45 the pair.

Armoire: An oak bridal armoire, made in Normandy, C. 1830. $7,500.

Lamp: 1902 green glass and brass hurricane lamp, $350.

Floor: Exquisite French terra-cotta tiles, $20 per sq. ft.

TOTAL: $1,857.00

Curtains: Cotton/poly print, $4.50 a yd.

Baskets: New Chinese wicker, $12 each.

Table: Brand-new pine, a straight-lined classic as timeless as the antique version, $240 at Conran's.

Covered tureen: Oriental import, new, $12.

Plates: All new, from import stores, $6 to $10 each.

Chairs: Unfinished reproductions of French provincials, $450 armchair, $300 side.

Figurines: Ceramic partridges, new, $12 a pair.

Floor: Quarry tiles with a terra-cotta look, $2.50 per sq. ft.

Armoire: A made-today unfinished pine wardrobe, adapted with molding from the lumberyard and embossed wood carvings from a specialty building-supply store, about $400.

Lamp: A new green glass shade, $30, atop a glass spirit lamp, $8.

TONGUE IN CHIC: Positively Post-Modern

Can you take a thrifty turn on something as sybaritically stylish as post-modern?

Indeed you can. Playful spin-offs of classical architecture come in high/low versions, too.

Check out the first-generation print, then compare it to the high-resolution repro.

Column: Lightweight aluminum, comes in Doric, Ionic, Corinthian, et al., $200.

Lamps: Undulating ceramic wall sconces, $255 each.

Gargoyle: Female head of terra-cotta once graced a buiding facade, $250.

Birdcage: Victorian wirework, modeled like a house, $650.

Mirror: Angelo Donghia's "broken pediment," in unpainted pine to suit today's tastes, $2,300.

Dresser: Dark and deco, but made today, $1,095.

Coffeepot: Limoges "Cathay," $160.

TOTAL: $5,165.00

Column: Same as above.

Lamps: Plastic half-globe sconces, $105 each.

Gargoyle: Plaster cast version of an architectural relic, $35.

Photos: Peter Vitale

Birdcage: White-sprayed wicker, $22.

Mirror: A crafty copy of the designer original, made with $20 worth of wood, some scraps of crown molding and a $50 piece of mirror.

Dresser: Three plastic "Stack Five" storage units by Kartell, side by side, $110 each, topped with a surfboard-shaped piece of ¾" plywood.

Coffee service: "Kabuki" by Mikasa, cups $6, saucers $4.50.

TOTAL: $804.00

TONGUE IN CHIC: Newport News

It takes audacity to do a carbon copy of a look as proper and aristocratic as this one—very yacht-i-da. Outside the French doors, polo games, tea dances and lawn tennis may be in progress, but inside we're taking a nervy twist on the decorator/moneyed look.

Table: Ten yards of Schumacher's peach satin, $34.50 a yd., cinched with Scalamandre's coral silk tassels, $1,003 the pair.

Chairs: Sheraton bamboo chairs in dark tortoiseshell finish, $720 arm, $560 side.

Dishes: Limoges "Cathay," $154 per place setting.

Flatware: James Robinson's "Queen Anne" silver, $2,300 for four sets.

Glasses: Crystal clarets, $31.50 each.

Decanter: Cut glass, George III style, $875.

Candlesticks: Frosted palm trees, $175 each.

TOTAL: $6,735.00

Table: Ten yards of synthetic satin at $25 a yd. saves about $100 and still looks peachy; the tieback is $12 from the dime-store notions department.

Chairs: Sheraton knock-offs, $219 each.

Dishes: Mikasa's "Kabuki" pattern, $35 a place.

Flatware: Queen Anne pattern in stainless, $50 a five-piece place setting.

Glasses: Garden variety wineglasses, $5 each.

Decanter: Orrefors' "Julia," $110.

Candlesticks: $20 from a gift shop.

Photos: Peter Vitale

TOTAL: $1,190.00

TONGUE IN CHIC: The Decorator Look

Prissy and precise, the quiet little table in the corner has become a collector's classic. The diminutive painted enamels, the understated birdcage and other accents hold court on a draped table of the finest fabric. Top designers charge a fortune for this trendy look. You can have the same symbols of status by substituting affordable collectibles for expensive ones.

Lamp: The very "right" ginger jar with fluted linen shade, $550.

Birdcage: Of slimmest bamboo, $200.

Painting: Enamel floral on stand, $425.

Boxes: One, cut velvet, two, leather with gold leaf, $250.

China: Oriental blue and white pedestal bowl, $425; teapot, $240.

Shells: The chambered nautilus, still "in," each $15.

Tablecloths: One simply *must* sleep and eat off Porthault. From France. The rust undercloth, $260; the hand-scalloped overcloth, $185.

Wall: The requisite and original tortoiseshell, $400.

Decanters: They are status if they are crystal and Baccarat. These are: $320, $200, $180. Wineglasses too, $190 each.

Sterling Silver Tray: Vintage, $250.

Chair: Chinese Chippendale updated, lacquered, $1,200.

TOTAL: $5,620.00

14

Lamp: The ginger jar. At five-and-dimes, $45.

Cricket Cage: A delicate oriental import, $5.

Painting: Cardboard print, import store, $2.

Frame and Box: Pseudo shells, or pasta shells to be exact. Frame, $2; box, $5.

Other Boxes: Some covered with adhesive paper, $1. Others, tea boxes, $3.

Teapot: Terra-cotta oriental import, $12.

Shells: The kind used for Coquilles St. Jacques, two for $2.

Tablecloths: Top, one square yard of fabric, $4. Beneath, a sheet of course, $20.

Wall: Simple small fans make a statement. Not too weighty, perhaps. But nice. And cheap. Fans each $1.

Decanters: Real liquor and liqueur bottles, free if you drink the contents. Or if you buy them full: left, Anis Del Mono (Spanish anisette) $9; Amaretto di Saronno $12; rear, Gilbey's Vodka $8; right, Pippermint Get (crème de menthe) $8.

Corks: $1 for a bag of eight.

Straw Tray: Oriental, $6.

Chopsticks: Rich-looking tortoiseshell finish, eight for $6.

Chair: Imported leather and slats, $95.

Photos: Bradley Olman

TOTAL: $257.00

TONGUE IN CHIC: Pattern-on-Pattern

Blue-and-white, pattern-on-pattern, collector's chic—this luxury look has always been "in." The custom version at left is filled with one-of-a-kind antiques, fragile porcelains, intricately patterned rugs and fabrics and oriental accessories. You can put it together for less—much less—with ethnic finds, plastics, wicker and a sense of style and humor.

Fabric: Hand-screened and shirred on brass rods, it makes a luxurious backdrop, $500.

Plant: Elegant palm, $95.

Chair: The white plaster look is very Southampton. This chair is molded from a special composition of plaster, polymer and Fiberglass, reinforced with steel, $765.

Pillow: A made-to-order treasure, $65.

Lamp: The base is a nineteenth-century Chinese porcelain vase, $325. Shade and wiring adds $75. Total, $400.

Side Table: Beside the chair is a graceful John Rosselli drum-shaped porcelain piece, $1,400.

Table: Oriental inspiration, twentieth-century craftsmanship. Straw table is $1,200.

Goose: It is porcelain and might well cook your budget, $795.

Rug: Intricate geometrics, and subtle, muted colors. This custom 6' × 9' Canton dhurrie, $1,155.

Etagère: Museum quality antique display, $2,220.

Accessories: Top shelf, bamboo box, $250. Here is an ironic twist—Karl Springer's $1,335 box is inspired by the look of everyday Bennington pottery. It is lacquered, suede lined, with silver inlay. Rabbit from shards of antique Ming pottery, Karl Springer, $350. Blue and white platter, John Rosselli, $180. Matched Chinese vases, John Rosselli $160 each. Smaller box, Karl Springer, $650. Bottom shelf treasures: nineteenth-century Fu dog, $1,350. Smaller pair $450.

Dishes: Royal Copenhagen means quality. "Blue Flowers" cup, saucer and dinner plate, $84. For the pattern-on-pattern look, John Rosselli platter under all, $45.

Food: Coquilles St. Jacques—lobster, shrimp, crab and scallops in a rich cream sauce—makes the perfect after-theater supper, $36 for four. China shells, $3 each. All on a Royal Copenhagen platter $55. Total, $103.

Elephant: Handwoven from split bamboo, then lacquered, hollow box, $600.

TOTAL: $14,017.00

16

Fabric: Indonesian cotton stretched over three Fome-Cor panels. These took 5⅓ yds. at $36 a yd., plus $33 for Fome-Cor.

Plant: Fat asparagus fern, $5.

Chair: Bamboo director's chair with lots of class, for $73.

Pillow: Cover a form ($5) with a handsome dish towel, $3.50.

Lamp: The same whited-out look for less. At department stores, $40.

Side Table: Import store basket ($45), topped with glass ($32), stacks up to the custom-made kind.

Accessories: More oriental lovelies: fan, $1, coral, $3, cup and saucer on stand, $6, small and medium plates, $5 and $3, butter-fly, $3. Larger Mikasa plate, $15.

Goose: Gladys glows with 25 watts. Whimsical and functional, one or a gag-gle, $25 each.

Rug: 6′ × 9′ multicolor cocoa mat rug from import store, $75.

Photos: Armen Kachaturian

Etagère: Smooth and plastic for display or books, $50.

Accessories: Take another look at everyday stuff: goblets, $9 each. Restaurant supply plate ($7) and tureen ($12). Ersatz objets d'art from import stores or a Chinese grocery: China bird, $5. Elephant, $9. Ring of geese, $15, stand $9. Stacked baskets, $22. Frame any handsome fabric scrap, 11″ × 14″ frame, $11. Chinese soup tureen, $12. Super sake bottles, $4 each, $2 for each stand. Rice bowls, $2 each. Bottom shelf holds carved wooden box, $9. Basket/tray, $12. Five-and-dime lion frightens away the evil spirits, $22. Hiding underneath, dime-store tureen, $10.

Dishes: A trip to China-town never hurts the wallet. Saucers, $2 each; ginger jar, $18; chopstick holders, $1 each. Then hit restaurant supply houses: oval dish, $10; platter, $12.

Food: No need to use high-priced fresh shellfish for Coquilles St. Jacques. Frozen or canned (fillets, clams, shrimp) stir up quickly. $16 for four servings. In natural scallop shells from Katagiri, $3 for four.

Elephant: Wicker and sculpture in one. Oriental import store, $75.

TOTAL: $936.50

TONGUE IN CHIC: Thirties Deco

Nothing was more modern than Moderne—wood and chrome, sharp edges and zig-zag curves. Called Art Deco, it represented a machined streamlined style that appeared in European design. Its development—about 1910—continued until the mid-thirties. Characterized by a developing technology, stylized motifs, often Egyptian, and other geometrical patterns, Art Deco got an added boost in the early 1920s following the opening of Tutankhamen's tomb. In the early seventies there was a resurrection of the Deco look—retro Deco, really—and it came out of the attic and back into fashion. It is now all quite pricey but, as we show you here, it is possible to approximate the look of the Moderne mode.

Wall: Gray vinyl car upholstery fabric, 8 yds. at $20 per, trimmed with auto chrome strips, $1 a foot, $176.

Framed Piece: Painting by Robert Flinn, $400; frame, $150.

Floor Lamp: Chrome torchère with glass rims, $250.

End Table: It is marble all around, $275.

Table Lamp: Vintage chrome with enamel stripes, $285.

Statue: New Lalique crystal, $350.

Candy Dish: Cobalt glass, chrome, $75.

Candy: Imported bonbons, $10 lb.

Sofa: Chrome and wood—super S-curve arm—upholstered in Ultrasuede (7 yds. at $50 per yd.), $350 total.

Rug (on sofa): Geometric area rug, $250.

Animal: Gazelles epitomized the strength and grace of the period. In fiberglass, $185.

Magazine Rack: Chromed steel, Bakelite handle, $125.

Plaque: Lacquered fiberglass cast of Diana and the Hound, $185.

Pedestal: Lucite column with illuminated base, $300.

Vase: Cobalt glass slips into sterling base, made by Kensington, $165.

Flowers: Silk magnolia blossoms, $300.

Table: Metal designed Ray Patten for International Nickel Co., $250.

Glasses: Ruby glasses with antelope motif, $1 each.

Sugar and Creamer: Chrome from Manning Bowman, $45.

Clock: Cobalt mirror surrounds face, $125.

Pitcher: Chrome with black wood trim, $65.

Cocktail Set: Cobalt glass, chrome details, $125.

Bottle: Cobalt glass again, $45.

Coffee Table: In fact, the birth of the coffee table. Lacquered bow base with cobalt mirror top, $300.

Glass Balls: Cobalt thingamajigs, $20 each.

Lamp: Frosted glass cube by Sabino, $250.

Animal: German ceramic antelope, $85.

Vase: English pottery by Carter, Stabler and Adams, $135.

TOTAL: $5,308.00

Wall: Just gray latex paint—with wood molding strips wrapped in Mylar tape, $25.

Framed Piece: An Icart reproduction (on mirror), $60.

Floor Lamp: Shower rod, glass shade (painted black) and more, $33.

End Table: Quick as a flash, plastic and glass, $57.

Table Lamp: Great look for a stack of plastic parts, silver paper and stars, $28.

Statue: Harlow likeness in plaster, $45.

Candy Dish: Formerly an ice bowl, $12.

Candy: Good'n Plentys, $1.

Sofa: Sweet and simple but of questionable lineage (maybe from a bus station), covered in good gray denim (7 yds. at $6 per yd.). Frame, $25, from Goodwill. Total $67.

Rug (on sofa): From new rug remnants and samples, cut and fit, $20.

Animal: New plaster yard art, $10.

Magazine Rack: Two hubcaps ($12 each) blocked together, $24.

Plaque: Large photocopy made from a drawing, $35.

Pedestal: Three Plexiglas tubes, two Plexiglas disks, $80.

Vase: An old cocktail shaker, $18.

Flowers: Plastic, $22.

Table: Thrift shop kitchen table, polished and painted, $30.

Glasses: Woolworth's, circa 1955, $1 each.

Chrome Cups: Plastic, $2 per package.

Clock: Runs a little late but has a kind face, $5.

Pitcher: 1950s hammered aluminum, $8.

Blue Bottles: New from Bromo Seltzer, Noxzema . . . cost $7.

Coffee Table: An unfinished wood Parsons table, $60 (lacquer it black) topped with blue Plexiglas mirror, $42.

Glass Bulbs: Lightbulbs and porcelain sockets (all new), $10.

Lamp: Glass brick with bulb, socket and wire underneath, $9.

Animal: Plaster dog, solid white, $7.

Vase: White with blue flamingos—no pedigree, $12.

Photos: Thomas Hooper

TOTAL: $733.00

TONGUE IN CHIC: Turn of the Century

Take a turn on the Turn-of-the-Century—cozy and patterned. Grandmother's looking-glass look—Early Room-at-the-Inn—has lived on as an interior institution. What were common everyday furnishings in the 1900s (brass beds for $11) have become valuable and expensive today—(brass beds, $650), carved oak rockers, pier mirrors and oriental rugs. By using similar patterns, replicas and ornamentation, you can make Granny still feel at home.

Wallpaper: $21 a single roll, total $126.

Framed Print: Maxfield Parrish's *Daybreak*, original, $195.

Frame: Gilded gesso on wood, $75. C. 1900.

Picture: T. Roosevelt campaign poster, $75. C. 1900.

Commode: Solid oak, perfect condition, $250. C. 1895.

Lamp: Green tinted glass, $125, handpainted shade, $150. C. 1892–1910.

Clock: Single bell alarm, black face with moving eyes, $235. C. 1905.

Jar: Crystal with sterling top, $65. C. 1897.

Comb and Brush Set: Celluloid, six pieces for $65. C. 1908.

Dresser Cloth: Linen with drawn thread embroidery, $30.

Bowl and Pitcher: Staffordshire ironstone from England, $280. C. 1898.

Rug: Kerman, Persian, hand tied, 9' × 12', $2,000. C. 1924.

Curtain: Handmade lace, $185. C. 1890.

Curtain Rod: Spiraled oak, $55. C. 1897.

Pier Mirror: Oak with beveled mirror, a buy at $350. C. 1888.

Scarf: Gentleman's, embroidered silk, $60. C. 1906.

Hat: A straw boater, $45. C. 1890s.

Portrait on Shelf: Admiral Dewey on celluloid photo album cover, $85. C. 1898.

Packages: Four rare tin containers, $225. C. 1895–1928.

Bed: Classic simplicity in brass, not a nick, $675. C. 1912.

Quilt: Lonestar pattern, all handwork, $425. C. 1920.

Pillowcases: Lace trim. Check fabric boxes in thrift and antique shops. Two for $70. C. 1890.

Pillow Sham: Embroidered cotton with applique, $45. C. 1908.

Pillow: Silk sewn into a heart shape, $35. C. 1922.

Tray (and contents): $350

Rocker: Oak with pressed carving, Sears' finest, $185. C. 1896.

Cushion: Needlepoint in ten colors, $75. C. 1900.

TOTAL: $6,536.00

Wallpaper, $55.

Framed Print: Maxfield Parrish's *Daybreak*, $24; frame, $35.

Frame: Plaster, from a ceramics shop, painted gold, $10.

Picture: Take a portrait of a pal, print it sepia, $22.

Commode: New unfinished pine cabinet, $79, hardware, $8; stain, varnish and wax, $12.

Lamp: Reproductions are everywhere. Base $23; new shade, $38.

Clock: Big Ben, $32.

Jar: Cotton dispenser from medical supply, $6.

Comb and Brush Set: Pseudo tortoise (new), four pieces, $12.

Dresser Cloth: Salvation Army, $3.

Bowl and Pitcher: Greenware, paint it yourself, $17.

Rug: 6' × 9', rayon/cotton, $115.

Curtain: "Machine-made" lace tablecloth, $12 at Goodwill.

Curtain Rod: New spiral dowel and two finials; stain and add curtain rings, $14.

Pier Mirror: An old oak door, mirror trimmed with new molding (stained), a small shelf and brass coat hooks. Total $80.

Scarf: A five-and-dime special for $2.

Hat: Costume shops have hundreds, $4.

Portrait on Shelf: John Philip Sousa on sheet music, $3.

Packages: New powders, soaps, fancies, all for $12.

Bed: It is iron; manufactured for three decades, very findable, painted with Bronze Spray Plating, $65.

Coverlet: A project: Collect thrift shop doilies, pot holders and other crocheted pieces (about 85 for double bed) and sew them to an open-weave fabric. Total $90.

Pillowcases: From Sears, $7 a pair.

Pillow Shams: Antimacassars ($9).

Tray (and contents): $28.

Rocker: Made yesterday, $66.

Cushion: Thrift shop doily ($1) over a small pillow, $5.

Photos: Thomas Hooper

TOTAL: $926.00

MUSICAL CHAIRS: Twisting History

Tall and twiggy, like the secretary on the left—an eclectic mix of country-cured maple and Victorian bamboo—or solid and chunky, like the workhorse of a cherry-wood dresser on the right, both nineteenth-century knock-offs succeed in a setting that's historically a mixed metaphor. While the major pieces take us back to the turn of the century in a flash, the ceiling fan, potted palms and torchère lamp summon up Casablanca.

The dark cherry-wood finishes of the drop-leaf desk and dresser provide dramatic counterpoint to creamy walls, the blonde bentwood rocker and the muted Navaho rug.

Whether this comforting corner on the left is used for writing letters or primping before the wishbone mirror on the right is purely personal: Choose the form that follows your function.

MUSICAL CHAIRS: Turning Tables

These deformalized dining rooms, inspired by the back patio and the local diner, prove that eating arrangements don't always have to be a standard 29 inches high.

At left, the garden party moves indoors with a metal-and-plastic table that is 4 inches lower than the norm and proportionately low-slung, tilt-back chairs. It all folds away when the party is over.

The plastic laminate table at right can be lowered via lever for after-dinner coffee. Banquettes may stir memories of burgers 'n' fries, but this time they're elegantly upholstered in cream-colored cotton canvas, not cold vinyl.

Just because there's a fine oriental rug on the floor and a set of grandly proportioned doors doesn't mean you have to take tradition and run with it: Flying in its face is visually stimulating and a lot more fun.

MUSICAL CHAIRS: Swapping Sofas

The sofa/sleeper used to be a luxury—a place to put extra guests when the guest room was occupied. Guest rooms? Today, sofa beds *are* our guest rooms. And—thanks to technology and a heightened sense of style—we now have hideaway beds that give us night-after-night comfort—for ourselves, not just for our guests.

Two classic sofa designs have been successfully adapted to sleeping and combine high style with high utility—plus, they are attractive and convertible enough to fit into any setting. The traditional Chesterfield sleeper at left is covered in soft corduroy, handsomely designed with deeply buttoned back, rolled arms and beechwood bun feet. A rattan convertible? Sure. The bright print at right —riding on top of a rattan-paneled frame—lets a most contemporary style work double time.

MUSICAL CHAIRS: Shuffling Chaises

The chaise—whether it was in Marie Antoinette's boudoir or Bette Davis's bedroom—used to be for swooning and resplendent relaxation. When homes got smaller and budgets got tighter, the chaise was one of the first pieces to go. Now it is back—but for different reasons than the first time around. Chaises are now an alternative or addition to the sofa—they combine high style with high comfort.

These two stellar versions come from similar traditions but got separated en route due to updating. The one at left—a classic version with old-country charm—disarms a setting that mixes traditional with contemporary. The chaise at right—complete with bun feet and a madcap modern print—makes a more fun-loving impact in the same setting.

As for the rest of the room, the fabric shutters and curtains shed light while ensuring privacy. The natural wood and light fabric complement the soft lines of the chaises.

MUSICAL CHAIRS: Changing Seats

Two extremes work extremely well in the same setting. And what two styles could be more disparate than low and modern, and tall and traditional? Both chairs fit well in this environ-ment. Just as blue jeans are now appropriate with quilted smoking jackets so too these chairs.

The low-slung foam chair and ottoman at left has a zip-off, dry-cleanable cover. Well priced and chameleon in char-acter, they work anywhere. At right, a traditional wing chair is "easy" and comfortable.

The setting comes together with primitive patterned paper, marble plant-stand-as-end table, Victorian shelf, large palm and a lamp made from an inexpensive oriental parasol and a bamboo pole.

ROOMS THAT LIVE

The apartment living room has to act like many other rooms—the garden and utility room, the guest room, the workroom, the backyard. And sometimes all at once. Plus, it has its own life to lead.

Such demands could give any room an identity crisis. But with a sense of challenge and a little common sense, today you can let your living room live the way you do.

We are no longer defined by the possessions that once possessed us. We are augmented by them. We have been finally exorcised of mandatory color coordination and everything-must-matchness. Now fun and function are as important as pure aesthetics. We put up a picture over the sofa not because it "goes" but because it "pleases." And that coffee table has to do more than serve coffee. It has to support: dinner? feet?

And as the way we live has changed, so has our furniture. We call it "furniture that works," and that means furniture that lives right along with you. In days past it seemed that the living rooms of our childhoods should have been set off with velvet cords —*look, but don't touch*. They were Drop Dead chic—the Urban Cathedral, the Subur- ban Sistine, into which guests filed, paying homage to each venerable object, price and bloodline duly noted. Muse- umlike.

Now we do not want our friends to come in and Drop Dead. We want them to drop in. And we want the living room to communicate that welcome.

But how? The chic design publications tell you that home happiness will come your way if you only use the requisite prints and patterns, coordinated colors and this season's hottest decorator. They would be out of busi- ness, though, if they said what we do—that nothing is "stylish" anymore unless it is your own style.

On the following pages you will see many exciting rooms with one important thing in common: They are all totally realistic. Some might appeal to you more—your taste might favor "New Antiques" rather than a minimal look—but all these rooms and all the projects in them are possible and practical. You will see rooms that comfort, rooms that seem to explode with color and energy. Rooms that take you back—and forward—in time. Rooms that take you outdoors and back in.

Rooms that disguise and surprise, that raise the ceiling and lower the floor. All of them offer possibilities for making your living room whatever you want it to be.

If you are a collector, set up the room so you can live with your goods. Let work in progress stay out in the open. Bring craft projects out from the back room. Now the back room *is* the front room.

On the next pages we take you by the hand from room to room. The photographs are different but the message is the same: Take the best of *everything* —a piece here, a window there, the best concepts and ideas—

and apply them to the way you live. Remember: The living room is for living.

A Few Easy Pieces
A little acts like a lot when you use only a few dominant furnishings instead of an assortment of sofas and tables that can overwhelm a small— or even a large—space. A Few Easy Pieces means leaving space free and clear of the things that can get in the way of the way you live. But it does not mean sacrificing anything. The point is to strip your room to the bare essentials and let the simplicity speak for itself.

Naturally Neutral

The nomads knew how to make a place cozy in no time—with natural materials, an abundance of textiles and the glow of firelight. The same easy ethnic artistry at work here creates a room as warm and enveloping as a nomad's tent.

The plump, rolled-arm sofas are sectional units hooked together and set up face to face, their off-white upholstery a blank canvas for showing off the simple surrounding accessories: a few antiques, pots of tulips, baskets of exotic potpourri.

Sturdy, neutral industrial carpet underlies areas anchored by flat-weave Caucasian rugs, visible through the glass top of the coffee table.

Strategic lamps for reading and a few dramatic spots under the trees are amplified by candles grouped for impact.

A depressing black fireplace is lightened up with new terracotta tiles, its too-serious mirror relieved by strips of humpback door molding.

The stripped pine hutch, below, does buffet service as well as houses stereo equipment, with two lower doors newly hinged together for easy access.

Photos: Thomas Hooper

Jaunty Angles

Snazzy and self-assured, this pastel glow of a room looks like it's been art-directed. And it is all done with a few basics, confidently applied.

The real creative coup is underfoot. The red-and-pink ceramic tile floor is a bold checkerboard on which many different design games can be played.

Note the furniture placed at calculated angles: The floor forms a grid against which the modular seating units are juxtaposed. The superseating starts with a canvas-covered four-piece combo of generous, loungeable proportions. Quick change is factored in—the modular pieces slide with a push

across the glazed tile surface. Add to that a plump, quilted club chair and ottoman in screaming cherry red and a couple of serviceable surfaces—a smoked glass coffee table with oak trim and a sturdy black plastic rolling cart set up for stereo.

Accessories include a vase-shaped torchère lamp recalling the fluid forms of the fifties and exotic peony-print pillows. Three wooden masks from Bali form a grinning totem on the wall. A framed poster of tropical islands rising out of the mists is an ethereal image at interesting odds with the right-angled realities of the room.

THE ISLAND

BILL THOMAS

Photos: Peter M. Fine

Shoji the Way

Out of the Far East comes this understated design system, which manages to be casual, elegant and unpretentious all at once. The ultimate in Zen simplicity, it is based on two traditional Japanese elements: the rice paper and wood shoji screen (today, fiberglass often replaces the rice paper) and the futon mattress.

Shoji screens are translucent multipurpose wonders that can diffuse bright light from a window, hide an ugly view, divide rooms into areas or partition a loftlike space. They can be put on sliding tracks to form walls or closet doors, or hinged together and used as freestanding screens. They come in standard heights and widths or can be ordered custom-made.

Futons are emerging in the eighties as popular, comfortable, colorful alternatives to conventional beds and sofas. Filled with layers of cotton batting, they also come in a "westernized" version that includes some foam. Roll them into sausages, fold them into sofas, spread them out or kick them out of the way—futons are available in various sizes and thicknesses, colors and prints. Smaller zabutons (traditional hand-tufted meditation cushions) and pillows filled with buckwheat hull are authentic accessories available at futon dealers.

Heightening the oriental mood in this room are natural wood floors brought to a lacquerlike sheen with several coats of polyurethane.

Block-shaped tables of white plastic laminate with recessed bases and sturdy lamps with handmade rattan bases keep things low to the ground.

The New Classics

This living room has a mind of its own. The attitudes of the past are the antecedents of the new pieces—a comfortable sofa, lounge chair, traditional table. All of it has an updated twist and a tip of the hat to technology. The result is a pure and fresh living space that is airy without putting on airs.

The focal point is clearly the sofa, a super easy chair that lounges the way you do. This kind of fat upholstery abounded in the thirties. It worked then because it was comfortable. The new classic version is still voluptuous, but now svelte.

The lighting in this room is notable because it is hardly noticeable. Whereas yesterday's lamps were permanently planted in place, these new ones travel, moving around as your needs do. Clamp-on, flexible lights combine pared-down beauty with high function. Our lighting aesthetic has expanded in recent years. The beauty of lighting is not only what it looks like, but what it does.

Adding or hiding more light are the curtains—not dreary draperies that turn a living room into a hideout, but fresh fabric on attractive wooden rods that make an open and shut case.

At right are storage cubes (which use overlooked floor-level space). The clean lines of the square box, plus the add-on options of doors, drawers and shelves greatly increase storage possibilities. They look built-in —and, in a sense, they are, since you arrange them yourself.

The dining table serves work as well as dinner. This one is butcher block, combining the best of nature and science. Around the table are molded plastic chairs. Easily used with a myriad of styles, they can stack, come in many colors, are inexpensive—and are engineered in a shape that could only happen in plastic, which is no longer imitation anything.

The lounge chair, combining metal and canvas, is a logical extension of the classic director's chair, another outdoor piece moved inside.

The storage unit (at left) comes from commercial sources and was originally used as retail display. It is easy to assemble, and creates a grid that adds interior dimension. Made of chrome tubes with masonite shelves, the unit is easily added to or knocked down.

The oversized poster is accessible, affordable and, when blown up big and hung alone, is a grand option to little clusters of pictures. These days our finest contemporary art often comes printed large on paper with someone else's message. Communication is the new key.

A kilim rug sits confidently on a white tiled floor.

Photo: Bradley Olman

The Convertible Living Room

Because the new family portrait is often children with interchangeable parents, the everyday living room and occasional office must also be the weekend bedroom. You can take custody of a room quickly and deliver yourself from lagging delivery dates with mass-market furnishings that have longtime durability, plus style that will stay put as long as you do.

The pieces that make this room so adaptable are the sofas —one that quickly converts to a bed while the other groups and regroups, thanks to lightweight, high-quality polyurethane modulars. With a forward flip of the back panel, the bed-sit-sofa serves for sleeping. The molded plastic tables are coffee tables by day, bed stands by night.

The windows represent another instant option: Shades are retractable art, with contemporary chintz fabric adding color and character. When the shades are down, the room is filled with light from fixtures around the room. Lighting that consistently works best happens to be lighting that worked first to shed light. The green glass shade from offices past, the Luxo lamp, late of artists' drawing tables, track lighting and some recent fixtures are all elegantly simple.

The table at the back is a modernization of the seventeenth-century trestle base in chrome with an ash wood top for durable dining/desk space.

Underfoot, a sisal rug—originally summer mats for porch rooms—comes indoors. Super-textured (like diving-board mats), sisal rugs come in a variety of styles, always well priced.

White on White

Minimal is the maximum in this room. Because it is small, furnishing with a few functional yet high-styled pieces is better than crowding it.

A few overriding principles help transform this room from a space to a place:

When using only a few furnishings, multiple-choice pieces like these modular units give you greater flexibility. These are covered in plain white canvas, making their simple lines even cleaner.

Leave the modulars out in the open—not jammed against the wall—for breathing room.

Like any good graphic design, this room needs a strong focal point, and that is what it gets with the striking fabric mural hung over the fireplace. Leading up to it is a practical fiber rug, readily available at many oriental import stores.

Bare windows give the room a sense of lightness. Those boxes hung above each window are really stereo speakers, covered with loose-weave fabric and mounted onto the wall.

Because this room is small, the floor should remain as uncluttered as possible to give the illusion of space. Rather than floor lamps, all lighting has been hooked up to a track so that no cords show. Track lighting offers both uniformity and flexibility. Those austere white industrial lamps are available at hardware stores and are easily hung. The track lights over the fireplace throw spots in any direction, and each has separate circuits that can be controlled individually.

Graceful, white molded plastic pieces are both light looking and lightweight for easy moving. The table and magazine rack have origins in high Italian design but are now being manufactured in affordable versions. The piece at left doubles as a serving cart that can roll into the kitchen or bedroom (the holes below are for wine and liquor bottles).

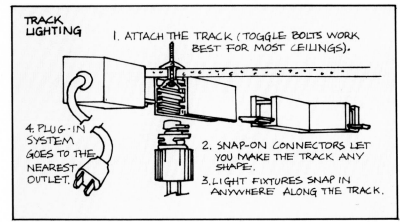

TRACK LIGHTING

1. ATTACH THE TRACK (TOGGLE BOLTS WORK BEST FOR MOST CEILINGS).

2. SNAP-ON CONNECTORS LET YOU MAKE THE TRACK ANY SHAPE.

3. LIGHT FIXTURES SNAP IN ANYWHERE ALONG THE TRACK.

4. PLUG-IN SYSTEM GOES TO THE NEAREST OUTLET.

Design: Stephen Habiague

Minimal Modular

A new rule: Furniture that works is designed for the way people live today—for good looks and multiple functions. Modular systems are especially flexible and are available in many styles. Here the sofa makes the whole room. Its simple lines, extra comfort and overscaled (yet graceful) design allow it to live happily in a modern studio as well as in a Victorian town house.

These particular pieces are all part of the same seating system —wave-quilted with a matching end table and coffee table. It all happens in three basic shapes (see diagram): a square, a square with a back and a square with a back and an arm (the corner piece). The ottoman (partially visible in the fore-

ground) is made of two matching pillows stacked together.

But minimal is not the end of it. There is a striking balance of Victorian and sleek modern in various round-the-room pieces: Light comes from a streamlined metal sculpture lamp and a well-priced paper Japanese hanging shade. Natural light comes from the windows, hidden only by plain, natural-finish shutters with the louvers open to let in the light. A horizontal strip of natural wood molding tacked on the walls just below window level adds classic wainscoting quickly. A few bold plants, prints, pots and pillows fill out the room. A handsome kilim flat-weave rug projects softness and warmth. This room is not modern; it is classic.

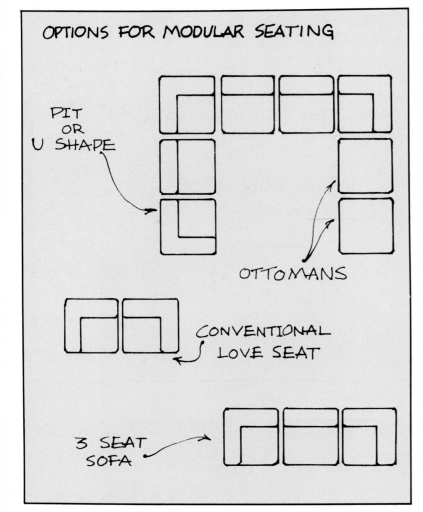

OPTIONS FOR MODULAR SEATING

PIT OR U SHAPE

OTTOMANS

CONVENTIONAL LOVE SEAT

3 SEAT SOFA

Walls: Natural wood molding
Lighting: Simple and sculptural
Windows: Natural-finish
shutters

Photo: Bradley Olman

Two-Piece Suite

Floor: Woven sisal area rug

Window: Wicker screen

Walls: White molding, warm walls

Instead of the usual facing sofas, this room works by exchanging one sofa for a chaise. Both are exquisitely upholstered and formally flank the fireplace. Other surprises: The sofa conceals a double bed and the chaise doubles as a single bed. Pushed together, the units make a deep seating island, an L or any other configuration that pleases.

In the past, furniture—especially sofas—had to point the way to a room's focal point—usually a fireplace, étagère or window. Here the seating units are flexible and stylish enough to offer several options—and changeable focal points: a steady, sturdy, white molded plastic Italian table; a wicker screen as window treatment; an overgrown (but not overbearing) palm tree; and a simple, but substantial, woven sisal rug. Pillows are thrown around for comfort.

The New Traditional

In the late sixties anything that was not old enough to be "antique" was put down as "bad." Plus, many interior designers seemed convinced that Good Taste came only from the sleek and modern, from chrome and leather, from fantastic plastics and the austere white-on-white. A whole heritage of furnishings seemed to disappear right out the door—the classic curves and fine old lines as well as the vintage pieces of our near past: the wooden hutches, the curly-backed chairs with cabriole legs.

Well, we have gone around yet again. But this time—and this is the key to the New Traditional—we haven't thrown out the new as much as we have readmitted the old. No longer is it either the cold industrial look *or* grandmother's parlor. It is a way of living that combines the comforts of old with the trendiness of today, saying that old style does not have to mean old fashioned; that anything goes if you like it enough. The New Traditional spells comfort and a sense of home that welcomes you with furniture that is faithful in reproduction of authentic versions.

The New Traditional apartment has all the advantages of today without turning its back on all the good things from yesterday.

Salon of the Eighties

50

You *can* play dice with history—put the various eras in a cup, shake them up and come out a winner. What's come up here is emblematic contemporary decorating: an audacious mix of classical references, Victoriana, Deco sensibilities and current furnishings, which all add up to opulence.

What makes the disparate elements work? In this scheme, the background color is an important unifier. White was too stark, so a tony wicker yellow was used, set off by a band of white at the ceiling. The crown cornice molding is a period touch still available from today's tinsmiths in patterns of the last century. (Check the Yellow Pages under "Metal Ceilings.")

The pastel palette is carried through, from the rosy rug and bubble-gum pink lamps to the mint green draperies, generous panels of cotton canvas knotted at the sill in playful imitation of yesterday's heavy brocades. The clean, classic lines of the white convertible sofa give the room the freedom of expression it needs to traverse the decades.

The ironic Ionic column, newly made in lightweight acrylics, is a witty potshot at the architectural formalities of the past. Other eccentric accessories that work because they're presented with pizazz: the "zebra" throw, a hand-painted canvas fake; a pair of mismatched plant stands, one American art pottery, one Adirondack twig. A folding screen made of painted plywood gives guests privacy.

The Drawing Room Updated

Traditional design and furnishings are reinterpreted here in a room that does not take itself too seriously.

The comfortable camelback sofas—inspired by English Chippendale and Hepplewhite, but more plump—are made today. The Louis XV armchairs are left natural, making them seem contemporary without discarding their classic eighteenth-century lines.

Holophane lamps, unbreakable, prismatic glass-shade fixtures, make elegant hanging light fixtures.

The sitting ducks on top of the Welsh sideboard are not folk art but new wooden ones used for decoupage.

Lacy curtains on wooden rods replace the heavy draperies expected in a period room. The geometric fretwork of the new bamboo screen suggests the Chinese imports so favored by the Edwardians.

Below: A collection of favorite objects takes on importance because of the charmingly deliberate manner in which it is arranged. It doesn't matter that nothing in this display would fetch a high price at auction— the items are precious because they are clues to a personality. Put your own bottles, jars, seashells and boxes on display. Play with arrangements by color, shape and material until a satisfying grouping emerges. Don't cram things; give them breathing space. And when it all grows stale, change it!

Photos: Bradley Olman

On the wall a Metropolitan Museum reproduction of Oliver Tarbell Eddy's *The Ailing Children* is framed with decorative molding. Use a miter box to cut the frame's corners and then leave it unfinished.

And more new antiques: the country English pine blanket chest, Scandinavian hurricane lamps (on the coffee table), and new American fern stands. The green-shaded brass lamp on the blanket chest is a fine reproduc-tion of an old classic. In the back of the room, a rococo English baker's rack (green painted metal instead of the traditional wrought iron and brass) gives stereo equipment an elegant housing.

In yet another corner of the room, the indoor palazzo has terra-cotta figures and tile de-signs so timeless that they can not be labeled. This small area, set off by the tile, makes a room within the room.

Photos: Bradley Olman

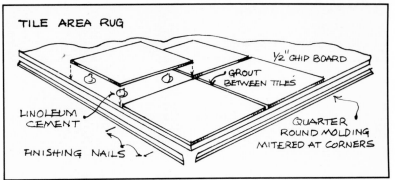

TILE AREA RUG

½" CHIP BOARD

GROUT BETWEEN TILES

LINOLEUM CEMENT

QUARTER ROUND MOLDING MITERED AT CORNERS

FINISHING NAILS

HOW TO DO IT

Tile: Cut chipboard to fit tile size. Glue on tiles, then grout. Edges are finished with ¼"-round molding nailed to the chipboard.

Vintage Relaxation

Straitlaced rules of living do not apply here. This room tilts toward the traditional but its message is Relax. It is okay to put your feet on the coffee table or pull up any chair.

While many of the furnishings have a rich traditional look, they have been updated for function.

The camelback Chippendale sofa is no longer stiff or foreboding because it is covered in natural canvas. The slick and serviceable coffee table is strictly modern. Unlike dainty models of another day, this one is roomy enough to serve dinner for four.

Conventional wisdom might restrict these Italian-inspired light sculptures to a strictly modern space but they work well here. They are easily made by seaming stretchy white fabric; slipping it over a wire frame and fastening both to a plywood base. Screw a porcelain ceiling socket to the plywood base. The fabric can be secured with drawstrings to change bulb. A pair can divide a room or provide soft lighting anywhere.

Instead of wallpaper, a fabric-covered wall or two does the job —and camouflages bumps, cracks and the old peeling wallpaper that afflict many older apartments. First, the walls are padded with polyester batting. Then the fabric is stretched around a lightweight vinyl frame that is tacked to the wall's edges.

Two painted metal outdoor chairs are covered in easy canvas. A pair of ottomans stretch the comfort.

Country Comfort

You do not have to live down on the farm to have the charm of it. Here are some homemade homespun ideas.

In the corner the Hoosier cabinet (the kitchen pantry of old) is used as a bar and serving piece.

That picture frame is really an old window sash. Old photographs, seed catalogs, botanical prints or anything that looks right to you works.

An old bed becomes a sofa with comfort provided by fat pillows made from feed sacks. Just iron and stuff (polyester fiberfill works well) to make the pillows.

That end table is a pickle crock with a pine top cut to fit. If you add a plywood disk to the underside of the pine top, it acts as a "lip," or wedge, to prevent the top from slipping.

Barn boards, picked up on a scouting expedition, were used to build that sturdy corner unit at left. It is made to look like an old corner cupboard but lacks a back. Make it by cutting shelves at 45-degree angles on both sides. Screw wooden cleats into the vertical sides, spaced to support the shelves. Then add wood strips top and bottom; everything unscrews to move. You will need 50 clean feet of boards.

Other country comforts: a cobbler's bench coffee table; a new, reproduction gas lamp; a round cheese box as end table; and a hickory branch settee handmade by southern craftspeople (available by mail order).

Walls: Old window sash as picture frame

Window: Dishcloth curtains; old house shutters as screens

Floor: Dime-store rugs sewn together

Storage: Barn-board corner cupboard

Unexpected materials can cover a window inexpensively and attractively. These are squares of dishcloths, sewn together and clipped with drapery rings.

A braided rug is really a shortcut patchwork of small, inexpensive dime-store rugs joined together. Machine sew together, join the strips with heavy cord.

Photos: Bradley Olman

Home Is Where the Hearth Is

Everything here is clearly a period piece—yet the period is *now*. All these classics are new reproductions—modified a bit but always true to the ideas that made these furnishings great in the first place.

The pieces—not the room—are overstuffed. Borrowing from the "white and light" school of decorating, the room maintains white walls, several well-chosen large plants and sheer dotted Swiss fabric over the windows.

The sofa is an overstuffed version of its thirties ancestor, with ruffles around the pillows, as well as a gathered skirt on the bottom—a plushy and cushiony place to flop. Covered in pale blue velvet, at left, is a Lawson chair whose familiar lines have been around since the late twenties. Even the new leather recliner is surprisingly good looking.

Two substantial pieces of golden oak give solid dimension to the room. Yes, you can find a reproduction rolltop desk, complete with nooks, crannies and cubbyholes. Made today too, the turned oak coffee table still displays fine detailing.

Highlighting the prevailing blue is an American-made oriental rug. Other accessories include an oak framed mirror and a brass fireplace screen.

A Place To Come Home To

This room is home—not so much as we remember it—but as we want it to be. It is warm and wonderful, an inviting place that gives you permission to relax. One secret of this welcoming comfort is the fabric, descended from English drawing rooms through early American homesteads. The tricks are a basic two-color scheme and all-new furnishings, though they look vintage.

The softly rounded, modular sofas and chaise are upholstered in fabrics reminiscent of William Morris's nineteenth-century English patterns—reinterpreted by Laura Ashley. They restate the romantic feeling prevailing for years in fabrics, with one important exception: These new fabrics are not pompous like their predecessors. They are old in style but contemporary in every other way.

The wallpaper and the fabric on the screens near the window complement each other in design and color.

The originality of this room comes from the way traditional design has been reinterpreted and mixed with contemporary styles. Look at the details: the bark chair (made of hickory) could have been lifted from the front porch of a house in the Blue Ridge Mountains a hundred years ago. Actually, it is made today in North Carolina. The Queen Anne table, covered with lace cloth, is also a faithful reproduction, down to its gracefully turned legs.

The hanging lights in the corner are only half old. Made from antique glass shades that have been wired to new fixtures and hung from the ceiling, they fill the corner with a cluster of charm. The window, treated with a wooden molding frames the lacy tablecloth. Screens, covered in a compatible fabric, provide a setting without hiding all the light.

62

Walls: Paint, chair-rail molding and wallpaper

Lighting: Cluster of old glass shades

Window: Stretched lace tablecloths and fabric on wood frames make screens

Homemade wainscoting is achieved by painting the lower walls shiny burgundy, tacking on natural-finish chair-rail molding and wallpapering the wall above. A Matisse poster and a striking geometrical rug finish this room.

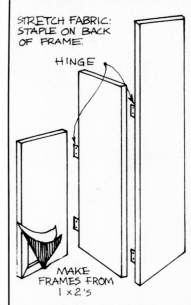

STRETCH FABRIC: STAPLE ON BACK OF FRAME.

HINGE

MAKE FRAMES FROM 1 x 2's

HOW TO DO IT

Screens: Make frames from 1 x 2s or canvas stretchers. To prevent light leaks, stretch black fabric over frames before you staple on the finished fabric. Stretch the fabric and staple onto the back of the frames. Hinge where shown (see drawing).

Photo: Thomas Hooper/Design: Ben Lloyd

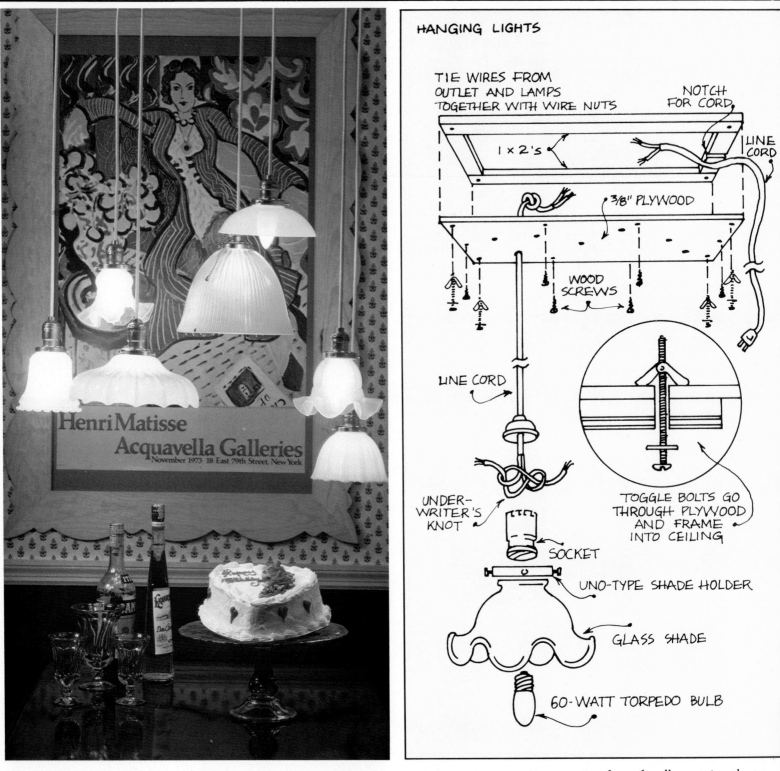

HANGING LIGHTS

TIE WIRES FROM OUTLET AND LAMPS TOGETHER WITH WIRE NUTS

NOTCH FOR CORD

LINE CORD

1 x 2's

3/8" PLYWOOD

WOOD SCREWS

LINE CORD

UNDER-WRITER'S KNOT

TOGGLE BOLTS GO THROUGH PLYWOOD AND FRAME INTO CEILING

SOCKET

UNO-TYPE SHADE HOLDER

GLASS SHADE

60-WATT TORPEDO BULB

The updated Victorian lamps above prove, once again, how we can rummage through the past and find new solutions. Hiding among the old are lots of brand-new ideas. For example, these turn-of-the-century lampshades are updated by using a display window trick and hanging them in a cluster. And at right, a very modern white-lacquered chest and glass shelves take a turn on an old farm dresser arrangement.

Walls can be papered, painted or paneled or, as here, all three. Wainscoting used to mean a lot of expensive wood paneling, often hand carved. You get the same look (above and right) by gloss painting the bottom three feet of wall, papering the top, then finishing the divide with chair-rail molding that is left natural. The Matisse print (above) is framed with scalloped gingerbread wood molding, left unfinished.

A Singular Collection

Venerable rooms are often made, not born. This comforting space is the result of careful collecting—rugs, fabrics and a special new/old coffee table made for an era that had none.

The coffee-table trick: Simply take an old wooden five-panel door and cut it down to size.

A kilim rug warms the floor and the Saltillo woven Mexican rug enriches the back wall. Needlepoint, Pennsylvania Dutch patchwork, old photos and vintage paintings all have a place. Soft peach-colored walls are romantic and warm, making an otherwise unremarkable space something special. The lines of the fanback rattan chair (with yet another pattern covering its pillow seat) and the rich wood of the great-great-grandfather clock balance all the cozy patterns.

HOW TO DO IT

Door Table: Find a wooden five-panel door from an old house or salvage yard. Saw the door into three pieces so that the three center panels become the tabletop and the two end panels make the sides. (Sometimes the lower panel is a little longer than the others but you can cut it down a bit to match the other end, which is usually about 16".) Four shelf support brackets hold the panels together underneath. Sand the door and stain it—or if the original finish is beautiful, go over it with fine steel wool and add a coat of wax.

Systems

Furnishing by system is more than an organized arrangement of sofas and chairs. It's a single grand gesture—one principle that will solve most problems. The answer can be modular seating that is lightweight and flexible. Or it can be a wall unit that serves for dining and work space. It could be arrangements of bookcases and mattresses that sleep, sit, store and serve. Most importantly, a system is a psyched-out space plan that fits the style of the people who live there.

Platform Anatomy

The elements: A magnificent park view. A cavernous bowling alley of a room.

The problem: The room eats up the view, when the view should eat up the room.

The solution: Platforms—don't lower the windows, raise the floor.

An ingenious bi-level system of platforms puts everything on a higher plane and creates brand-new living areas, while the majestic view comes in and makes itself at home. The two new levels add some real shape to an ungainly space. The floor near the windows is raised so that you can see outside, sitting or standing. The graceful curves of the lower platform break up the space and lead you into the main seating area. Carpet covers all, a rich synthetic for plushness and durability.

A painted stripe at the ceiling and a strip of contrasting picture molding give dimension to the all-white walls.

The furnishings run along traditional lines, but with an overstuffed fatness that redefines them for today.

Two squishy chaises, strategically placed for gazing contemplatively out at the world, are an undeniably luxurious touch.

They are larger than their Victorian ancestors and done up in plushy velvet.

The track lights illuminate the pictures on the walls and also cast enough indirect light to brighten the seating area.

The ornately carved mirror over the mantel, the Deco hanging fixture in the left rear corner, the tapestry-covered footstool and the kilim rug in the foreground are all old.

A quirky treatment for a non-working fireplace: Transform its black hole into a light-box sculpture with a lining of plastic mirror cut to fit and fat candles for reflected fire.

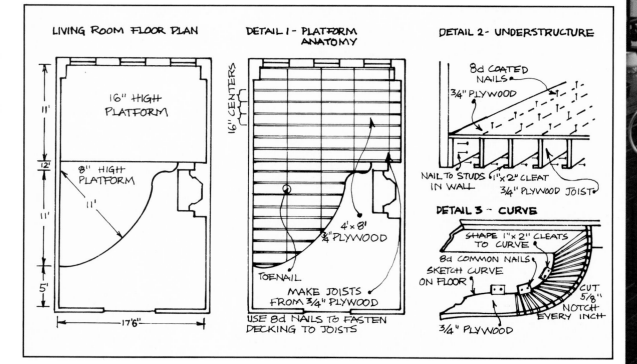

LIVING ROOM FLOOR PLAN

16" HIGH PLATFORM

8" HIGH PLATFORM

11'

11'

12'

11'

5'

17'6"

DETAIL 1 - PLATFORM ANATOMY

16" CENTERS

4' x 8' ¾" PLYWOOD

TOENAIL

MAKE JOISTS FROM ¾" PLYWOOD

USE 8d NAILS TO FASTEN DECKING TO JOISTS

DETAIL 2 - UNDERSTRUCTURE

8d COATED NAILS

¾" PLYWOOD

NAIL TO STUDS IN WALL

1" x 2" CLEAT

¾" PLYWOOD JOIST

DETAIL 3 - CURVE

SHAPE 1" x 2" CLEATS TO CURVE

8d COMMON NAILS

SKETCH CURVE ON FLOOR

CUT 5/8" NOTCH EVERY INCH

¾" PLYWOOD

HOW TO DO IT

Platforms: A split-level room like this one can be a bit overwhelming—just how do you build all those mysterious things? But the philosophy is basic-box simple.

Think of each platform as a system of modules: each module is a box made of ¾" plywood—with the open side down. (The crosspieces underneath are also ¾" plywood.) If you do not want to cut all those plywood strips for the bottom supports, you can get by with construction grade 2 x 6s or 2 x 12s.

If the platform covers up electrical outlets, you can move the outlets higher on the wall or install them in the platform. (Check with an electrician if it is necessary to extend wires or conduits.)

Staple carpeting (over padding) to the platforms. You can also use carpet squares, vinyl tile or two or three coats of polyurethane.

Photo: Thomas Hooper

Graphic Design

This design system is squarely suited to any small, plain white box. The idea is to go for a few simple—yet highly sophisticated—graphic effects.

That said, remember that any design problem has an infinite number of solutions. There are no right answers, only interesting possibilities.

Here are some guidelines for plotting a small, boxy room according to functions: The super graphic: It is a tape-on-the-wall grid that is the perfect canvas for setting off clearly defined shapes of simple furnishings. Adding a pattern on the walls can relieve small space awkwardness and pull all the pieces together. The furniture is on the square too—seating is provided by channel-quilted modulars that fit the room's compact size. As a bonus, these well-upholstered foam units do a quick conversion to lounging and sleeping platforms. Tube-framed director's chairs have rounded squares that look intriguing against the right-angle grid.

The two small laminate tables —used as a coffee table—mimic the latticework walls and the Raynaud poster. Also, the draperies echo the quilted seating units. These channel-quilted "window blankets" keep the cold out from ceiling to floor; the blanket lets a small window reach new heights. Lighting that makes a counterpoint: Vary the pattern and add high-rise lighting—from photographers' umbrellas mounted on shiny metal light stands. Both

found in photo supply stores, they convert in a flash with porcelain sockets and standard bulbs. Storage on display: Classically styled cabinets of warm honey pine are slim enough to give you room to move while still providing open and closed storage space. Plastic triangle shelves at right show off glassworks. Heavily textured sisal matting is neutral and wears well.

You can tape a room in a few hours even if you cannot draw a straight line (get someone to help you with the measurements).

To mark a horizontal across the middle of the wall, hold a spirit level against a straight edge. Then draw your guideline above the straight edge in light pencil.

Cover the pencil mark with 1"-wide duct tape, also called gaffer's duct tape. You will find it at hardware stores and photo supply shops.

Repeat the procedure for all horizontals, spacing the lines 9" apart.

For verticals, start in the middle again. Use a ladder to draw a line from ceiling to floor. After marking, cover with the tape. Repeat the procedure, spacing verticals 9" apart.

Note: To avoid taping yourself into a corner, remember to work your grid from the middle of the wall toward the edges. That way, you can adjust for possibly sloping walls at the corners instead of repeating a slanted line across the wall.

Windows: Quilted "blanket" draperies

Lighting: Photographers' umbrellas

Walls: Duct-tape grid

Floor: Textured sisal matting

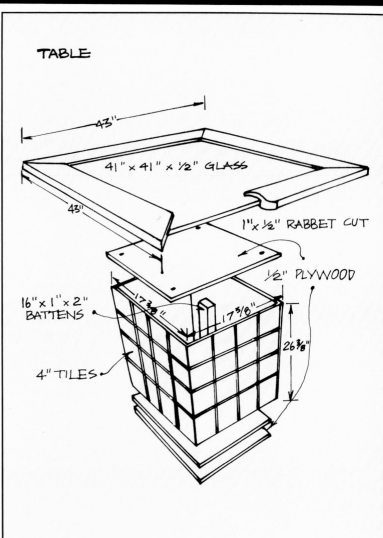

TABLE

43"

41" × 41" × ½" GLASS

43"

1" × ½" RABBET CUT

½" PLYWOOD

16" × 1" × 2" BATTENS

17⅜"

17⅜"

26⅜"

4" TILES

HOW TO DO IT

Tile Table: The square root of this versatile table is merely bathroom tile glued to a wooden box. Build a box—have the lumberyard cut four pieces of ½" plywood to length for the sides after you have decided on your dimensions (figure a multiple of the tile dimension plus grout or 4" for a standard tile): three plywood squares (the double bottom and top); and four 1 x 2 battens for bracing (see drawing). Nail and glue the sides, battens, top and bottom as shown.

Tile it: Secure 4" tiles with tile adhesive, spacing tiles ⅛" apart. Grout after adhesive has dried.

Top it off: A 41" square of ¼" glass will do the job, or build a mitered picture frame for the glass with four 1 x 3s cut to length. Cut a groove along the lower edge (called a "rabbet") that is ¼" deep and 1" wide. Miter the corners and fasten with white glue and mending plates.

Finishing touches. Place felt circles at each corner of the base to protect the glass. Rest glass on base and place frame over it.

Here is a closer look at the graphic design elements at work. Two small laminate tables have a pattern that complements not only the grid wall and poster but the heavy channel quilted material on the sofas and rounded director's chairs.

Room Within a Room

Think in broad strokes when planning a room. This super system—with its seventeen working parts—shows how one overall solution applies to all problems.

Here in yellow and white is a system for sleeping, sitting, eating and storing. Eight store-bought bookcases (painted yourself) frame nine foam slabs (75" x 30" x 5") and inexpensive bed pillows. These slabs have been covered in cotton so they can be easily changed and washed. Hinged shelves were added to the bookcase fronts; when they are down, they work for closed storage; in the up position, they can be used for eating and working. By removing the pillows, guests have a comfortable place to sleep.

Everything else in this space has been planned with the system in mind. Formica Parsons tables can be moved around for eating and are sturdy enough to put your feet on. Against the wall: a white table, which doubles as a desk and buffet area. The white folding chairs become functional art when hung on the walls for storage. The windows are framed with 1" x 6" boards, with fabric stretched and glued around them. Even the white carpet—supplied by the landlord—helps highlight this ingenious system.

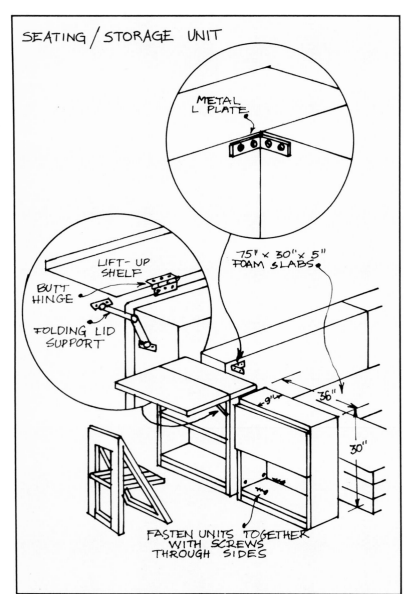

SEATING / STORAGE UNIT

METAL L PLATE

LIFT-UP SHELF

BUTT HINGE

FOLDING LID SUPPORT

75" x 30" x 5" FOAM SLABS

9"

36"

30"

FASTEN UNITS TOGETHER WITH SCREWS THROUGH SIDES

Success on Many Levels

Most people change their living space by rearranging furniture instead of attitudes. Start discovering diverse ways to make the room fit into your life. Think of the space as a canvas—paint your own needs on it.

That is exactly what has happened in this room. The standard apartment fare—white walls, shag carpet, predictable windows—were transformed into a many-leveled room, simple and spare, with exceptional flair. Here's how:

The multilevel landscape raised the seating level to the view, making the outside cityscape visible from every part of the room. Platforms were covered in the same heavy-duty industrial carpet as the rest of the room, for visual uniformity. Each level was built to fulfill a function—dining, sitting, working.

With the spaces now so varied, white walls seemed all right again. The raw pine, baskets and natural earthy tones warm up the room.

Easy-to-build multi-use table surfaces make for high function in this room. The tables are sturdy and have a uniform look. (Except for the dining table, they are all easily made.)

Bare windows further heighten the airy lightness. At night, standard venetian blinds assure privacy.

The soft, modular furniture can be shuttled around at any time. That slatted bridge connecting the two living-room areas is fun but not essential. The slats are nailed to a piece of plywood and then the bridge is bolted to wooden 2 x 4 strips underneath.

In a room as minimal as this one, the accessories must be especially well thought out. Several substantial plants were chosen for warmth and color contrast. A simple industrial lamp overhanging the table combines clean lines with good light. A basket of fruit creates an artful still life. There are no pictures or posters—just several simple hanging baskets.

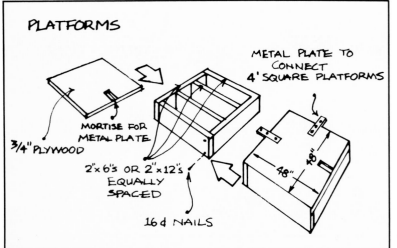

PLATFORMS

METAL PLATE TO CONNECT 4' SQUARE PLATFORMS

MORTISE FOR METAL PLATE

3/4" PLYWOOD

2"x 6's OR 2"x 12's EQUALLY SPACED

16d NAILS

48"

48"

HOW TO DO IT

Platforms: The drawing shows the general construction method for platform plans tailored to any situation. Keep the platform units no larger than 4' x 4'. Make 4 x 4 boxes fit the system that fits you, then custom-make smaller ones to fill in. Join the boxes together with metal mending plates, recessed into the surface of the plywood. A sharp wood chisel and a hammer make short work of it. When the boxes are all joined, staple on carpet or use self-adhesive carpet squares—or have the carpet installed.

Photo: Armen Kachaturian/Design: Jerry Ross

HOW TO DO IT

Modular Seating: There is a wide range of modular seating now available in all price ranges and styles and fabrics, but you can also build it yourself. Use simple cubes padded with foam (footstools made the same way double as extra seating). Add backs to the others. Group the units to make a sofa.

Materials:

    3 1 x 12s 28"
    2 1 x 12s 26½"
    1 ¾" plywood 26¼" x 26¼"
    4 6" x 6" triangular corner
braces of ¾" plywood
    2 metal straps ⅛" x 2" x 16"
    6 yards 48"-wide fabric
    1 piece 5" high-density foam
26¼" x 26¼"
    1 piece 5" high-density foam
26¼" x 12"
    2/3 yard 1" foam 36" wide
    2 yards ½" foam 36" wide

The secret of the softness and comfort here is to wrap the wood box construction with foam. A nubby loose-weave fabric cover wears well and hides any mistakes because of the built-in irregularities of the fabric. Hand sew the corners as shown on the base and the back. Wrap and staple the corners of the seats. Also cover 5"-thick foam forms for back pillow chairs.

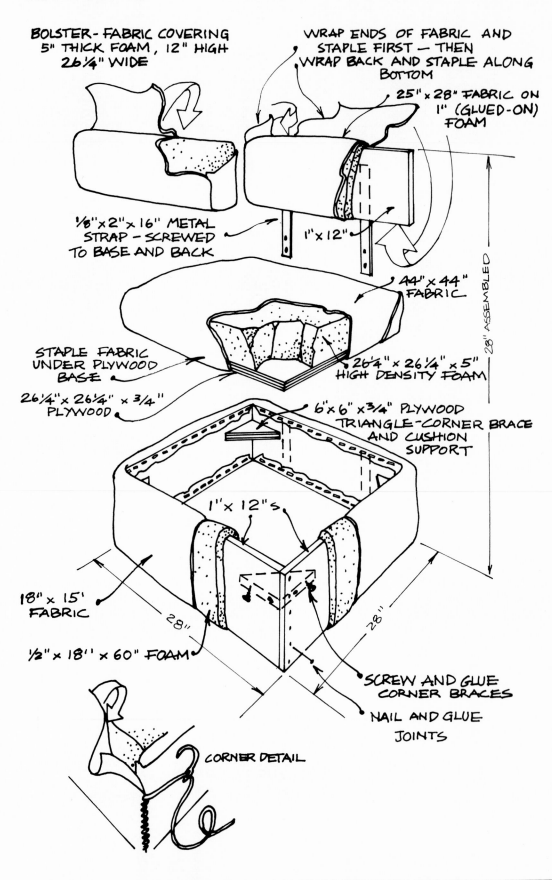

MODULAR SEATING

BOLSTER- FABRIC COVERING 5" THICK FOAM, 12" HIGH 26¼" WIDE

WRAP ENDS OF FABRIC AND STAPLE FIRST — THEN WRAP BACK AND STAPLE ALONG BOTTOM

25" x 28" FABRIC ON 1" (GLUED-ON) FOAM

⅛" x 2" x 16" METAL STRAP - SCREWED TO BASE AND BACK

1" x 12"

28" ASSEMBLED

44" x 44" FABRIC

STAPLE FABRIC UNDER PLYWOOD BASE

26¼" x 26¼" x 5" HIGH DENSITY FOAM

26¼" x 26¼" x ¾" PLYWOOD

6" x 6" x ¾" PLYWOOD TRIANGLE-CORNER BRACE AND CUSHION SUPPORT

1" x 12"s

18" x 15' FABRIC

28"

28"

½" x 18" x 60" FOAM

SCREW AND GLUE CORNER BRACES

NAIL AND GLUE JOINTS

CORNER DETAIL

HOW TO DO IT

Coffee/End Table: This table is built by gluing all the joints together.

Materials:

  22 1 x 2s 22⅛" (As and Bs)
  4 1 x 2s 25⅛" (Cs)
  8 1 x 2s 11" (Ds)
  4 1 x 2s 9" (battens)
  2 1 x 2s 13" (fold-down supports)
  4 2" butt hinges
  White glue

Buy several small C clamps to clamp the joints while the glue dries. Put the two leg frames (Ds) together first (legs are set 1½" in from edge of tabletop). Then glue on the tabletop pieces (As and Bs). Glue on the end flaps and attach with hinges as shown.

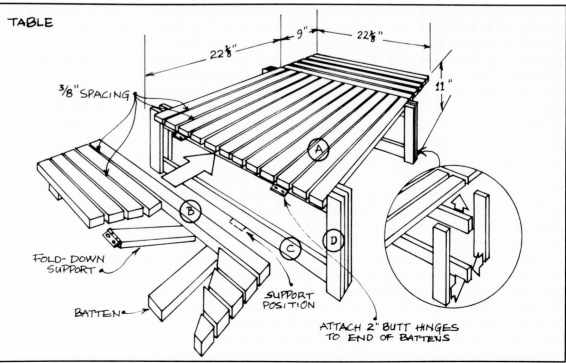

TABLE

22⅛"   9"   22⅛"

11"

3/8" SPACING

FOLD-DOWN SUPPORT

BATTEN

SUPPORT POSITION

ATTACH 2" BUTT HINGES TO END OF BATTENS

A B C D

Blonde on Blonde

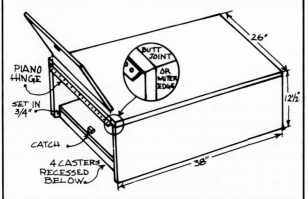

HOW TO DO IT

Coffee Table: It opens on one side and is large enough to stash a few folding chairs for unexpected guests. Have the lumberyard cut the wood to the dimensions in the illustration. The pieces are glued together with white glue, then screwed with 1¼" wood screws. Selby hinges are shown in the photo, but they can be tricky to install. A piano hinge is easier.

Photos: Bradley Olman/Design: Dennis Freedman

Humble plywood is the basis of this spare, sophisticated, built environment. This deceptively simple system packs multiple functions into its spare scheme. The ocean-liner-sleek furnishings, with the blonde finish so popular in the 1940s and 50s, are all easy do-it-yourself projects.

Storage is where you make it: Here it's hidden inside the coffee table, under the sofa cushions and in the glass-topped end of the sofa unit.

Top-grade birch plywood (about $50 a 4' x 8' sheet) is used for the parts that show: the basic box coffee table and the hefty dining table.

The dining table looks as if it's made from massive slabs of wood, but it's all illusion: Strips of glue-on wood veneer tape matching the blonde color of the birch plywood conceal the fact that the legs are simply two pieces of ¾" plywood layered together. The impressively thick top is 1 x 2s screwed underneath a piece of plywood, the joints again covered with veneer tape. One important poster on the white wall, a turn-of-the century original, brings color and life to the entire space. Accordion-pleated shades that open from top or bottom block a boring view but welcome the light.

Blonde on Blonde

HOW TO DO IT

End Table and Platform: You can get away with a cheaper grade of plywood for the sofa unit and its appended end table, which are meant to be covered. In this case, a neutral flat-weave industrial carpet is the upholstery of choice.

The recipe calls for three 4' x 8' sheets of ¾" plywood (you'll have some left over), about 25 feet of 1 x 2s, lots of 1¼" wood screws and 1½" finishing nails. You'll need to build two boxes —an end table/liquor cabinet and a long rectangular platform—then bolt them together. Divide the long box into two equal compartments, nail a partition in place and cut a trap door to fit over each compartment. Use a utility knife to cut the carpet to size, then glue and staple it to the boxes. Finally, make (or have made) four cushions to fit.

Right: Carpet the platform and table before installing the oak doors. Add piano hinges and touch latches (which have no knobs to show). Then have a piece of ¼"-thick glass cut for the top.

Far right: The under-the-cushion doors are supported by 1 x 2 braces screwed onto the front and sides of each compartment. Piano hinges along the back edges make for easy access.

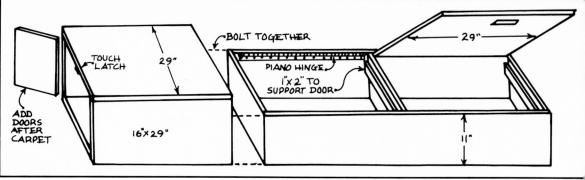

The Indoor Patio

The Indoor Patio is a style of furnishing that is much more than one windowful of plants or even a big tree in the corner. It is an attitude about the outdoors—and an attitude about the indoors—that suggests nature without trying to imitate it. This can be done with fabrics, colors, organic and natural furnishings. Too often, apartments—not just high-rise and not just urban—are victims of the shut-in blues. Here we show you how country greens can give your place a feeling of the Great Indoors. You'll see wicker and rattan, bamboo and sisal mats, plants and clever lighting—all working as useful furnishings. The Indoor Patio—like other styles—is also about breaking boundaries. It's about setting up the atmosphere you like. You can hang a hammock in a living room—or any other room—because, although at first it looks "unexpected," it does add grace and a natural feeling. Wicker, rattan and other straw-woven materials traditionally have been relegated to the veranda and porch. Now they are being updated and upholstered and are comfortably stylish indoors.

Beachy Keen

The blue of the ocean, the white of the sand, an abundance of reeds and grasses—this is the seashore reinterpreted for indoor, all-year-round consumption. This house in a beach community was a vintage firehouse in its former incarnation—the crisp white living room once a dingy garage in which fire trucks stood. After a complete rehab drained the owner's bank account, inexpensive new-fashioned solutions had to be found for seating and serving in the old-fashioned space.

For sprawling, three twin-size mattresses are professionally upholstered in cotton canvas, complete with buttons and contrasting piping, then stacked on sisal-covered plywood boxes. A profusion of Indian cotton pillows are multiple variations on the ever-popular, always-pretty blue/white theme.

Low-slung basket-weave folding seats come out for company, slide back under the coffee table to reclaim floor space.

The bleached pine table is sturdy enough to support supper and can also serve as a display surface for the irresistible collectibles of the waterfront: shells, rocks and sea glass.

A pine plank floor, painted white, was laid over concrete during the rehabbing process. The tongue-and-groove paneling original to the firehouse was also whitewashed. Ugly wall paneling is the plague of many beach and seasonal houses. You don't have to live with fake-wood grains or somber tones: A coat of whitewash is the freshest solution.

Windows: Canvas roll-up shades

Walls: Tongue-and-groove wainscoting

Floor: Pine planks, painted white

Photo: Bradley Olman

The Sunshine Room

You do not have to remain in the dark if your living room does not have plenty of natural light. Careful furnishing can turn it into an indoor sun porch —with a little help from golden colors, light rattan and wicker furniture.

By day, sunshine takes the place of pictures, draperies, rugs and heavy furniture. Wicker and rattan pieces give an atmosphere of elegant informality while underscoring the casual flavor of the space. A wine crate becomes an end table here when it is placed between two porch-style chairs.

The light bamboo and glass table at right is a desk during the day, a dining table at night. Cardboard file boxes stacked beside the table are camouflaged with the same coordinating East Indian fabrics that cover the cushions in the seating area. The "Casablanca" fan chair also is used as a desk chair. The basket hassocks (some of which double as plant stands) can be pulled up for extra seating.

Above: Even without natural light, this room glows at night. White floor spots illuminate the corner pots and the tree fern.

Lush bromeliads, each enthroned on its own basket hassock, define this corner of the room. Strategically placed lights cast weird and wonderful shadows on the screen and wall.

Crate Expectations

Here the unexpected takes a turn for the terrific. Crates—the kind that oranges, melons and pianos come in—become fun and functional furniture. These contemporary primitives make sense with their no-nonsense looks and high utility.

All it took was minor reconstruction to get these sturdy, knotty-pine pieces ready for living-room use. So what if the joints do not exactly dovetail? That is part of the charm. Here is how it happens:

The coffee table took no reconstruction at all; it is just a big wooden skid, cleaned up and given a few coats of polyurethane (but you can paint it instead).

The end table is a larger skid, cut down, sanded and again coated with polyurethane.

The bar is simply a packing crate with a couple of alterations. A little quick work with a saw created a door, and a plywood shelf set inside doubled the storage space.

Crates created the little love seat, but with a painted finish this time for variety (the dimensions of the piece have been stenciled on). The cushions came from an old sofa, with quick slipcovers made from new yard goods. Bed pillows and cases can also be used.

The sofa is a found oldie given a quick make-over with a lace tablecloth tucked over the old upholstery.

A long pine board has been placed over the radiator as a holding platform for plants.

The wonderful blue-sky window shades are just lengths of fabric stapled to wooden shade rollers. Narrow hems are sewn along the sides, plus a deep hem along the bottom for a length of wooden molding.

A hammock (at right) swings from the ceiling to the wall.

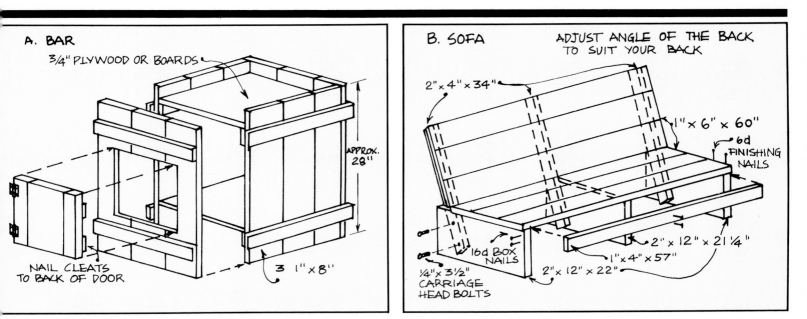

A. BAR

3/4" PLYWOOD OR BOARDS

APPROX. 28"

NAIL CLEATS TO BACK OF DOOR

3 1"×8"

B. SOFA

ADJUST ANGLE OF THE BACK TO SUIT YOUR BACK

2"×4"×34"

1"×6"×60"

6d FINISHING NAILS

16d BOX NAILS

1/4"×3 1/2" CARRIAGE HEAD BOLTS

2"×12"×22"

2"×12"×21 1/4"

1"×4"×57"

HOW TO DO IT

A. The Corner Bar: Buy construction grade pine or fir. If you can hunt around, pick the pieces with sound knots and lots of grain. Cut the door opening with a saber saw.

B. Sofa, So Good: The dimensions for this sofa are shown in the illustration but you can adjust the overall size to fit any cushions you already have and want to use.

C and D. Tables: Both tables are built the same way, except that the coffee table has a couple of 2 x 6 cleats across the bottom to make it a little taller and stronger.

E. Hammock: Sling a big hammock across the corner of a room but measure first to make sure you have the space. Hammocks are always longer than you would guess—a fact of life. Make sure too that you find wall studs to anchor both ends. Drill a pilot hole in the stud. Hang with a sturdy screw hook.

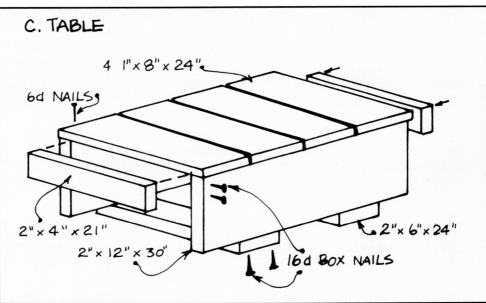

C. TABLE

4 1"×8"×24"

6d NAILS

2"×4"×21"

2"×12"×30"

16d BOX NAILS

2"×6"×24"

D. TABLE

3 1"×6"×14"

16d BOX NAILS

2"×12"×16 1/2"

2"×4"×11"

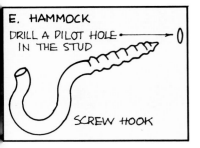

E. HAMMOCK

DRILL A PILOT HOLE IN THE STUD

SCREW HOOK

A Year-Round Summer Place

Windows: Hand-painted curtains

Lighting: Crafty chandelier

Floor: Bathroom tile

This glamorous gazebo—all cool tile, slick wicker and breezy latticework—has the whiff of decorator cachet, without the price. Borrow a few ideas from this roomful of clever tricks:

The Mexicali border zigzagging around the room is painted on strips of poster board with an $11 stencil kit.

The basic black-and-white floor tiles are the cheapest available (about $2.25 a square foot), laid with an imaginative, odd-shaped border.

The three-panel lattice screen comes from a commercial display house.

The posh look of the dramatic dining area is born of more deception: The peachy table is draped with ten yards of a satinlike synthetic, gathered with a dime-store drapery tieback and paired with reproduction Sheraton chairs.

The curtains at the rear are homemade versions of a chic, pricey pattern: semigloss latex applied to cotton canvas.

Five unpainted furniture legs turned upside down, wired and secured to a central baluster post create a Newportlike chandelier.

The wicker pieces are widely available at import stores. Spray-paint them white or leave natural, as the Victorians did.

New Antiques

An antique is usually considered to be any object more than a hundred years old. New Antiques, however, are different sorts of relics—things from the turn of the century, from the twenties and thirties, even from the fifties. And along with these new discoveries comes a new philosophy: Just because they are old and not aged does not mean they are not as beautiful or worthy as their ancestors. Plus, New Antiques can be functional; never thought precious enough for showcases, there is no reason why collectibles should not work too.

Art Deco chrome, Fiestaware dishes, golden oak pressed-back chairs, Hoosier cabinets—these are just some of the finds that flourish in thrift shops, garage sales and attics. Collecting furnishings that work makes a lot more sense than living with a museum full of nonfunctional things. Another plus: investment value. Someday they will grow up to be Real Antiques.

A Room with Roots

Country comfort is the object here—not slavish allegiance to a particular period or museum-like reverence for the artifacts of the past. Beauty before age, you might say. "Period" counts for less than looks, comfort and style. These New Antiques—mostly thrift shop finds—run from Victoriana to early last year.

The rolled-arm sofa and chair are modern versions of the thirties overstuffed look, plumped up with pillows made from vintage drapery panels. The wood-and-wicker armchair is an old porch piece of uncertain ancestry. The glass-topped coffee table with its deer antler base, though new, harks back to the

mid-nineteenth-century rage or furniture made of horn.

The walnut hallway mirror brings home the interior architecture of the 1880s, while the floor lamp with its parchment shade is a homey reminder of 1920s middle-class taste. As it increases in popularity, American folk art is getting increasingly expensive and hard to find. The 100-year-old wooden rocking horse in the bay window is a prime example.

Below: An ornate Victorian wicker chair coexists comfortably with a simple, stripped pine bed, handmade before the turn of the century.

Photos: Thomas Hooper

Putting Collectibles to Work

Give collectibles a job; hire an heirloom. Do not let your period bits and pieces hide under glass looking pretty—let them work for you as well. That will give you space for more of them too.

This room combines twenties to forties design with comfort and utility. All the new antique pieces are readily available today by scouting flea markets and shops and have been made livable with old fabric pillows and new covers. The rundown:

Both 1920s chairs in the foreground are of durable reed construction, comfortable enough to sink into.

The framed mirror was salvaged from a thirties oak dresser.

Rich velvet draperies came from an estate sale, and are hanging on new fat wooden rods and wide rings, stained dark.

The sofa and table bases are well-crafted rattan. New pine boards were added for the table.

A much-worn oriental rug was cut up and used for pillow covers. The four stained-glass window panels were salvaged from a house that was being demolished as was the old leaded, stained-glass valance hung from the ceiling.

The lamp is a recent marriage of a bronze base and a silk-lined metal shade.

Unique curves, period details, humor, architectural bits—even the oversized rubber tree—all add humor and personal style.

Photo: Erik Arnesen

Instant Heirloom

In a roomful of bamboo and oak new antiques, the newest—and brightest—is an irresistible rag rug, made today to look like yesterday. In the truest sense, this rug is a case of rags to riches. Once make-do floor coverings, rag rugs have become American folk art and, nowadays, you are lucky if you can unearth one for less than $600.

But by using the old potholder principle, you can turn your own rags into rugs. Recycled materials—old bedspreads, draperies, tablecloths, shirts, slacks, towels, flannel bathrobes—are the strips.

HOW TO DO IT
Rag Rug: Building the Loom
The only tools you need are a screwdriver, tape measure and hammer.

Materials:
4 6' 2 x 2s
300 3" finishing nails (get some extras in case you bend a few)
8 3" wood screws

First screw together the 2 x 2s into a square. Then reinforce the corners with braces. Mark off each inch (72 per board) with a pencil. Drive the nails into the marks, about 1" deep.

Tear or cut your fabrics into 4" or 5" strips. In all, you will need about 50 yards of 45"-wide fabric. Half the strips should be sturdy, nonstretchy fabrics—cotton, flannel, corduroy, upholstery material—to make the warp. These strips are strung on nails to make a base to weave through. The weaving strips should be stretchy fabrics such as nylon, acetate, double knits or matte jersey.

To make the strips easier to handle, sew the ends together to make 8 to 10-yard lengths. Roll up the strips as you go along, folding under the edges.

You will need about 30 10' long rolls of the stretchy fabric and 35 8' rolls of sturdier fabric (it gets too bulky if the rolls are too long). Tearing and rolling the strips is time consuming, but it is better to have them ready before you begin.

Begin to weave. Warp the loom with the sturdy fabrics. Loop the fabric, going back and forth around each nail, sewing on each new strip as you need it. (Be sure the raw edges are turned under.) One important rule: Do not pull the fabric too tight—it should be slack enough to lie along the floor. Also keep your eye on the rug as a whole. The warp is the pattern of the rug so plan the colors and textures before you begin.

When you start weaving, it gets a bit tricky—the stretchy strips go through double. To measure the first double strip, lay an unrolled strip of stretchy fabric across the loom, grabbing it a few inches beyond the edge of the loom. Hang onto this loop and take the strip back to the other side; start weaving. Hook the loop on the nail when you finish each row, then measure and weave again. Sew on new rolls as you need them. If a row bulges too much in the middle, skip a nail on each side.

Finish off the edges by pulling a doubled strip of fabric through a series of loops. To get started, unfasten a loop from one of the corner nails; either tie or hand sew the end of a stretchy fabric strip to it. Then use a crochet stitch: Taking off one loop at a time, push the edging strip through this rug loop and make a new loop (about the same size). Push it through the loop you have just made. Take the next rug loop off its nail and start over again. Continue around the rug. Hand sew the tag end.

Deco Heaven

This red-hot room sizzles with the flash and glamour of Hollywood in the thirties. When you analyze the components, though, you'll find as much brand new as vintage. It's Deco-tech, really—a happy melding of Moderne and industrial utility.

The wall-to-wall mirrors, the palms and gladiolus, go a long way toward re-creating the aura of a star's dressing room.

The floor in the dining area, heavy-duty ceramic bathroom tile with a snazzy black border, pays homage to all the black-and-white thirties musicals ever made.

The bar angled in the corner was once a somber brown cabinet sitting forlorn in a second-hand store. Glossed over with cream-colored lacquer and punched up with new pulls, it stands ready again to shake cocktails.

The dining area's centerpiece is a stripped-down wooden table base, once married to a chipped and scratched porcelain top. Topped now with a half-inch-thick slab of glass and accompanied by new red-and-white metal chairs—stackable, lightweight and party-ready—it borrows from the past without bringing it all home intact.

The chromium-plated standing ashtray is a little bit Flash Gordon, a thirties original and a lucky flea market find.

The rest of the room is indebted to today's technology. The white wall sconces are industrial fixtures usually seen upside down over theater "Exit" signs. Buy them in lighting supply stores, cover the pipe connector with rubber exhaust hose and add curly plug-in cords. Easy-pull curtains are made from quilted movers' pads, using a grommet kit, shower rod and rings.

Photo: Thomas Hooper

Deco-rated

Windows: Skinny aluminum blinds

Lighting: Vintage shapes

Floor: Secondhand find

Below: Hotels and theatres about to be demolished are two more places where you can salvage old furnishings at old prices. Because so many public places were built or remodeled in the thirties, they are especially rich sources for finding the highly decorative, overstuffed, solid furnishings and accessories of the Art Deco period. For example: The chenille rug here came from an old movie house lobby; the sofa, recovered in red, purple and brown cotton suede cloth in a typically Deco pattern, used to hang out in a hotel lobby; the end table is an archetypal thirties nightstand from a hotel room. The hotel lobby coffee table's distinctive rounded legs spell thirties.

But not everything is old. The lamp on the nightstand/end table is new but descended from Deco tradition. The sleek neon standing lamp behind the sofa is made from a circular fluorescent fixture with a round base. The narrow slat venetian blinds are a modern version of the old wooden ones. Other accessories, on the windowsill and coffee table, are a discriminating mix of contemporary and secondhand finds.

Opposite: Along with a sense of wit and humor, collectibles can easily become part of your living room. The chairs, the tables —even the clothes hanging like art on the wall—are yesterday's funk and flash that have become another alternative for today's furnishings.

This offbeat mixture of Deco and forties findings breaks rules as it breaks with tradition. No thick velvet sofas with matching side chairs here. Instead, a delicate pastel mural painted on the wall, three one-of-a-kind chairs, pulled together by color, surrounding a modernistic fifties blond wood and glass table. The pillows on the floor—covered with discarded fabric remnants—now become their own seating.

The overstuffed chair is slip-covered in forties bark cloth, found in a thrift shop. The fifties rattan chair moves inside from the old front porch. The thirties standing ashtray—originally for trips on ships and trains—rolls around.

Fabrications

The blaze of warmth in this room comes from a lot more than the fireplace—it emanates from the fiery colors of the fabrics and fancywork from the thirties and forties.

Two sofas sit on both sides of the fireplace in the traditional manner—but mend their ways with a lot of hanky-panky pillows. Pillow forms are covered with lush, floral pillow covers in bark cloth and polished cotton. They are inexpensive and easy to find in secondhand shops; some even have zippers. Old drapery panels have the same vintage charm. Just cut the fabric for round or square pillows or stitch around the design for a one-of-a-kind shape.

What to do with the pillows? Try displaying them on a single bed (at left) with wedge-shaped bolsters at the back. Plants, prints and new antique collectibles make the pillows feel at home.

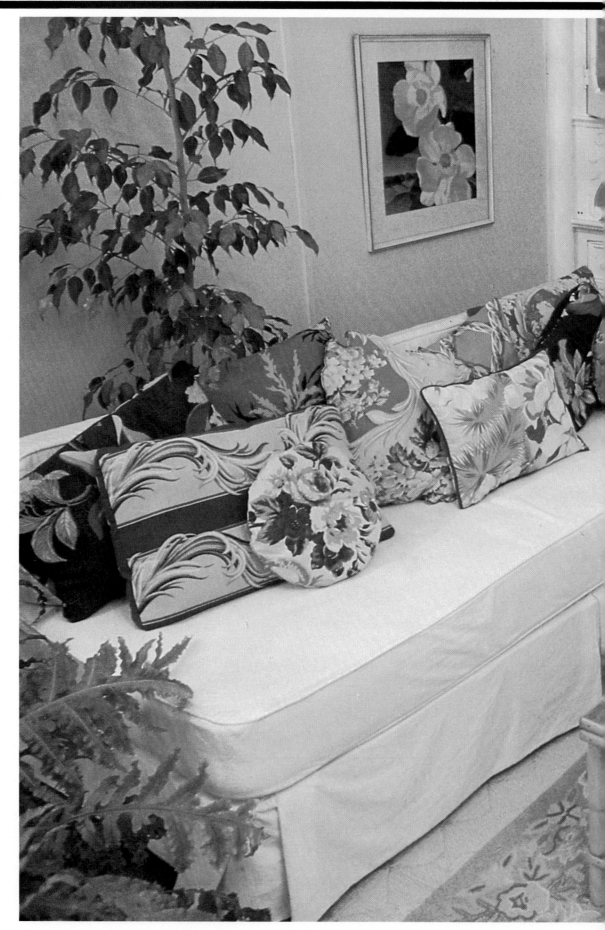

Photo: Thomas Hooper

Untiques

Legally, antiques must be over a hundred years old. But un-tiques—those American golden oldies that were machine or hand crafted within the last century—are still less expensive and more available. Treasures like these—found in salvage yards, estate sales, junk stores, attics, basements and points in between—can turn the most modern room into a collector's paradise.

The first task is to set the groundwork. Lay a new cotton import rug over the wall-to-wall carpet. New, lacy curtains, a 1910 steamer trunk, an old, stained-glass window (hung from screw eyes attached to the window frame on top), and an old auto sign camouflage a slid-ing glass balcony door.

A rescued, well-seasoned sofa from the forties has a colorful afghan on top hiding its bald spots. Next to it: multipurpose spool cabinet like the ones found in general stores. (The "O.N.T." drawer stands for "Our Newest Thread.") Behind is a handmade folding screen (which helps round out the room's sharp corners), a cast-iron lamp and other second-hand finds.

A round-back wicker rocker nods toward its country cousin, a farm house oak rocker that cost $7 in the 1905 Sears cata-log. You can still find them today. The secretary-desk unit to the right has everything: drawers, plenty of glassed-in shelf space, a drop-door writing surface, a mirror and fancy pressed carving.

Other collectibles provide imaginative accents: a 1900 trike, new folk art for warmth and whimsy. The metal and wood shoeshine parlor chair is quite at home here. The coffee table is really an old type-set-ting tray with letters still intact, set on a wicker table.

Photos: Bradley Olman

EATING PLACES

The dining rooms of our childhood were not exactly places to eat in. More often, they were stage sets—backdrops with props that came to life for role playing with relatives, acting out special scenarios or recurring family dramas. The dining room was a static formality of table proper and chairs reserved for company and holidays. And while waiting for that next occasion, the dining room was just a very fancy passageway to the warm kitchen.

Our eating habits have changed considerably. We snack and we eat on the run. We cook with a crowd and we taste-test as we go—which is as much a part of the meal as the sit-down courses afterward. We order in pizza and serve it on bone china plates. In homes everywhere, formality for meals and service is a choice, not a given. It is not that we have rejected the old for the new—we have simply synthesized and acknowledged our options.

Just so, our eating surroundings have changed dramatically too. Very few people can afford the space for a room that does just one thing, a room that sits around waiting for the next occasion. When space became a premium in apartment architecture, the dining room was the first to go. Some were replaced by euphemisms such as nooks, alcoves, ells, but these were swiftly transformed into guest rooms, children's rooms or offices.

Today's apartment dining rooms are defined by where you eat, not by the furniture, and it is never just one place. If friends arrive to watch a special television program, you simply turn the bedroom into an eating room by piling on the trays and pillows. If dinner is served in the living room, you wheel over a movable feast on a rolling cart. Instead of a table that just sits there and looks pretty, we have adopted the supertable: by day, a mild-mannered desk, additional work space or even a wall hanging; by night, faster than a speeding dustcloth, it becomes a flop-down, drop-down, fold-up, drop-in and sit-down eating surface for eight, buffet for sixteen or intimate dinner for two. These well-priced, functional eating units are today as universal as the old mahogany dining ensembles.

New materials have kept pace with our changing needs. Furnishings made from chrome, vinyl, wood or plastic are serving meals nowadays right alongside the more traditional setups. Simultaneously, stainless steel utensils are placed next to sterling; plastic plates mix with china and glass. Edibles turn into the new centerpiece.

With our developing flexibility and our growing demand for hardworking good looks, the contemporary dining room is a state of mind, not a room waiting in state.

High Spirits

Right: Here's a glitzy party set with all the essentials of first-class entertaining: soft, controllable lighting to fine-tune the mood and a bar/buffet that could almost be a stage for a miniature Fred Astaire to tap across.

The drop-down tabletop and pedestal light boxes are quickie at-home projects with high visual profile and maximum versatility. You can make them with inexpensive particle board topped with white plastic-coated hardboard scored with a black grid—the kind sold as trompe l'oeil bathroom tile. Pine lath strips form the frames.

With folding legs and a good, sturdy handle, the tabletop serves hors d'oeuvre, drinks or buffet dinner. Dropped flat against the wall, it joins with the plastic lucite mirror to complete an octagonal shape.

Atmospheric nightclub lighting is provided by simple light boxes—hardboard rectangles with Plexiglas tops—that work as plant stands or end tables, as well as moving around on command to create shadowy corners. The wall sconces come together in a few hours with white Plexiglas, lattice strips and lamp adapter kits. Curly red cords add extra punch.

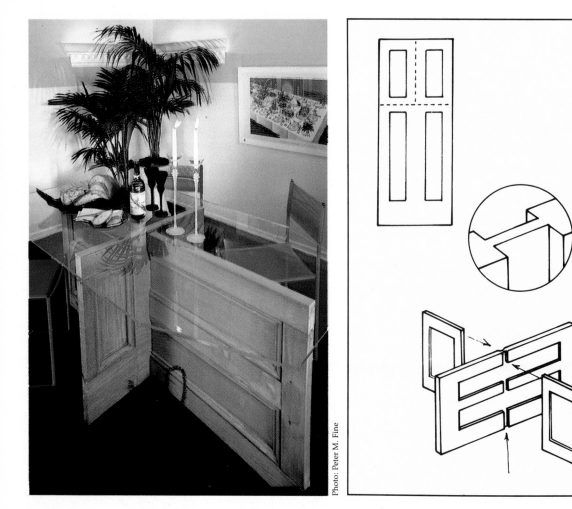

Photo: Peter M. Fine

Above: You can transform just about any old door into a terrific table base, though the procedure varies according to the configuration of the panels.

HOW TO DO IT
Glass Table: Trim the door to standard dining table height (29 inches) and strip it if necessary with paint remover. For a four-panel door, cut it in three parts as shown, with a circular saw.

Make notches as deep as the recessed panels (see illustration) with a handsaw, hammer and wood chisel or circular saw. Fit one of the short pieces into one of the notches and nail from opposite side. Then do the other side, nailing the two pieces together at an angle. Top it with ½"- or ⅝"-thick glass slightly longer and wider than the base.

110

Puttin' on the Glitz

112

Belle Époque

Left: It's all flash and mirror and guaranteed to impress your friends. Once you assess the elements, this bar à la Grand Hotel de Ville is not hard to reproduce. Two tiled shelves and a pseudo-window created from stick-on mirror tiles and strips of pine lath are all it takes to pull off the grand illusion.

Wineglasses rack up underneath the upper shelf. Illumination comes from a techy drafting lamp, found at artist's supply stores. Elegance is not all, however: When drinking's done, the bar serves sensibly as a breakfast counter, buffet or even desk-top duty.

Right: Talk about romance . . . If you've a penchant for opulence, you'll love this ice-cream sundae of a room. It's really not as luxe as it looks. Underneath that central concoction of raspberry-colored fabric lurks an unprepossessing card table, with a round top cut from plywood and yards of ruffled canvas fortified against stains with two coats of polyurethane. The white architectural elements—the fiberglass columns, the ceiling band, the harlequin tile floor—make sparkling good foils for the lemon-sherbet-colored walls. The carefully chosen accessories—a frosted glass French Deco chandelier, the poinsettia, the leafy corn plants dramatically lit from below—even little things like the black tableware and sculptured candlesticks—come on strong to offset the frill.

Photos: Thomas Hooper

Classics of Three Centuries

Photo: Peter M. Fine

Photo: Thomas Hooper

Top Left: Reproduction madness has struck in this cozy enclave of eighteenth-century ambience. All pieces are made-today takeoffs on traditional styles. The utilitarian hutch is "after the manner of" Pennsylvania German. The expandable table is Queen Anne-style, with graceful cabriole legs, while the chairs are classic Windsors. We know we're dealing with interpretation, not restoration, when we spot the ringed plastic light fixture. The walls sport panels where none existed before. Just nail narrow picture molding in rectangular shapes, paper within.

Below Left: This is down-home dining, late nineteenth-century style, a casual mood that meshes beautifully with the rehabs of today. The handsome oak table comes straight from the pages of a 1902 Sears Roebuck catalogue (via a flea market, most likely, and not nearly as pricey as its claw-footed cousins). The bentwood chairs are the real thing too, though current copies are readily available if the flea market fails to yield. Note the floor-to-ceiling window, formerly a door. It and its neighbor to the left were replaced with simple glass panels and framed with pine boards.

Right: The Bauhaus chairs that are the main design course of this clearly contemporary space are the classics this century calls its own. Still being manufactured after Marcel Breuer's original design, these chrome and wicker chairs with their cantilevered curves are free-flowing complements to the straight lines of the plastic laminate table.

The slim shelf along the wall stands ready to serve. While the ceiling track lights and convex elevator mirror shout "hi, tech," the old porch door reminds us of the past.

Window Dressing

Dinner's at eight, and the food looks great. The question is how to make the environment equally attractive. Here, two inspired suggestions for dealing with nonviews.

Left: Lightweight latticework shutters relieve the boredom and provide a geometric grid that sets off the sculptural shapes of the furniture. Do it yourself by gluing together one-inch-thick pine lath strips (from the lumberyard) at four-inch intervals. Hinge the shutters at the side for easy opening.

The huge slab of a plastic laminate table is a piece of everyday art that expands for more by adding a new leaf. The modern lines of the table are emphasized by chairs that are just the antithesis—Queen Anne reproductions, given a brilliant update via new coloration, red lacquer with gold-stripe highlights.

The ringed acrylic-and-chrome light fixture rises and falls on an adjustable cord.

Note the lab beakers and test tubes acting the part of perfect bud vases.

Right: A dreary outlook on the building across the street could have been concealed by curtains or shades, but that's the road not taken. Instead, a touch of ornate Victoriana lends some character to the bare-bones view. This piece of wooden gingerbread fretwork once served to divide the front parlor from the back in an old home. Now it sets off an all-square Parsons dining table and some New Classic chrome and cane chairs.

Antique stores and salvage companies usually offer a selection of rectangular shapes, from a couple of feet to 10 or 15 feet long. They hang easily from the ceiling with cup hooks and monofilament.

New World Splendor

Whoever said "Don't mix light and dark wood" has never seen this dining-area setup that runs the gamut from dark walnut to natural pine.

Those hand-carved shellback chairs (made-today imports from Italy) are comfortable with the glossy Parsons table or as extra seating anywhere. Plus the table is a clean, well-lighted place to work.

Stack-up storage units sit in front of an awkwardly placed kitchen door to add architectural interest. Another character builder is the wraparound cornice of embossed sheet steel.

Another natural, the latticework grid, deals with a no-view window.

HOW TO DO IT
Instant Architecture Cornice: Purchase the sheet steel from an industrial supplier (look in the Yellow Pages under "Metal Ceilings"). The metal is quite sharp and should be handled with work gloves. Cut the strips with tin snips.

Then attach the cornice to the wall, nail the sheet steel to two furring strips (1 x 2s nailed around the ceiling and walls). Seams should be overlapped. Mitering the corners can be tricky so allow an extra piece or two for errors. Tip: When you fit the miter, you do not have to work at ceiling level. Try it out in the corner at a more reachable height.

HOW TO DO IT
Hanging Lamp: Cut 30° grooves in two 12" 2 x 2s and two 18" 2 x 2s. (If you do not have a table saw, have a lumberyard cut it for you.) Miter corners and assemble frame with glue and L brackets as shown. Glue in centerpiece. Mount and wire porcelain sockets. Staple wire alongside vertical 2 x 2 (or rip the 2 x 2 in half and cut a groove down the center with a rabbet plane or table saw. Conceal wire inside groove and glue boards together). Secure pieces of Plexiglas to frame with epoxy glue. Hang lamp with eyebolts and S hooks and connect wires to ceiling fixture.

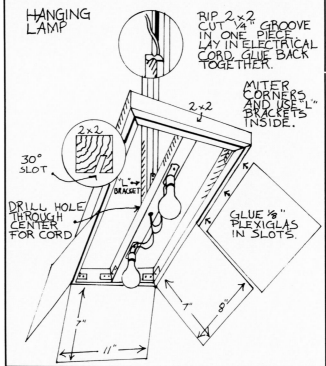

HANGING LAMP

RIP 2×2 CUT 1/4" GROOVE IN ONE PIECE. LAY IN ELECTRICAL CORD. GLUE BACK TOGETHER.

MITER CORNERS AND USE "L" BRACKETS INSIDE.

2×2

2×2

30° SLOT

"L" BRACKET

DRILL HOLE THROUGH CENTER FOR CORD

GLUE 1/8" PLEXIGLAS IN SLOTS.

7"

7"

8"

11"

Table Topping

With the mere swing of a table-top, you can turn any foyer or entryway into an eating room. Just add a side table that flips.

After a tabletop transplant, this small Parsons table gives you two tables in one: a working side table in the entryway, or enough sit-down seating for up to eight.

The other pieces in the room are just as inventive as the flexible table. Even with the apparent formality of a wall sconce, traditional drapery and a gilt mirror and picture light, the casual pieces fit in. Dishes and silverware are all high camp gear. Dish towels were pressed into napkin service. An institutional pitcher displays flowers, and plant pot saucers hold bread and fruit.

HOW TO DO IT

The Tabletop Transplant: Find a Parsons table (finished or unfinished). Take two plywood pieces, each the same size as the top (the one pictured here is 24" x 48") and hinge them as shown. Be sure to place the hinges so they will not scratch the tabletop. Cover the edges with wood tape. Finish the new top like the original table. Double the tops over on the tabletop (hinges hide in the back). For a sit-down meal, unfold the top, turn 90 degrees to create a 48" square table.

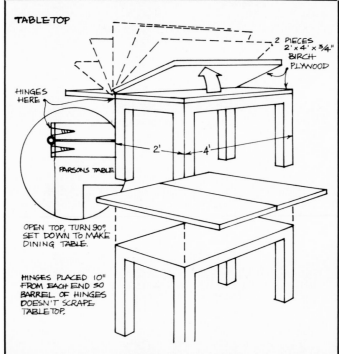

TABLETOP

2 PIECES 2' x 4' x 3/4" BIRCH PLYWOOD

HINGES HERE

2'

4'

PARSONS TABLE

OPEN TOP, TURN 90° SET DOWN TO MAKE DINING TABLE.

HINGES PLACED 10" FROM EACH END SO BARREL OF HINGES DOESN'T SCRAPE TABLETOP.

A Room in Bloom

Thanks to inexpensive lunch cloths—those colorful cotton tablecloths from the forties with wide borders of cherries, apples or flowers—this dining room bursts with color. Everything in the room—except for the plants and the food, of course—is a secondhand find. The old-time charm has been enhanced, stretched and assembled in new ways.

With some imagination and a little luck at the thrift shop, you can get a similar rich look for rag prices. Use several cloths layered as has been done here, and do not be troubled by contrasting patterns.

Of the same vintage: the embroidered tea cozy, dish towels and napkins. At the windows are starched, hand-embroidered dresser scarves, hung from tension rods. Wide hem tape has been sewn to the backs to make a casing for the rods to slip through. Everything on the tabletop—all still manufactured today—carries through the room's forties flavor.

Table Talk

Opposite: Anything with a leg to stand on can be the basis—and the base—for a dining table.

Plywood boxes and smart provincial fabric update the traditionally stalwart English trestle table. This one, unlike its ancestor, has a glass top, but a hollow-core door or a slab of butcher block can also effect the transformation. Chippendale chairs finished au naturel are a suitable update. The bar in back was originally an unfinished treasure chest—available from craft stores.

Above Right: The humble glass-topped sawhorse rides again, this time in the guise of slender but sturdy enameled steel trestles. Good-design home furnishings stores have them in several colors. The folding party chairs are classics, and you certainly can't quibble with the price.

Right: With one unexpected idea, an ordinary table can become surprisingly special. In this case, using chrome bar stool bases to hold up an oversized tabletop changes a white box space altogether. This table has a copper top but plywood would work as well.

Far Right: A dining area does not need to be an alcove: Any wall can be used to provide a table-shelf. Mount the table on corner brackets screwed into the wall.

Photo: Peter M. Fine

Photo: Bill Helms/Design: Demetrios Kontopoulos

Photo: Bradley Olman

Off-the-Wall Dining

This dining/wall unit, complete with storage space, includes its own nook for serving meals. The drop-down table is part of a four-stack bookshelf/drawer system that is easy enough to build over a weekend. There is even a perching place for out-of-use chairs; they are stacked behind the table housing.

The simple natural wood keeps the system contemporary and light while the blue table-top adds strong color contrast.

HOW TO DO IT

Dining/Wall Unit: Get all the supplies at a building supply dealer. Pick out a good grade of pine if you intend to leave the wood natural; it can also be painted. Have all pieces precut.

What to Buy: This list is for a unit 7' tall, 8'6" long and 14" deep (shelves are 11½" deep). The chest of drawers is a stacked set of three, each 28" high.

2 x 2s (actual size–1¼" x 1½")
8 pieces 7' for uprights
4 pieces 8'6" for top and bottom
7 pieces 14½" for crosspieces
1 piece 35" for tabletop crosspiece
2 pieces 30" for table legs
1 x 2s
1 piece 24" for table legs
34 pieces 11½" for shelf supports
1 x 12s
17 pieces 32" for shelves
Plywood
1 piece ¾" x 32" x 48" for tabletop
Plastic laminate for tabletop
1 piece 32" x 48" (optional)
Hardware
34 3½" x ¼" hex head bolts
5 5" x ¼" hex head bolts
Nuts and 2 washers each for the bolts
30" continuous hinge (for table)
1 pair 1½" butt hinges (legs)
1 cabinet catch
1 pound 4d finishing nails
1 pint contact cement (optional)

Bolt together the four up-rights and the crosspieces (7'-long 2 x 2s and 14½" crosspiece 2 x 2s). C-clamp the pieces in position, drill (with a ¼" drill bit) through both at once and bolt them together before removing the clamps. Then bolt on the 8'6" lengthwise 2 x 2s.

Stand the whole unit in place and nail on the 1 x 2 shelf supports, spacing the shelves at the best heights for your storage needs.

Make the table legs and hinge them to the tabletop. Bolt the 2 x 2 crosspiece on the front of the unit and attach the table with a continuous hinge. Screw a cabinet catch under one of the shelves to keep the tabletop folded up. Cover the top with plastic laminate or paint.

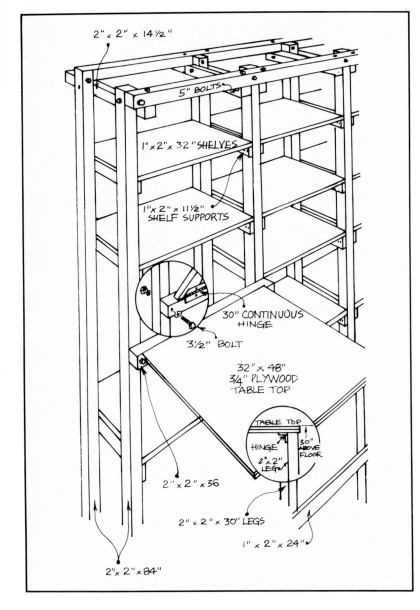

2" x 2" x 14½"
5" BOLTS
1" x 2" x 32" SHELVES
1" x 2" x 11½" SHELF SUPPORTS
30" CONTINUOUS HINGE
3½" BOLT
32" x 48" ¾" PLYWOOD TABLE TOP
TABLE TOP
HINGE
2" x 2" LEGS
30" ABOVE FLOOR
2" x 2" x 36
2" x 2" x 30" LEGS
1" x 2" x 24"
2" x 2" x 84"

The Groaning Board

Walls: Painted plywood paneling

Window: Natural linen shade

Right: This dining area—one end of a long living room—is a cross-fertilization of contemporary and country. A green industrial lamp oversees the solid walnut table. Flanking the table are made-today Windsor chairs and a space-saving banquette, which is actually a reupholstered old trolley car seat. The walnut table, like the banquette, was a secondhand find.

A traditional English butler tray, in front of the window, shuffles a bar around at your beck and call. And the country natural linen window shade is easy to make: Hem the fabric top and bottom and slip in 1″ dowels for weight. Tack up the shade and two pairs of natural linen strips (front and behind).

Opposite: Just because you like the look of turn-of-the-century golden oak doesn't mean you have to hunt out the real thing —even if you can find it. Those solid old pieces have become scarce and costly. The alternative is a new crop of reproductions. Everything in this room, from the Hoosier cabinet to the liqueur decanters, is new. Made today with the look of yesterday, the new-old furniture is surfacing because the design and utility are timeless. And as of old, these pieces are solid oak, well made and good looking, just manufactured with modern technology. This dining setting combines classic design with a very new twist: The old-style office chairs never gathered around a table before but now they offer all-day comfort. The round oak table—an endangered species among antiques today—is brand new. The glass display cabinet with mirrored back both stores and displays dishes and serving pieces. Overseeing the scene is another reproduction—a leaded glass Tiffany-style lamp.

Kitchen-Side Dining

Below: This dining/working/cooking area handles a big load with style even though the space is small. Ignore the tired advice of paint-it-white-to-look-larger. Instead, go for one bold stroke. High-gloss burgundy paint on the walls sets off the area dramatically—and makes that informal dining area just a bit more formal.

Wood, glass, plastic, metal and fabric coexist comfortably here. The light Russian plywood chairs and the plywood and white vinyl table keep the space visually uncluttered.

The window shade is quickly made. Buy simple spring-loaded shade hardware, staple fabric across the top; hem the sides; slip a lattice strip through a small hem at the bottom, or finish with a plastic strip.

The outsized mirror with its easily made cabinet molding frame reflects the kitchen area and the Victorian light fixture.

Right: Another big look for a small space, also adjacent to the kitchen. The turn-of-the-cen-

...tury telegraph table/bench adds ...tyle and a sense of humor to an ...rdinary area. It rests on an ...American Indian print rug that ...lays up the kitchen's American ...ndian artifacts. And the slots ...nce reserved for telegrams ...ow store napkins and utensils.

Photo: Bradley Olman

Photo: John Katz

Rooms with a View

Storage: Wicker shelving
Lighting: On-the-floor spots
Walls: Paint two-tone and lush

Left: This haven is on the fifth floor of a big-city walk-up and used to be rather shabby. The dramatic transformation owes more to imagination (and maybe Sydney Greenstreet) than to money.

The table, chairs and wall shelf are vintage forties rattan, found in antique shops that specialize in thirties and forties pieces (but similar new ones are available).

Real, yet not alive, the palm trees are dried leaves—permanently carefree. Small spots carefully placed in the trees are shot up through the leaves for spectacular, spiky shadows.

Dark walls (and ceiling) keep the atmosphere intimate and lush (and also hide wall irregularities). Old bamboo dining chairs sit atop a sisal rug.

Opposite: What if we told you that the view of your dreams is just an f-stop away? Formal gardens, Roman fountains, sunsets, skylines—the possibilities are yours to imagine.

The French door lending Parisian ambience to this dining area—arched window molding, terrace and all—is a grand photo-gesture, a custom blowup by a professional lab of a 35mm slide. To get the amazing fool-the-eye result, the camera was held at midway point of the door's height (about four feet) at a distance of 3½ feet. A wide-angle lens was used. The blowup, mounted on Fome-Cor, hangs six inches from the wall so it forms natural shadows. The foreground flowerpots (real) take the illusion a step further.

KITCHENS THAT COOK

The new kitchen is the kitchen extended, retaliating against rigid architectural boundaries by conquering space in unexpected places. The old kitchen was a place where one lone person (usually of the female persuasion) prepared food behind closed doors. But as cooking has become the new participatory sport, the kitchen has become the new playing field, spilling out into the dining area for extra work/play space. Our kitchens are now replete with tools lifted from commercial sources and they are stocked with ingredients from every ethnic cuisine of the world. There is even a new kind of kitchen clutter, which is a revolt against the antiseptic. It is clutter that is a sign of life.

More and more, kitchens are becoming adjunct living rooms, places in which to gather, to participate, to share secrets, to play. The old cliché about the kitchen being the "hub of the home" is more appropriate now than ever.

And the recipes are changing too. The old one used to be: Mix one stove with one refrigerator. Add running water. Apartment kitchens were mere afterthoughts of modern planning, and living in one meant little more than moving in, putting down clean shelf paper and taking pot luck. The galley kitchen—no storage, no window— was as tight as a ship, infinitely less imaginative, rivaled in size and utility only by the broom closet. That has all changed. Granted, the apartment kitchen has its own special problems, but it also has its own unique solutions.

You do not need to break through walls, buy a lot of new appliances or install expensive custom cabinets in order to ake your kitchen work.

In the last decade or so, basic itchen principles have been re-efined because of new values, ew demands in home living, ew technology and materials. Io longer is the kitchen a room ɔ hide in or shield with louver ɔoors and stand-up screens. ack then, meals seemed to appen as if by magic. Today, iere has been a definite shift in ensibility. From: 1. Yes, Vir-inia, there is a kitchen. 2. In act, why not come in and see ow it is done. 3. Listen, Vir-inia—as long as you are stand-ıg there, would you mind peel-ing that onion? 4. And, come to think of it, why not invite the rest of the guests in, too, so everyone can help.

And so the kitchen is now a room to behold and belong in, a room not just for one, but for guests and friends. With that change of attitude has come new kitchen/living ideas:

1. Use your eyes and trust your instincts. Break rules. Who says that the refrigerator, stove and sink must be placed in the perennial triangle pattern?

2. Get organized. You want to use every bit of space you can.

3. Do not be stymied by styles. Your kitchen can reflect your taste. *Personalize.*

As our choices have become more sophisticated, more inter-national kitchen activity has, ironically, gotten back to the basics. We have, once again, discovered the pleasures of making pasta and pastries, of making wine, and turning our kitchens into greenhouses— greenhomes—of herbs, even without the window box.

The new kitchen is a space in which to explore and experi-ment, a place in which to try and taste, create and relax, a room to share and savor.

Hardworking Hardware

This industrial-strength super-kitchen packs a bright red punch, then dazzles us further with design and storage ideas lifted from the diner, the doctor's office and the garden gate.

The room's anchor is an extended central work island, with a range at one end and a butcher-block countertop on aluminum pipe legs at the other. The cart underneath comes together with elbows, couplings, tee joints, casters and two tiled plywood shelves.

Existing wood counters (*below*) get a new, scratch-proof face with $^1/_{16}$" sheet metal cut to fit and applied with construction adhesive. The refrigerator, pushed into a rear closet, frees up three feet of floor space. Along the right-hand wall, open shelves come in three forms: pine, wire and glass pastry cases, available from restaurant supply stores.

See how well the enameled medical cabinet handles domestic duty; it's replaced the pine hutch of yore.

A section of chain link fence, ordered preassembled, holds aloft a gleaming arsenal of pots and pans.

The Extended Kitchen

This "kitchen" is not really all kitchen. It breaks boundaries and eats its way into the living/dining space. Title this one "The Kitchen That Ate the Plain-White Box."

What makes the transition are quarry tiles that float one room into another, extending the space by using pots, pans, storage, a table and other traditional "kitchen" collections.

The eating/work area has bentwood chairs coupled with a Formica Parsons table, a stylish alternative to the old-time regulation matching dining set. The table's deliberate lines are a sharp rebellion against its mahogany ancestors, yet there is dignity in the proportion of this version that expands and contracts with leaves.

In 1857 Michael Thonet fashioned the bentwood chair of wood steamed and molded into curves. Le Corbusier designed the first of the updated armchairs in the twenties. Lightweight enough for any movable feast, these chairs are affordable, accessible and adaptable.

Overhead, factory lights are a democratic alternative to the chandelier.

The wall storage system (below) was once found only in expensive European-engineered and often custom-made furniture. Like all good radical ideas, the wall system has filtered down through extremist layers into the mass market, losing a bit of its machined quality, a lot of its priciness, but none of its workability.

Photos: Bradley Olman

The Extended Kitchen

Work space is everywhere. Any workroom requires order, easy access and storage space. And every surface is eligible. This kitchen gets its organization from stainless steel grids, hooks, bins, boxes and baskets —all now standard in any kitchen that works. We've learned a few lessons from restaurant kitchens, like hanging pots from ceilings and making the walls work without (or in spite of) standard kitchen cabinets.

Good-looking, durable and easy-to-care-for molded plastic is a new kitchen material. The stacking plastic drawer units function in any room, but in the kitchen they are the handy depository for all those easy-to-use, but hard-to-store conveniences—hand-held appliances, aluminum foil, plastic wrap, pot holders. The stacking drawer units also support sturdy butcher-block counter space.

A flexible metal lamp—long ago borrowed from the architect's office—offers high-powered illumination over this kitchen work space.

A rolling cart—made from heavy-duty stainless steel wire and covered with a slab of butcher block—is a floating worktable that doubles as storage space when stationary. Industrial-looking cooking ware, professional in inspiration, is now widely available from the country's best and biggest housewares manufacturers.

Kitchen Lib

No behind-closed-doors for this kitchen. No sleek/chic pretensions either. This is a kitchen committed to openness—a friendly, welcoming place that looks natural and organic without looking dated. Perhaps it's relaxed because it's been liberated from the problems of cabinet doors that stick, don't close properly, hit you in the head and waste precious moments of cooking and chatting time. Open shelves everywhere—tucked in all the odd little spaces like over the built-in oven, above the refrigerator and under the countertop range—make clear glass jars of beans and grains look as appealing as the penny candies of childhood.

Pine lath strips on the wall are cheap and clever hanging storage for pots and utensils. The central work island, fitted with a bar sink and electrical outlets, doubles as a snack bar.

Mexican tile covers the floor, the counter fronts and tops, even climbs halfway up the wall to form a spatter shield behind the range.

Baskets are useful, decorative and totally in keeping with the natural materials mode.

Home Cooking

An industriously industrial-looking kitchen need not be a cold, uninviting place but it should be a highly functional room where anyone can find a space to work or at least a place to sit and watch. Here the layout and the equipment combine to make the room both comfortable for watching and efficient for working.

Most of the old cupboards and doors were removed and replaced by a commercially inspired butcher block-top cart (next page), floor-to-ceiling painted pegboard, plastic drawer units and pine shelving —much cheaper than custom cabinets and unique. The result is three flexible work areas with open and closed storage

above and below, unified by clean looks, factory lights and a single color.

When it comes to pegboards, all manner of brackets, hooks and supports are now available at hardware stores and lumberyards.

In the work area (below), two narrow pieces of pine shelving placed side by side cost less than a single wide board. Protect them with two coats of satin polyurethane, and set the shelving across stacked plastic drawers.

The shelves over the refrigerator are supported on metal wall brackets screwed into the wall studs. Glass and white dishes add to the airy effect.

Photos: Bradley Olman

Home Cooking

Above: Yet another extended kitchen creates even more unexpected work space (this one stretches right out into the living room, outside a narrow galley kitchen). Pots and pans hang from a suspended chicken coop; more storage fits on a shelving unit placed in front of the window. Mexican chairs replace regulation wood or metal ones. *Right:* Restaurant/ industrial design has definitely come home. Functional commercial wire shelving fits right into kitchen spaces—and big wheels roll the wagon right to the center of the cooking scene.

The Erector Set

There is more than one way to extend a kitchen into another room. Sometimes you can even do it on wheels.

Strong and square, a sturdy building block with a solid foundation, this erector-set unit was built in just a few hours. It is representative of the new philosophy of extending kitchens: Storage and work areas need not remain shut away in the kitchen. Put them anywhere you need them.

Inexpensively assembled, this unit will expand your kitchen area into the dining room or living room.

The system is made from slotted angle irons, available in industrial supply or machinery stores and usually used for industrial shelving. Mesh chicken wire and hooks hang up pans and utensils, and a butcher block surface is substantial enough for chopping and slicing.

HOW TO DO IT

Erector Set: The dimensions of this unit can be adjusted to fit any space. This one is 6' high, 28" wide, 30" deep. Use galvanized sheet metal and painted angle irons. Cut and bolt together the angle irons with $5/16$" x $3/4$" bolts.

Materials:

4 slotted angle irons, 6'
8 slotted angle irons, 30"
8 slotted angle irons, 28"
40 nuts and bolts, $5/16$" x $3/4$"
4 locking casters (3") with corner brackets; nuts, bolts, washers
2 pieces 1" x 2" wire mesh, cut to fit top and back
Cut to fit inside frame (about 28" x 30"):
2 pieces $1/2$"-thick plywood
2 pieces 16-gauge galvanized sheet metal
1 piece butcher block (or Formica-covered plywood)

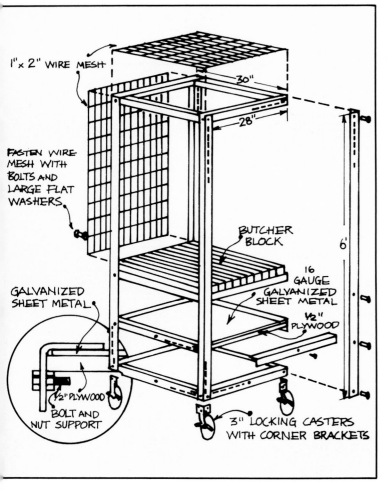

1" x 2" WIRE MESH

30"

28"

FASTEN WIRE MESH WITH BOLTS AND LARGE FLAT WASHERS.

BUTCHER BLOCK

GALVANIZED SHEET METAL

16 GAUGE GALVANIZED SHEET METAL

$1/2$" PLYWOOD

6'

$1/2$" PLYWOOD BOLT AND NUT SUPPORT

3" LOCKING CASTERS WITH CORNER BRACKETS

The New Pantry

Ceiling: Glued thin wood strips
Storage: Natural pine cabinets
Windows: Salvaged stained-glass panels

There is more to today's functional kitchen than good design. Layouts and appliances may be modern but the feel—and many components—can be old. This kitchen's warmth radiates from genuinely old accessories, old-look stained glass and plenty of natural wood.

The open display of packaged goods changes with every shopping trip, adding a new dimension to functional art. The cupboards and stained glass are both homemade as is the wood-covered ceiling, which is built from a kit of 3"-wide mahogany strips, thin enough to cut with a pair of scissors.

The combination of open display with the rustic warmth of pine brings a special quality to any kitchen. How-to: To build the cupboards, decide what you would like to store/display; then sketch your plan on the wall. Starting from the bottom, use small angle irons to fasten the shelves to the wall and screw the vertical dividers to the shelves.

The Old Pantry

If you are living with an old kitchen and the appliances work, you do not have to modernize it. Let it live back in time, when it once was young. Flea markets, estate sales, auctions, thrift shops, salvage yards—these are the new five-and-dimes for the new antique kitchens. What's more, many kitchen wares haven't changed since Betty Crocker wore braids. You still can find the old dependable shapes and materials new in department stores and cookware shops. There is nothing depressing about this Depression-era kitchen.

The old-time stove sets the style. Most storage is contained in the vintage freestanding Hoosier cabinet. And all the colors here are the perfect prescription for the Depression blues.

Below: An old medicine cabinet works well for spices. The mix of old and new packaging and jars adds color and zest.

Photos: Erik Arnesen

Mother Knew Best

A kitchen to remember. Too often relic kitchen appliances are the booby prize that comes with old-world charm: stained sinks, ovens that must be lit by hand, refrigerators that look as if they have been waiting a decade or two for the iceman. Gut, modernize and renovate? Not at all. If the stove and refrigerator work, and if the water runs hot and cold, the rest of the room need not be snazzy modern. It can be preserved. What you add can complement the design that has existed for years.

Everything (except the appliances) in this room is new, all commercially available today. Inexpensive and designed for function, these pieces were not acquired for nostalgia value but because they are timeless. They are still around because they are still good.

But the room does not stop there. It takes obvious, everyday items—the match and laundry starch boxes, for example—and turns them into design statements.

Color can also unify. The main color in this room is blue, just as it would have been forty years before. Blue was billed as the "kitchen color" then, and it still lives on in vintage spatterware dishes, utensils, old-time fabrics, tiles, and cobalt blue canisters.

Country charm and staunch utilitarianism are provided by cast-iron pots and pans, a classic mixer, general-store canisters, porcelain cabinet pulls—even the chocolate chip cookies. All have made a well-deserved comeback. The dish drainer— often hidden in so many kitchens—looks right at home here.

Photo: Bradley Olman

Dining à la Cart

What makes this shining example of a table-cum-cart such a freewheeling wonder? Let us count the ways. It is (1) a commodious work surface that turns itself into (2) an elegant dining table with the flip of a hinge and (3) still has room to spare for below-decks storage. It almost builds itself with the help of "post caps"—metal flanges bolted at strategic intersections that are also an important design feature.

HOW TO DO IT
Dining Cart:

Materials:

4 2 x 4s, 22½" long, for legs

2 2 x 4s, 30" long, for top end rails

2 2 x 4s, 45" long, for top side rails

2 2 x 4s, 41" long, for shelf side rails

2 4 x 4s, 27" long, for shelf end rails

2 1 x 12s, 30" long, for table leaves

1 ½ x 14 x 41" chipboard for bottom shelf

1 ½ x 45 x 27" chipboard for tabletop

2 1 x 2s, 45" long, for top supports along sides

2 1 x 2s, 25½" long, for top supports at each end

2 1 x 2s, 41" long, for bottom shelf supports along sides

2 1 x 2s, 12½" long, for bottom shelf supports at each end

12 "Teco" #1 post caps

100 ¾" galvanized sheet metal screws

1 30 x 48" galvanized sheet metal, 1/16" thick for top

2 30 x 11¼" galvanized sheet metal for leaf tops

2 30-inch piano hinges

4 plate-type, swivel rubber wheels, 2" diameter

1 pint contact cement

4 table leg support brackets

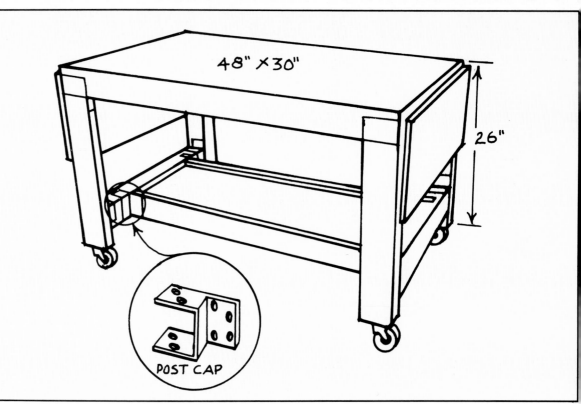

POST CAP

Paint all wood components first with high-gloss enamel. Build frame of 2 x 4s and 4 x 4s, using post caps at intersections. Add 1 x 2 strips to inside of rails to support recessed top and shelf. Screw chipboard top and shelf to 1 x 2 strips. File edges of sheet metal and cement to top and leaves (wear gloves). Screw piano hinges to leaves, then to 2 x 4 rails at end of table. Attach folding support brackets. Add heavy-duty rubber casters to bottom of each leg.

High-Level Storage

Those pots and pans and wine-glasses swinging from the rafters are a grand example of form following function. The plain white box apartment kitchen has been swiftly transformed into a literal showplace —everything in the place shows. And not by accident.

All the wood pieces were specifically engineered to accommodate these hanging wares. Small shelves are carefully measured to be the perfect size for spices. The same holds true for the racks holding the wineglasses.

The interior architecture of the space emerged not only through the wood construction but also through the gentle lines of all the objects—curved goblets against straight wood, tall slender spice jars alongside round, fat crocks, dark enameled pots below pale wicker baskets. The result: Scandinavian in texture, oriental in feel, with every inch functional.

It was all simply constructed. All that is needed is to adapt the dimensions to the design of your room. Pine shelving replaced the ordinary kitchen cabinets. (They were removed and stored.) Meat hooks, available at gourmet shops, hold oddly shaped tools such as the Chinese skimmer at left.

Yucca and spider plants offset the crisp look of the pine. Even a simple wooden tray is of interest when hung on the wall.

Glass Act

This stunning array of bottles and jars takes its design cues from the old apothecary shop. It is just the Rx for a disorganized collection of herbs and spices—not to mention pasta, grains, beans and candies. With a condiment cabinet like this, you'll never again be held up by a search for saffron while the bouillabaisse boils over.

This is laboratory chic carried to a glorious extreme: All the beakers, test tubes, flasks and dressing jars come from hospital supply houses (check the Yellow Pages under "Laboratory Supplies and Equipment")—and it's amazing how well the products of the lab translate to the kitchen. Nowhere can you get as good-looking a mortar and pestle for garlic-crushing or as serviceable and durable a jar for showing off the shapes of pasta.

The basic box is made of inch-thick redwood (pine is possible, too), with a hardboard back and adjustable shelves. You can custom-make a similar one to fit the space you have. Remember to make the inside shelves two inches shallower than the cabinet to accommodate the spice racks mounted on the insides of the hinged doors. The racks themselves are simply 2 x 2s with holes drilled into them with a spade bit. Store-bought wire, wood or plastic racks can work just as well.

Photo: Peter M. Fine

Out and Out Storage

Left: Use and improve every inch of a narrow apartment galley with these space-conscious ideas:

Closet pole ceiling: Lengths of unfinished closet pole (from the lumberyard) are attached to the wall with pole sockets.

Screw large cup hooks into poles where needed.

Open cupboards with painted edges—doors off.

A rolling cart (in the foyer/pantry) expands storage and work space. Carts abound with bins, shelves, drawers.

Cover countertops with dime-store cutting boards. They are the same length as a standard counter is deep (24″).

Store and display utensils on lath strips studded with cup hooks. Search out wood or wire racks for everything that moves.

Right: In this *almost* impossibly tiny galley, steps are a luxury there's no room to take—except for those that maximize style and efficiency, for example:

A smooth cooktop set into a butcher-block counter is augmented by a convection oven niftily tucked into the overhead cupboard. Doors are removed for a feeling of air and space.

The half-refrigerator beneath is a necessary compromise (there's a second one in a hall closet for extra beer and Perrier).

A quick and easy grid system uses every inch of the left wall and reduces clutter. Make it out of ¾″ dowels squared off at six-inch intervals and joined from behind with 1¼″ screws. Cup hooks and S-hooks both work.

Tasteful basics keep the look clean and simple: a bamboo window shade, an inexpensive paper lantern, simple white dishes.

Short Takes

Design: Stephen Habiague

Left: Don't get locked into labels. Just because bamboo shades are sold to be hung on windows doesn't mean they can not be used elsewhere. Here they have replaced paint-encrusted cabinet doors. The inexpensive matchstick blinds are available at most oriental import stores. A scissors or sharp knife will cut them to exact size. Fruit baskets and large wicker trays, quickly hung under the cabinets, keep the natural look going. The dish drainer also hangs on the wall, adding yet another texture and more work space. Another disguise: A hanging vine veils an unexciting window view.

Photos: Bradley Olman

Left: The lighting strip mounted over the sink adds the extra light you always need over any counter space. The multiple outlet strips are available at lighting supply stores; light bulbs screwed into plug-in adapters bring drama to even the most basic salad preparation.

Above: You can completely revitalize dingy and dirty cabinets in about the same time it would take to wash them off—and with the same tool. A sponge dipped into blue paint (or any other color, semigloss or gloss), then dabbed onto the cabinets results in a spatterware look.

The Galley Gallery

Photos: Maris/Semel

In other times kitchens were decorated only with insurance calendars on the walls and a magnetic pot holder or two dangling from the refrigerator. Today kitchen accouterments are much more artful. These two kitchens are galleries—galley galleries, to be sure—with a Pop Art mixture of the fun and the functional.

Left: Country comes to the apartment kitchen with a warm combination of antique butcher block, old wooden bowls, pine, copper and pottery, giving the whole a look of organized chaos. The high shelving unifies the space and stores good-looking but seldom-used objects. The wall displays the art of the everyday: cooking utensils, pots, pans, posters, papers. Over the sink and refrigerator are larger shelves and cabinets for food and dishes.

Right: This kitchen-as-show-room uses open shelving to display culinary sculpture. Favorite posters and prints hung from floor to ceiling—as well as an American flag, in a wave to nostalgia—carry the gallery motif right to the top. An off-beat storage design: scarves and hats tossed on an antique chair hung on the wall. This room proves again that anything—from stuffed animals to old chairs—can become art when the frame is your frame of mind.

SLEEPING PLACES

Traditionally, the bedroom's been a space reserved for retiring, a place where we escaped from it all, a room for dressing and undressing (and a few things in between), but mainly it was the victim of a stern Victorian closed-door policy.

We have come a long way since white sheets and bedroom furnishings could only be bought in sets—ensembles—those suites of beds, along with an elaborate headboard, matching dressers (a tall one for the man, a short, fat one for the woman) and two matching night tables for a pair of ever-so-matching lamps. In 1952 those bedroom ensembles hit their peak (or nadir, some would say) when a furniture manufacturer sold one million "I Love Lucy" bedroom sets (just like the one on the show) in just ninety days.

Bedrooms are finally beginning to wake up. These Rip Van Winkles of apartment life have finally learned to do other things besides sleep. Now, for a variety of reasons from limited space to a new sense of place, bedrooms have become the alternate living rooms.

Now that the lights are on and the door is open we have changed our notions about comfort and utility. As you will see, there are many ideas that can solve the problem bedroom. Multifunction pieces solve stor-

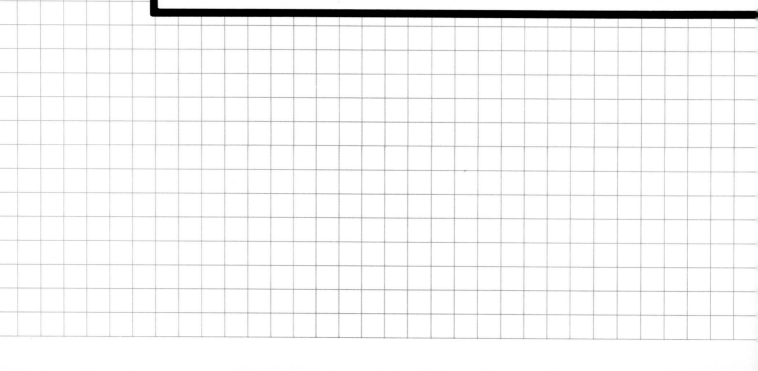

age problems: Beds now behave like sofas, desks become dressers, bolsters hold yesterday's and tonight's linens. It is often more handy to hang up jewelry on hooks out in the open, which makes for functional art. You will see how you can even hang your clothes on the wall. (If they look good on you, think what they will do for your walls.)

The old prescriptions for Proper Bedroom Decorating Etiquette have finally and mercifully run out. Now anything goes: chrome carts, wicker baskets, tall trees, wave-quilted movers' pads, lamps that formerly felt at home only in the office. Our bedrooms have blossomed into growing gardens, galleries of art and sufficient storage both in and out of the closet. And bed linens—printed and patterned in every hue, all with enough character to reflect ours, no matter whose initials are on them.

Bedrooms are no longer just bedrooms. They are offices and eating areas and anything else. Because more than any other room in the apartment, the bedroom gives you permission to kick off your shoes and make yourself at home. Finally, the bedroom has learned something from itself: to relax. And if you use your imagination while you are awake, your bedroom can make for pleasant dreams.

Cottage Industry

This room-to-wake-up-in is a sunny morning—clear, bright, simple and precocious—all friendly checks and geometrics. Its white is as fresh as Jersey eggs—not stark, but crisp—almost nautical when teamed with bands and boxes of bright blue. It is naïve in the best sense, consciously nostalgic, with all the wit and charm of the old Sunday funny papers.

And it is filled with crafty ideas you can pull off in a trice, without being a whiz in the needle-and-thread department. The no-sew country quilt is nervy enough to use this obvious-but-do-I-dare shortcut: all-purpose white glue. Six yards of white felt, 75 inches wide, and one yard of blue felt will do it. The blue gets diced into 184 3 x 3" squares, applied with a thin bead of glue around the edges of each square and an X of glue in the center. Stick in place; press with a warm iron. The white felt is cut in half, one piece for the top, one for backing. You can even get away with gluing the two pieces of white felt to each other if sewing seams is too daunting.

Instant country quilt—and it will stand up to dry cleaning. The glass canisters with the country-store look are from the five-and-ten, stenciled at home with cherries and checks.

Below: A gallery of fabric-framed family snaps. Fabric scraps (men's handkerchiefs, here) are stitched into tubes, stuffed with polyester fiber and sewn together at the corners. For a rigid backing, use cardboard sandwiched between two layers of felt.

Walls: White

Floors: More white

Windows: White pleated blinds

Lighting: Paris Metro lamps, twin-mounted for reading in bed

Photos: Thomas Hooper

Pining for You

Everything in this countrified bedroom is yellowed—and mellowed—with age. It matters not that the individual pieces span some 75 years of history. Their common bond is the warmth they emanate. A carved Art Nouveau mirror hangs without apology over a plain pine chest, and a down-filled chaise of Roaring Twenties vintage cozies up to a fine bamboo parlor table of the 1890s. Even the two pine pieces are different styles, though both are of English ancestry. The dresser on the left is mid-1800s; the wardrobe at right is turn of the century. With carving, molding and tasseled pulls, it's somewhat fancier than most pine you'll find.

Compared to French and American, English pine is the most available and the most affordable pine around. The old cupboards and catchalls of the working classes have become what golden oak used to be: hotly sought after, this time for unpretentious beauty and hardy utilitarian design. In fact, oak's poor country cousin is now priced higher than oak itself.

Filtering the daylight are curtains fashioned out of old and not-so-old lace panels, every one a different pattern, and so what?

Dark linen fabric stapled to the walls does a superb job of camouflaging badly cracked plaster.

Walls: Linen fabric hides cracks

Windows: Unmatched lace panels

Lighting: Reproduction ceiling fan incorporating lamp

Photos: Thomas Hooper

Dream Schemes

Forget the Puritan ethic—even if life can't always be a bed of roses, your sleeping quarters certainly can. What you see here is romantic fantasy, the stuff sweet dreams are made of.

Right: Four swirled Nouveaulike wooden posts, bought for next to nothing in an antique store specializing in architectural salvage, become existential bedposts—they don't support anything except the fantasy. (Shorter sections of fence or porch posts could become terrific table legs or pedestals for plants or sculpture.) Become an urban archaeologist:

Seek out old house parts at auctions, antique stores, estate sales and wrecking companies. Porch posts, railings, balusters, windows, panel doors, mantels and sections of gingerbread molding add instant distinction to a space short on history. The bedposts shown here are attached to a frame around the box spring made of lengths of 1 x 6. The airy canopy is a piece of canvas stapled to wooden dowels and hung from the ceiling with cup hooks and monofilament. A complete matched set of pillow shams, dust ruffle, comforter and sheets in a pattern that recalls the cabbage

roses so profuse in the past enhances the sense of lingering nostalgia. Bamboo side tables, hanging lampshades made of paper parasols and a new rug that faithfully captures the hooked handiwork of the 1920s lay on the period charm.

Below: A glorious little sleep house is constructed of easy-to-cut pine lattice panels from the lumberyard or garden supply center. The mattress rests on a plywood platform framed with more lattice panels.

Garden-variety bed linens are a relatively inexpensive way of bringing the room into bloom.

Photo: Thomas Hooper

Vanilla Crash Pad

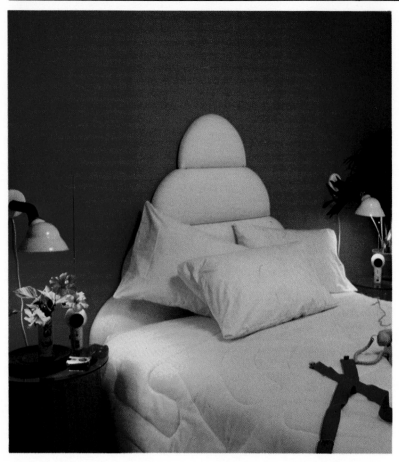

A bedroom that's mostly bed—a true crash pad for nightly splash-downs and early-A.M. launchings.

HOW TO DO IT
Ice-Cream Bed:

Materials: Start with two box springs surrounded by a padded bed frame. For bed frame and headboard, you'll need:

  4 1 x 8s to fit box spring sides
  2 1 x 8s to fit box spring foot
  4 1 x 8s cut with curved ends to shape the headboard
  4 4" corner braces with screws
  18 6" mending plates with screws
  2½" thick polyester foam

Build a bed frame 2" wider and longer than box springs (to allow room for bedding). Staple foam to edges of each board, Wrap each board with fabric (sheets are fine) to get the rounded effect; staple to the back. Assemble padded boards

with four mending plates at sides and three at foot; use two braces at each corner.

For the headboard, use a saber saw to cut curved ends on four boards; cover with foam and fabric (see illustration) and assemble with mending plates. Hang on wall or attach to bed with 1 x 4s nailed to headboard and springs.

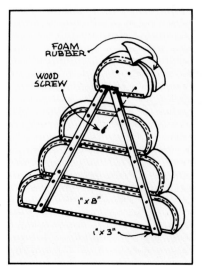

Walls: Hot red; neon letters from demolished supermarket sign

Windows: Mover's pad curtains on wooden rod

Lighting: Industrial lamps

Photos: Thomas Hooper

Murphy's Law

You remember Murphy beds, those drop-down mattresses that provided such a wealth of gag material for the Marx Brothers and the Three Stooges—but did you know they're still around? Today's store-bought Murphy beds take up only 18″ of precious floor space in their upright position. With an easy one-handed boost, this one springs to attention against the wall and hides there behind tieback drapes made from two flat sheets. The drapes slide along a curved piece of plastic water pipe on large wooden rings. The bedroom that waits in the wings is complete to the last detail. Two fabric-shaded fringed lamps, a very slim wall poster and a cylindrical plastic night table all fit inside, so when night falls you don't have to reshuffle.

Outside the enclave, the ornate ceramic mirror, secondhand pedestal table, small-print wallpaper and masses of gladiolus purvey that boudoir ambience—as does the abundant dust ruffle, which you can make yourself.

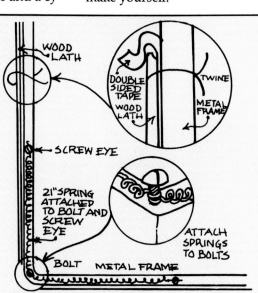

HOW TO DO IT
Double Murphy Bed:

Materials:

50 yards of gauze or mosquito netting, 45″ wide

2 rolls polyester batting, 36″ wide

3 8′ pieces of 1″ lath

25′ of twine

1 roll (about 20″) 1-inch double-stick foam tape

5 sash springs, 21″ long, from drapery store

6 1″ round head bolts, ⅛″ in diameter, with nuts

5 1″ eye bolts, ⅛″ diameter, 1″ long

Cut the lath to fit the foot rail and both side rails of the bed frame. Apply double-stick tape to one side of each piece. Stick the lath to the outer edge of the rails (press hard) and tie with twine at 1-foot intervals. Cut polyester batting in half to make it 18″ wide; fold so it's three layers thick and about 6″ wide, and staple it to lath strips around the bed frame. Next, drill holes for the small bolts through the top of the metal frame in each of the four corners (see illustration). On each side of the bed frame, drill three more holes, one 18″ from foot, one 37″ from foot and one 55″ from foot. Drill another hole through top of frame in center of foot rail. Use two sash springs per side and one at foot of bed. Stretch them out, thread them through eye bolts and fasten at ends with nuts and bolts. With springs in place, loop fabric over top of spring, push it between spring and bed and drape it to the floor. Continue around entire frame, making large circles with fabric, pinching and looping around spring, draping to floor and up around spring again.

Photos: Thomas Hooper

Sleep Island

Sleeping on this bed is like floating in a restful sea of gray. The "island" is a carpeted plywood platform. What's great is that it's completely self-contained—doing away with the whole complicated question of night tables, headboard and bookcases in one fell swoop. It is even wired for a clock, a radio and some inexpensive clamp-on architect's lights, which work ideally for reading in bed. The bed is sunken into the freestanding platform, with mattress and box spring resting on the floor.

The wooden chaise is an exact replica of the deck chairs used on transatlantic crossings in the days when great liners regularly plied the sea.

The poster on the left wall is an oft-reproduced French Art Nouveau advertising poster by Alphonse Mucha, accorded unusual star treatment here with behind-glass mounting and a gilt frame.

HOW TO DO IT

Island Bed: With the mattress and box spring on the floor, build a U-shaped frame of 1 x 12s around the sides and foot of the bed. Nail the frame to a headboard made of 1 x 12s and ¾"-thick plywood. An indentation for books and sundries can be made to the dimensions shown above or altered to suit your needs (allow for carpeting in your measurements). Run electrical outlets up through both sides of the headboard and drill two holes on top for lamps. You can carpet it yourself with adhesive and a heavy-duty staple gun, or hire a professional installer to deal with all the tricky corners.

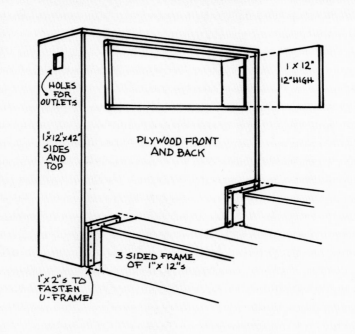

HOLES FOR OUTLETS

1"x12"x42" SIDES AND TOP

PLYWOOD FRONT AND BACK

1 x 12" 12"HIGH

3 SIDED FRAME OF 1"x 12"s

1"x 2"s TO FASTEN U-FRAME

Walls: Classic gray

Floor: Industrial carpet to match platform bed

Lighting: Techy tracks

Window: Narrow blinds

Photos: Peter M. Fine/Design: Kevin Walz

The Wall-all

Split levels worked for suburbia, and they can work for city bedrooms, too. Here, half the room is raised to meet the windows. Dividing the higher "bedroom" from the ground-level study niche is a headboard/wall with three shelves—a long, curved one on the study side and two small rectangles on either side of the bed. Covered in rich-colored plastic laminate to match the plush carpeting on the platform, the wall becomes a piece of interior ar-

chitecture where once there was merely air. It may look like a job for a master craftsman, but it's really just a simple, waist-high 2 x 4 stud wall faced with ¼" plywood.

The massive, carved bookcase/desk is a made-today number with designs on classical architecture. Continuity between the study and sleep areas is maintained by a steady flow of butterscotch-colored walls and warm textures, from the oriental rug to the quilt.

The Complete Retreat

This bedroom looks luxurious —and that is exactly the point. Yet it is also an office, a study and a second living room.

White-on-white gives this room its fresh look—particularly because of the comforter, draperies and shiny white metal lamps.

More easy mixing: rattan end tables, a clean-lined four-poster of natural elm and a velvet recliner. The bonnet-topped secretary is an eighteenth-century English reproduction.

At the window is a soft, unfussy version of the Austrian shade, with a Mylar reflector to let in double sunlight and give a boost to the low ceiling.

HOW TO DO IT:
Curtain: Each window takes a piece of fabric 6" wider than the window and 2½ times as long. Hem the bottom and sides by machine. Sew on three strips of Austrian shirr tape (a double-thick twill tape encasing a drawstring). Finish the top, allowing a 1½" channel for the curtain rod and 2" for the self-ruffle. To shirr the curtain, pull the cords together, tie them and tuck inside folds.

HOW TO DO IT
Reflector: Make a frame of 1 x 2s and fasten with L brackets. Pull the Mylar taut around the frame. Staple in place. Rest frame on windowsill and nail top corners to ceiling.

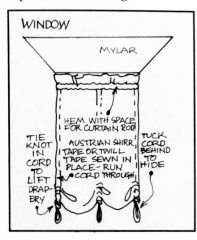

Photo: Bradley Olman

Tenting Tonight

Right: Typical apartment problems—veiny walls, shriveled shag and peeling window frames—can be inexpensively and quickly solved with some obvious solutions: sheets, simple rugs and thinking twice about things you never considered.

First the walls: Without any of the fuss of paint or spackling, hanging up patterned sheets will instantly alter the atmosphere with one showy stroke. First a strip of wood lath was tacked where the wall meets the ceiling. The sheets were stapled to the lath, making loose pleats. (Double flat sheets are exactly 8′ long—the same height as most rooms so no cutting or hemming is necessary.) Overlap the sheets where they join and make sure they meet over a window so you can tie back the "curtains."

The comforter is made from the same sheets (matching comforters can often be purchased) and the bolster covers are made from yet another sheet. With what is left over, make a dust ruffle that can be attached to the bottom box spring with Velcro fastening strips (so the ruffle can be easily removed for cleaning).

Two rattan headboards make a sitting place out of the bed.

Unexpected charm from unexpected places: a child's chair works as a night table; a wicker wine rack on the windowsill holds plants and magazines; sisal matting on the floor covers up unsightly shag, without losing softness underfoot.

Below: The wardrobe is little more than two metal utility cabinets with four panels of lattice screen doors. To put it together: Hinge two panels of lattice screen together and attach to each side of the cases (you might have to put two shelving units together). Cut legs of the screens (be sure to adjust bottom shelf to fit flush with bottom of screen). To hide the sides, ¼″ tempered hardboard panels are bolted to the 1 x 2 frame with finish washers and stove bolts. If the screen is a tad narrow, screw 1 x 2s where the doors end. Finish off with wooden pulls, magnetic door catches and clear plastic storage boxes.

Photo: Thomas Hooper

George Washington Slept Here

A city-slick high rise can feel like a country inn. It is a matter of reinterpreting a style without reproducing a stamped-out carbon copy.

The canopy gracing the new four-poster looks old—but it is really a lace tablecloth stretched over the poles. Country green and white wallpaper matches the lace-edged fabric that covers the inexpensive bedside lamps on either side of the bed. The rocker was bought unfinished, then painted white and given dime-store decals for instant heritage.

Prefab 4 x 8 sheets nailed to the wall quickly offer farmhouse paneling. The chair-rail molding for the wainscoting is made of 1 x 4 boards, wide enough to be used for extra shelf space.

Near the window (drapery-less but framed in handsome painted molding) hangs a porch swing. (Make sure it is firmly fixed into the ceiling joists.) The pillows involve more cutting than sewing (a doily sandwich of fabric circles and batting, stitched inside the edge of a large lace circle). Overhead, flowering plants bloom in market baskets lined with foil.

Photo: Thomas Hooper

A Turn on Tradition

A crossbreed of new and old—old ideals mixed with new ideas—is what makes a room more reinterpretation than reproduction.

Although everything here looks old, it is all new—either store bought or homemade. This room is kept clean looking by furnishing with restraint.

The most traditional fabric of all—linen—is seen everywhere but the twist is that they are all linen dish towels.

A trip to a building supplier will get you a bed. Buy turned spindles and then assemble them into a stately bed frame.

All wood pieces are stripped to their natural essence. The reproduction ash armoire and bedside commode are classic eighteenth-century French Provincial—the simple folk carving is the key to their beauty. Unfinished window shutters keep the light in as well as out.

HOW TO DO IT
Bed: To make the upright bedposts, use turned spindles. They are anchored at the top with closet poles and at the bottom with boards.

HOW TO DO IT
Linen Quilt: You will need: Dish towels. For a double bed quilt (finished size 80" x 88"), use 12 24" x 33" towels.

A sheet to use as a backing. Or buy twice as many dish towels and make it reversible.

Polyester fiberfill quilt batting. (Comes in sheet-size dimensions—buy as many as you want for fatness. Nine were used here.)

Colored yarn for tufting. To make the quilt: Sew the dish towels together in a giant patchwork. Then seam the patchwork to the sheet backing (cut to the same size) right sides together, around three sides.

Pile the layers of polyester

batting on top of the big wrong-side-out cover and loosely hand-stitch batting to the three seam allowances and along the top edge of the open side (do not sew towels and sheet together). Turn right side out, and hand sew the opening shut.

For tufts, cut yarn in 8" lengths and, using a wide-eyed needle, sew from the top, through the batting and sheet backing, and back up and out. Knot and tie bows. Tuft either in a random pattern or spaced geometrically.

To make pillowcases: Simply sew two dish towels right sides together, leaving one end open.

HOW TO DO IT
Dust Ruffle: Dish towel fabric or dish towels.

An old sheet large enough to fit the top of your box spring. To make dust ruffle: Use 1½ to 2 times as much fabric as is needed to fit around three sides of your bed. Cut it wide enough

to hang from the top of the box spring to the floor, allowing for a ½" seam at the top and a hem at the bottom. Cut the sheet to fit the top of the box spring, plus ½" seam allowance. Machine-gather the dish towel fabric along the top edge; adjust gathers to fit around the sheet. Sew the ruffle to the sheet, right sides together.

HOW TO DO IT
Dish Towel Shutter Inserts: Buy shutters that have spring-tip rods on the back at the top and bottom to allow fabric to be slipped on (or you can staple or thumbtack the fabric to the backs of the shutters). Measure the length from rod to rod and cut your dish towels to that length, plus 3" for hems. For width, cut the fabric 1½ to 2 times as wide as the opening.

Sew a 1" casing at the top and bottom of the fabric, slip the rods into the casings and fit the rods back on the shutters.

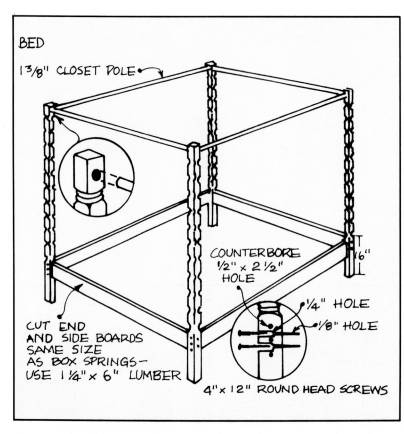

BED

1 3/8" CLOSET POLE

COUNTERBORE ½" x 2½" HOLE

CUT END AND SIDE BOARDS SAME SIZE AS BOX SPRINGS—USE 1¼" x 6" LUMBER

¼" HOLE
⅛" HOLE

6"

4" x 12" ROUND HEAD SCREWS

Photo: Bradley Olman

Sweet Retreat

What was once a tiny maid's room is now an efficient (though still tiny) hideaway, with all elements down-scaled to squeeze in a maximum of function and charm. Peeling plaster and dark corners are disguised by a provincial print fabric stapled to the walls. The pale color and delicate print open up the space without overwhelming it. Moldings painted coordinating beige soften the room's hard edges. Lengths of pine shelving are painted beige to match the woodwork for a custom, built-in look. Natural wood shutters at the window and on the bathroom door open on bi-fold hinges for space efficiency.

The furnishings are of necessity diminutive, but that doesn't cramp their style. The nineteenth-century polished iron Directoire bed measures even smaller than a single, making a comfy curl-up-and-read spot or an extra bed for not-too-tall friends. A panoply of pillows supports the illusion of abundance.

Below: The Louis XV-style desk, with cabriole legs, a pull-out top and six little drawers, was chosen for its small size. Even the 1800s fruitwood side chair is proportionately petite.

Walls: Small-print wallpaper

Floor: Wall-to-wall carpeting

Windows: Natural wood louvers

Lighting: New, but old-looking

Low-Slung Sleepers

This bedroom doesn't seem to have been designed so much as art directed—a typically small and predictable bedroom transformed into a working beauty—not through expensive fabrics and furniture—but through a few new ways of turning boring into bold.

The first thing to go was the old metal frame mattress/box spring combination. In its place is a frame built from three painted hollow-core closet doors (and a 1 x 4 crosspiece on the headboard side that doesn't show). Instead of a headboard, the wall is painted the same color as the box—a space saver that lets the dramatically bold black flow right up the wall. (It also nicely frames the Jim Dine poster.) The bedspread is really well-priced prequilted fabric used for ski jackets. The fabric was stitched at the quilting lines, making the seams invisible. Like the bedspread, the room is tucked in, wrapped up—neat and uncluttered.

Inexpensive plastic cubes, secured with Molly bolts, float on the wall, providing bedside storage that doesn't waste floor space. A wooden cube holds not a piece of sculpture but a cactus, showing it off in the best possible light.

A bright red plastic chair highlights the black, as does the cupid poster, which receives an extra large frame to give it breathing space.

HOW TO DO IT
Bed Box: Build the frame from three 15"-wide hollow-core doors and a 1 x 4 crosspiece. Paint with semigloss enamel; set mattress inside on the floor.

Below: If your sofa has to lead a double life, at least let it be a romantic one. This good-looking rolled-arm convertible is covered in tough corduroy on the outside, done up in soft pink linens within.

The standing lamp, with its opaque sea-shell shade, casts the glow right where you want it. Plant stands glossed up with fourteen coats of blazing red lacquer are ever-ready occasional tables for all-the-time use.

Three-dimensional étagères—freestanding units that look good from every angle—defy storage definitions by housing dishes, books, bar supplies.

Photos: Bradley Olman

Cocoon

Scaled-down furnishings do not necessarily make a smallish room seem any bigger. If you take the opposite tack, like the one spectacular bed here, the small room will open up to accommodate the design, particularly if that piece is as dramatic as this contemporary four-poster bed. After setting the stage with one eye-catcher, think carefully about the room's graphic design.

This bedroom works with squares. To balance the strong-lined, stately bed, a few smaller engineered pieces fill in the square.

Start with a desk—cleverly put together from a hanging shelf with a stack of roll-out plastic drawers tucked below. It is a smart way to stretch space while getting around an awkwardly placed heating unit. A mirror visually widens a narrow space while the frame echoes the four-poster lines. Nearby, the hanging globe fixture and gooseneck pharmacist's lamp provide curves for contrast, and pick up the shape of the horn poster.

HOW TO DO IT
Hanging Desk: Have a lumber-yard cut a ¾" piece of plywood 18" x 36". Cover exposed edge with ¾" molding tape and paint. Screw two L brackets to the wall 28" up from the floor. Screw hooks or eyebolts to the outer corners of the desk and to the ceiling. Screw desk to wall brackets and run wires from ceiling bolts to desk. To secure, wrap wire around bolt.

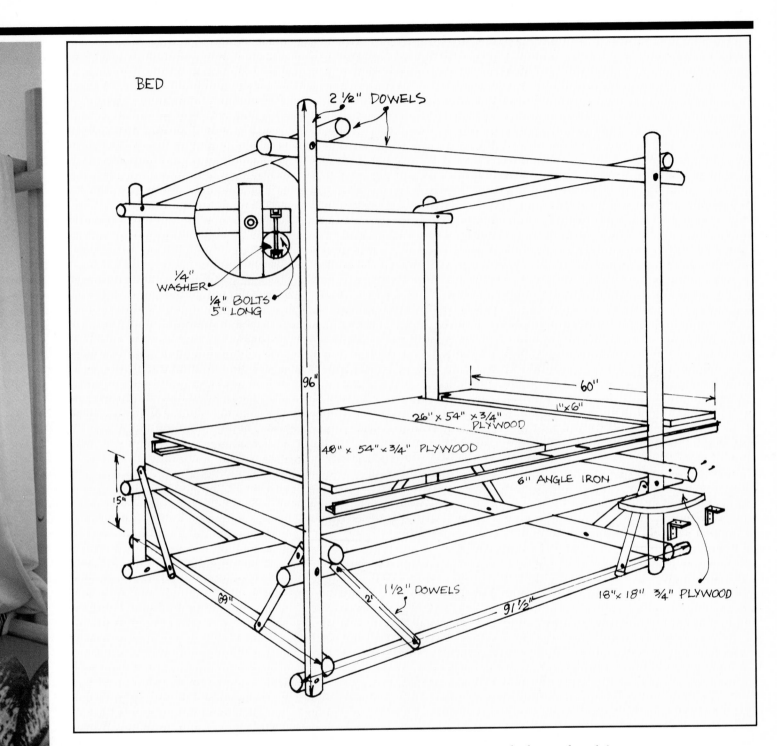

BED

2 ½" DOWELS

¼" WASHER

¼" BOLTS 5" LONG

96"

15"

6' ANGLE IRON

26" X 54" X ¾" PLYWOOD

48" X 54" X ¾" PLYWOOD

60"

1" X 6"

69"

2'

1 ½" DOWELS

91 ½"

18" X 18" ¾" PLYWOOD

HOW TO DO IT

Four-Poster Bed: Built from sturdy 2½"-diameter pine dowels, this grid-system bed is really three horizontal frames held together by four uprights. The bottom two frames are braced by short dowels. When bolting it together, it will help to have a friend around to hold the uprights steady.

To make it easier, have the lumberyard cut all dowels to length (see measurements in drawing). Use 5" stove bolts (¼" in diameter) to bolt together each of the three rectangular frames and to attach them to the uprights. Drill holes as shown and countersink the bolts. (Be sure to line up the holes carefully.)

Secure the short dowels (1½" diameter) with 4" stove bolts (¼" in diameter). Screw in 6' sections of angle iron for support on the long sides of the bed. The bed board is made of two pieces of plywood, one cut to 26" x 54", the other to 48" x 54". The foundation dowels at the side of the bed will extend several inches past the head. To fill this space (and keep pillows from slipping), build a shelf from a 60" 1 x 6 board. Cut it to fit around the dowels and lay flat. For the canopy, hem and wrap mosquito netting.

Oldies but Goodies

Style is where you discover it; especially in everyday items waiting to be used in new ways.

It is hard to believe that something right under your nose—the handkerchief—could look so stunning, but look again. This hanky quilt—stitched together from dozens of secondhand printed kerchiefs—splashes on a whole style from disparate parts. The crazy-quilt quality here (all over the room, not just on the bed) has transformed an average space into an intriguing place with warmth and coziness throughout.

HOW TO DO IT
Hanky Quilt:

You Will Need: Hankies (about 54 for a double-bed quilt, finished size 80" x 88"). If you can not find inexpensive old ones at the thrift store, try new brightly patterned dime-store handkerchiefs, washed several times.

A sheet to sew the hankies to and a plain backing sheet (or collect twice as many hankies and make it reversible).

Polyester fiberfill quilt batting (comes in sheet-size dimensions). Use up to nine layers for serviceable warmth.

How to Make It: Lay the hankies on one sheet in any pattern you like and stitch them down by hand or machine. Sew the hanky sheet to the backing sheet, right sides together, around three sides, about ¾" from the edge. Pile the layers of batting on top of your big wrong-side-out case and loosely hand stitch batting to the three seam allowances and along the top edge of the open side. (Do not sew the hanky sheet and the backing sheet closed yet). Turn the quilt right side out and hand sew the opening shut.

Calm and Collected

Another myth buried: Antiques do not always come in clutters. In this invitingly open space the temptation to add just one more piece was resisted. All the vintage pieces are showcased in this setting, yet the result, far from looking museumlike or untouchable, is comfortably warm and livable.

Turn-of-the-century brass beds (actually a brass sleeve around a steel core), once a staggering $11 in the Sears catalog, are now hard to score bargains on. Prices go up with every twist and turn of detailing in knobs and etched rings on the spindles, curves, four-posters—the fatter the better.

The oak-framed, beveled-edge mirror is a contemporary of the bed and was originally the top of an old dresser. Milk glass chandeliers (easy to re-wire) lit schoolrooms for decades; find the best prices at wrecking and salvage companies.

Old quilts are also getting pricy. Look for good condition, color, design and intricacy in the pieces and quilting.

The floor is left bare, in keeping with the spare plan.

There is no need to keep antiques segregated into periods. The accessories, like the bedside lamp and clock, are thirties and forties specials, found at secondhand shops.

Photo: Erik Arnesen

The Bed in Red

Walls: Repeat pattern wallpaper—Victorian feeling, contemporary design

Floor: Greek Flokati wool rug

Windows: White pleated blinds

Take off on the old four-poster with a red metal tube-framed bed. It's station central for sleeping, reading, lounging, typing, and watching TV.

Bed linens in forest green add depth and drama to the room.

The night tables on either side of the bed are office files, reconsidered.

A supergraphic poster of a benchmark Modernist chair echoes exactly the colors and angles that pull the room's other elements together. A lacy palm softens the setting.

190

Kids' Space

One thing that hasn't changed much since the fifties is the off-screen voice of the parent yelling, "Clean up your room!" Children's rooms tend to be organizational nightmares of constantly multiplying possessions. It starts in earliest infancy with playpens, swings, changing tables—and takes off from there.

As kids grow, so grow their parents . . . desperate for storage solutions for all the toys, books, records, puzzles, easels, boots, bicycles, souvenirs, tutus and trucks. The best you can do is provide a place for everything, even if everything is not always in its place.

What *has* changed since the fifties is that kids' rooms are more kid-size, with low shelves accessible even to toddlers. Keep storage child-scaled and you'll all have at least a chance of keeping things in order.

The other thing that's changed is color. Pastels used to be *de rigueur.* Then psychologists decreed that primaries were intellectually stimulating, and there was a national wash of red, blue and yellow. Today, if you ask an older child what colors he or she would like, you may hear something surprising, like "black and white," or "pink and purple." So stay flexible, and don't baby-talk a kid's room.

But remember that a child's room is part of your home—it's okay to let it reflect your grown-up tastes as well as your child's needs . . . at least until the room's occupant is old enough to hold sway.

Kid Space

Rooms for children once meant endless little duckies and decals; cute was the order of the day. Somewhere between toilet training and puberty, the room went through at least three changes of scenery for the growing-up kid and three times the work and expense for the parent.

No more. There are alternatives today—thanks to new and available products and materials and a changing attitude about children's needs. Now it makes sense for a kid's room to grow up along with the kid.

This room, for example, is designed for the way children really live—not the way we would like them to live. They are messy, and they like playing around. And thus a room with furniture that works the way today's kids play. Here's why:

Kids need room for activities and space for imagination. That is why the bed is elevated and the bed/dresser/desk unit is compact so there is a lot of floor space in the center.

Remember that old apple tree for climbing and building tree houses? Here the bedposts and ladder are an urban tree; the bed, an indoor tree house.

Kids are tough on furniture and so this tube furniture is right for rough-housing, with no sharp edges.

Kids do grow up. Furniture manufacturers keep forgetting that. When the child is too old for the tree house, the top half of the bed comes off to be regular adult height; the chair adjusts for longer legs too.

Open storage is important for children's toys. Another open storage idea shown below: bright, easy-to-make canvas bags grouped on the wall.

Protection is needed for those many kid projects. Roll vinyl onto the floor and everything goes when anything spills.

The Weekend Room

The territorial imperative applies to children, too. They need their own space, even if it's half a room shared with a sibling or a corner of the living-room, used only for weekend visits to a single parent's apartment.

This movable unit—essentially a partition constructed of eight hollow-core doors, ply-wood shelves, hinges and casters—clearly defines the child's universe. The essence of sanity for the part-time parent and visiting offspring could be a room like this that says, in its specialness, "you live here, too"—something a makeshift bedding-down-on-the-sofa could never convey.

Flexibility is at the heart of the system's success. The hinged sections change shape to accommodate an extra sleep-over guest, a larger child or to condense the room when its weekend occupant is not there. It offers storage for belongings on both sides of the divide: parental ones displayed on the out-facing side (below), kid's things—needed only inter-mittently—within. All shelves and a desk for homework are adjustable via a hole-and-peg arrangement to keep up with changing needs.

A sofa that opens into a bed, a lightweight plastic desk chair, a stool on wheels and some stackable baskets round out the fittings. The total effect is a special space full of familiar objects that states its message clearly: "Welcome home."

Photos: Bernard Askienazy

Not for Infants Only

The basic premise behind this colorful bastion of babydom is simple: Everything in the room is attractive, indestructible and easily cleaned . . . but not easily outgrown.

Kids grow up fast, and so should their furniture. Buying a crib that converts to a youth bed or a changing table that becomes a desk requires only a little foresight. What works for an infant should work for a toddler—and well beyond.

The crib unit here (below right), double-decked out with storage drawers, is designed to grow into a child-size bed (below left). The presto chango: The crib bars go into storage, and the trio of small drawers steps down to make room for a larger mattress.

The blue-and-white checkerboard on the floor is vinyl tile—handy, cheap and cheerful. Skip the rug; it turns spills into disasters and impedes the progress of riding toys.

High-gloss enamel on the walls is the number-one choice for ease of crayon removal.

Leave as much floor space in the clear as possible, even if it means pushing the necessities flat against the walls. That open space is often the city child's only rainy-day playground.

The multicolored heart and balloon prints and the blue-sky sheets are irresistibly childlike, but clear and simple. They're vastly better than the cutesy designs that used to be the standard for children's rooms and with which wallpaper and fabric companies still occasionally try to woo us.

Low, child-accessible shelves ring the room. When children can reach their own toys, it's more independence for them, less work for you. Save the higher wall areas for artwork and posters. Remember, a young child is low to the ground, and so should his or her room be.

Cloth pockets on the wall are convenient drop-ins for toys, dolls, art supplies. Fabric roll-up shades below the built-in shelf hide baby's belongings or an out-of-season radiator.

The diaper-changing area—a vital center of activity for the first year or two—has a cloth and clear-plastic-wrapped pad for now; later, it will take the load of an expanding library. Baskets that hold diapers will later contain building toys. The mini-closet pole carries baby smocks; later, small jackets and tops.

Even the yellow and white chair flips into a step stool when the climbing age sets in.

Walls: High-gloss paint for easy wipe-downs

Storage: Low to the ground

Floor: Vinyl tile checkerboard

Windows: Homemade curtains and wooden window guard

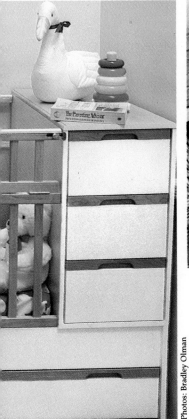

Photos: Bradley Olman

The Room That Grows Up

If you do a complete overhaul on your child's room with every other birthday, you'll be in the garage-sale business full-time. Instead, set up a space that is flexible enough to change with your child. The key: furniture that doesn't scream "baby!"

Below: Freestanding metal shelves from the lumberyard or hardware store harbor an array of brightly colored plastic storage bins for baby needs.

Plastic drawers stack up under hollow-core doors to make a changing surface that serves its fleeting purpose, then transforms back into still-useful components. The sofa sits by day, flips into a bed by night.

Pick a not-too-babyish fabric for curtains so they can hang around for a while. Likewise, the dhurrie rug in red and orange muffles noise, adds color, washes well.

Right: Same room, a few years later: The crib is replaced with bunk beds, and the nursing rocker's gone back to the living room, but everything else remains to serve another day.

The shelves go against the wall to open up more running-around space. The plastic bins are more useful than ever for stowing toys and the tens of thousands of plastic pieces that comprise them.

The drawer units split up into shorter stacks and, with two hollow-core doors, become a wide and wonderful play surface. The sofa, curtains, bulletin board and rug are still in place, keeping up the good work.

Old-Time Comfort Station

Somewhere along the line this bathroom had been modernized —made to look contemporary, despite the older fixtures, which have workable charm, and despite the older architectural details such as the wainscoting and medicine cabinet. This place needed "downdating" not updating. You can also install this more-or-less thirties look if you are renovating— good, old sinks, toilets and tubs can be found at salvage yards or demolition sites.

The rest of the room "downdates" just as easily: older wide, wooden venetian blinds from the twenties, and a new vinyl floor replaces the usual green tile.

The other surprise here is what is on the wall—old framed prints, family photographs, sheet music, magazine advertisements, lighthearted letters. The marble shelf in their midst is right at home. The old shaving mirror was rescued from a secondhand shop. Under the sink is an old wooden footlocker that handles the overflow of towels and toiletries.

All the accessories—the wooden toilet seat, the porcelain faucet handles as well as the soap dish and towel racks— abound at flea markets and thrift shops.

Band-Aids

Storage: Antique medicine cabinets

Lighting: Industrial goosenecks

Walls: Self-adhesive wall covering

Floor: Rubber-backed carpet

The worst fault of this white-box bathroom was its predictability—the fixtures, medicine chest, lights, flooring and walls were carbon copies of every other high-rise bathroom. There was some under sink storage but not enough.

The idea was to warm it up quickly, to personalize it with a slick and bright look. Now everything has that built-in quality, yet you can take it right along when you move.

The specifics:

Some things seem very permanent until you tinker around with a screwdriver. You can usually take down a medicine chest (check for screws inside at the back), then replace it with a cabinet of your own choosing. (If it is not screwed into studs, you will need to use Molly bolts to put yours up.) This antique medicine chest brings the warmth of wood into an otherwise very clinical room.

Inexpensive, industrial gooseneck lamps, or most any lighting replacement, can be hooked right into the same wiring as the old one.

You can disguise ugly ceramic tiles with a coat of epoxy paint (as over the tiles in the shower) and crisp, self-adhesive vinyl wall covering.

A variety of modular, on-the-wall storage units stretches the nearly nonexistent counter space. This green plastic system fits right into the mounting of the old holders and can be taken off for easy cleaning.

Blot out a floor you do not like with rubber-backed wall-to-wall bathroom carpet. Cut it to fit and lay it on top of the existing flooring.

Photo: Bradley Olman

Hot and Cold Renovation

This room—pre-revival—is typical of the bathrooms you are confronted with in older houses. Barely the bare essentials. Outdated—but still working—fixtures. No storage. Shabby and uncomfortable.

Now look at it. Built-in natural wood cabinets and walls restored to a beauty it never knew before.

Here is how it happened.

The wainscoting and flooring are made with tongue-and-groove fir strips. (Nail one strip into place; the next strip slips into the first, and so on. Four coats of polyurethane seal the wood for even the most humid household.)

Sink pipes are boxed in by paneling. The front swings down, like a bin, for extra storage. Enclosing the tub adds a custom, built-in look.

Vinyl fabric goes on the wall —and stays there—with vinyl fabric paste.

A D-ring shower curtain rod gives you privacy-in-the-round where none existed before.

The window opens onto an airshaft. Opaque Plexiglas keeps the view of you rated G. The window opens down for air.

HOW TO DO IT

Sink Enclosure: For the basic frame you will make a 2 x 2 frame enclosing three sides of the sink. Fasten this frame to the wall with nails (into studs) or with toggle bolts.

The sides of the box are like the tub's sides, alternating 1 x 2s and 1 x 6s spaced apart.

To figure the size of the frame: A 2 x 2 should run across the front of the sink and be lined up flush with the sink corners. Then butt the side pieces against the front 2 x 2 and run them back to the wall. Figure the height of the frame from the floor to just under the lip of the sink. (Caulk between the underside of the sink and the top of the boards.)

To make the drop-down, bin-like door: The top and the bottom boards on the front of the sink are stationary so fasten them as you did the side boards. To have something to attach the catch to, put a horizontal 2 x 2 inside the front. Then build a 1 x 2 frame for the door (as shown) that will fit into the opening, leaving ½" clearance on each side. Use a magnetic catch as shown to close the door. Use butt hinges and add a chain so it will not drop open all the way to the floor.

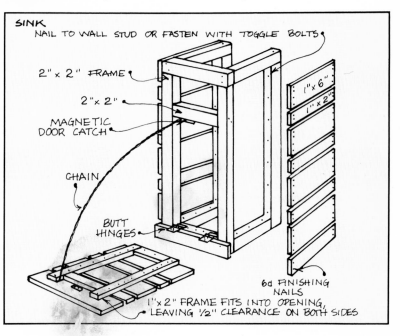

SINK
NAIL TO WALL STUD OR FASTEN WITH TOGGLE BOLTS
2" x 2" FRAME
2" x 2"
MAGNETIC DOOR CATCH
CHAIN
BUTT HINGES
1" x 6"
1" x 2"
6d FINISHING NAILS
1" x 2" FRAME FITS INTO OPENING, LEAVING ½" CLEARANCE ON BOTH SIDES

HOW TO DO IT

Bathtub Enclosure: Though complicated looking, if you reduce the box to its simplest elements, it is not so tough. The tub is surrounded by a frame of 2 x 2s on which boards are nailed to give it a finished, saunalike look.

First, you will need 2 x 2 pieces of lumber (fir was used here) the length of the tub, plus a foot or so. Cut the upright 2 x 2s to a height ¾" short of the lip of the tub. (The width, like the length, is up to you.) Then put the frame together with 8d finishing nails.

Nail 2 x 2s inside the top of the frame and just under the lip at each end of the tub. Cover the top with ¾" tongue-and-groove floorboards. Caulk between the lip of the tub and the boards.

For an interesting pattern on the sides: Use the tongue-and-groove boards again. Or alternate 1 x 2s and 1 x 6s, leaving a small space between each one to match the sink enclosure. Or simply nail 1 x 2s, 1 x 4s, 1 x 6s or 1 x 8s onto the frame (no spaces).

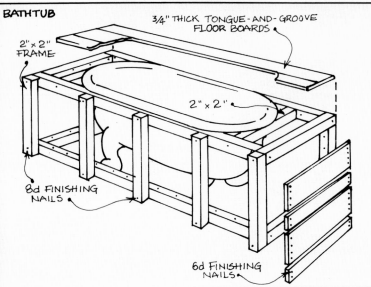

BATHTUB
2" x 2" FRAME
¾" THICK TONGUE-AND-GROOVE FLOOR BOARDS
2" x 2"
8d FINISHING NAILS
6d FINISHING NAILS

Urban Renewal

Under the influence of sleek industrial design, this small, square bathroom triples as a utility room and storage space as well.

Bring the turn-of-the-century look of ceiling tin (it is called sheet steel these days) down to eye level on the walls—a one-step tile effect without fuss. Three or four careful coats of polyurethane on both sides (before you handle it too much) are essential to keep the metal from rusting. Cut the tin to fit with metal cutting shears; then glue it up with panel adhesive.

Corner the space for storage: Triangular shelves are held up with wooden cleats. Plastic storage baskets stack underneath.

The tub is closed off with a simply constructed divider.

Opposite: You can fit everything into this bathroom, including the kitchen sink—literally. Why cope with a shallow bathroom model when eminently more functional sinks are available? Housed in this easily built, high-gloss white box (and supported by it), the kitchen sink looks right at home.

Over the sink: Lights that really work (you probably last saw them in a basement).

Below the sink: The chrome heater hangs on the wall to maximize floor space.

To the right, this wall-hung ironing board is designed for what you want from it most of the time—folded down out of the way. Take the legs off a small ironing board and hinge it to a 1 x 4 mounted on the wall (use toggle bolts or wood screws into a stud). Support the ironing board with a couple of flap-table hinges.

SINK

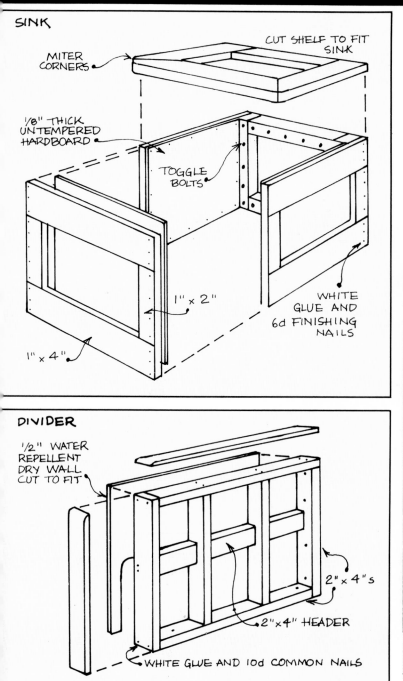

MITER CORNERS

CUT SHELF TO FIT SINK

1/8" THICK UNTEMPERED HARDBOARD

TOGGLE BOLTS

1" x 2"

1" x 4"

WHITE GLUE AND 6d FINISHING NAILS

DIVIDER

1/2" WATER REPELLENT DRY WALL CUT TO FIT

2" x 4"s

2" x 4" HEADER

WHITE GLUE AND 10d COMMON NAILS

HOW TO DO IT

Divider: To build the divider, first make a simple mini-wall—a frame of 2 x 4s with upright 2 x 4s inside. Add 2 x 4 headers in between the uprights. (Align the headers with the lip of the tub.)

Cut a piece of 1/2"-thick water-repellent dry wall to extend just above the edge of the tub lip. Nail it onto the headers. Nail dry wall on the other side.

Then put this wall at the end of the tub and secure it to both the floor and the wall. Use toggle bolts for the wall and 10d common nails for all but concrete floors. For concrete, drill 1/2" holes with a carbide bit, fill the holes with wooden pegs, then nail the mini-wall into the plugs.

To finish, nail a board across the open end and top of the wall. Use epoxy paint.

HOW TO DO IT

Sink Enclosure: To build the front and two sides: Each is a frame, consisting of 1 x 2s on the sides and 1 x 4s across the top and bottom. For the back: You will need extra support for the weight of the sink so build a frame of 2 x 2s. Glue and nail the four frames together, using white glue and 6d nails. Then cut the pieces of hardboard to fit the openings inside the front and side frames and attach them with 3/4" #16 brads.

Next mount the box on the wall with toggle bolts (or wood screws if you can find studs to screw into). Concentrate the toggles at the top of the frame so they will help support the sink's weight.

Make a shelf frame for the lip of the sink to sit on. (The size depends on how much shelf you want.) If you want rounded corners, cut with a jigsaw, then sand smooth. Fasten the shelf to the box with white glue and finishing nails. Fill the nail holes with wood filler.

Use epoxy paint for water resistance, then drop in the sink and caulk around it.

Short Takes

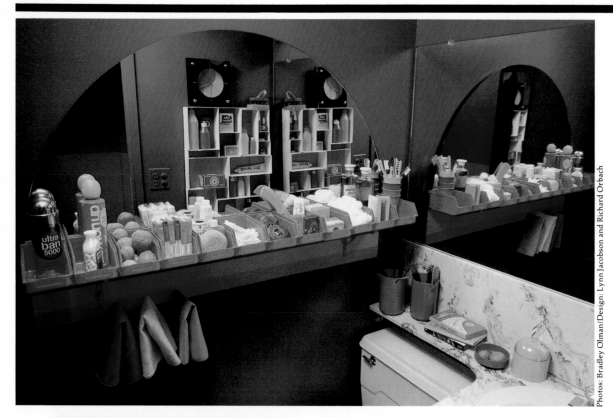

Photos: Bradley Olman/Design: Lynn Jacobson and Richard Orbach

Top Left: This bright bathroom storage solution brings those back-of-the-cabinet items out into the open so you can find them. Individual plastic bins set on a glass shelf keep everything handy. The stripe design under the shelf can be applied with paint but vinyl paper or fabric tape is easier. Dish towel racks, meant for the kitchen, work in the bathroom as well.

Below Left: Even the most ordinary bathroom can have flair along with function. The regulation medicine cabinet was removed here and replaced with a wall-length mirror and a homemade shelf unit. Plus a new ceiling—actually a fake. It is simply a single plywood board, hung on chains, anchored with ceiling hooks and covered with either self-adhesive mirror square tiles or stainless steel tiles.

Left: Put an end to gloomy bathroom lighting and give yourself an attractive display shelf at the same time. Build the shelf from two lengths of 2 x 10s, one for the actual shelf, the other for the vertical back. Cut the vertical back 1½" shorter than the horizontal piece. Nail them together and then nail a short board ¾" thick on each end. Screw a 4' fluorescent fixture to the back of the vertical 2 x 10 and wire it up. Add a line switch for turning the light on and off. Paint the shelf with gloss enamel, stain it or leave it natural. Next lift the whole thing into place and screw it into the wall through the two end boards.

Reflected in the mirror: A long ladder from floor to ceiling in front of the window doubles as combination towel rack/curtains.

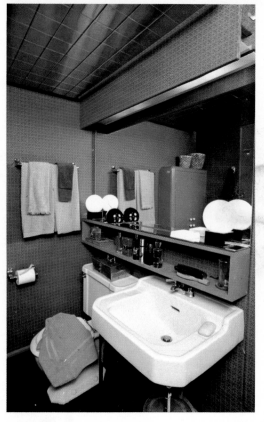

208

Left: When you are stuck with a set of ungracefully aging bathroom fixtures, it pays to do a little homework:

Slick up a chipped basin and tub with epoxy paint. Then add racing stripes with plastic tape.

The mirror is the better half of an old golden oak dresser. Simply unscrew from the bureau base. (Many mirrors are also sold separately.) Drill holes through the frame into the wall and secure with Molly bolts or expansion anchors.

Below: Most bathrooms suffer from high overhead—storage space is needed but no one ever thinks to look up. Here you can see what a few sticks of wood can do for the plain white-box bathroom. Use all 1 x 2s for the ceiling grid. Use narrow boards for the shelves. If you glue and screw the wood pieces together and use some ingenuity about wedging it all in, you can get by with very few holes in the walls, easily patched when you move.

Photo: Bradley Olman

Photo: Armen Kachaturian

Easy Being Green

Bathroom walls deserve photo play, too. Elegantly executed in all its details, this celadon green bathroom has one undeniable *pièce de résistance:* a 40-by-60-inch mural of a cherub-covered fountain in Madrid, which started out as an ordinary vacation slide.

Late afternoon sidelighting and a light rain emphasized the fountain and its details; a wide-angle lens kept the shape in proper proportion. The custom blowup was sent to a specialty company to be immersed in polyester resin and reinforced with fiberglass, a process that protects it from the room's high humidity and preserves color life. Then it was specially cut to parallel the curve of the background rainbow. Not an inexpensive proposition, to be sure, but the effect is well worth the effort.

The rest of the room matches the fountain's vintage—it's delightfully old-fashioned and worlds away from the coldly clinical. The wooden wainscoting, original to the house, is left intact, and practical ceramic wall treatments ignored in favor of respect for history. Claw foot tubs, if the enamel is in good condition, are highly prized for their looks and generous proportions. This one is repainted fresh white.

A Victorian-style lamp and a wall mounted soap dish add a touch of brass.

A collection of green-glazed vases, jars and bowls finds its perfect expression in this all-green room.

One last bit of drop-dead luxury: bath oils in a selection of glass decanters.

Walls: Original wainscoting left intact

Floors: Ceramic tile in checkerboard pattern

Photo: Bill Helms

A Prefab Rehab

Banish the basic boxy bathroom. Turn yours into a redwood retreat where moisture doesn't matter.

The requirements: waste-not, want-not efficiency, a puddleproof floor and lots of light.

The solutions: Prefab redwood sections (usually used for outdoor decks) make a floor that's easy to install and easy to dismantle. Tar paper protects the old floor from water. The prefab sections, from a lumberyard, are cheaper than individual redwood planks. They should be waterproofed with several coats of polyurethane. You may have to trim the bottom of the bathroom door for additional clearance.

Canvas-front cabinets under the counters mask stored essentials and plumbing pipes. Even the plywood medicine chest has a heavy canvas panel replacing the conventional mirrored door. Punch grommets at evenly spaced intervals and hang from cup hooks on underside of edge of counter. The canvas, which is mildew- and water-resistant,

comes from a fabric store. Grommet kits are as near as your local hardware emporium.

The suspended ceiling of translucent panels illuminates the room evenly by diffusing the glow of the fluorescents on the old ceiling. Plants love it!

Pre-packaged panels and hardware are available at building supply stores. The grid of T-shaped aluminum rails snaps together; drop-in panels rest atop the rails and the whole system gets support from bars along the walls and wires at-tached to the old ceiling.

More redwood deck sections make an instant counter along the left wall. The towel rack beneath uses up leftover pieces of redwood plus wooden dowels stained to match. Waterproof it all with polyurethane, then at-tach shelves to wall with L brackets and screw towel racks to shelf so dowel juts out a few inches. Top with glass.

The wall-mounted counter plus a sleek Scandinavian art-ist's stool sub superbly for a conventional bathroom vanity.

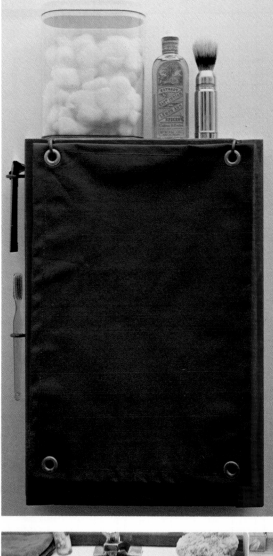

Back to Basics

Sometimes basic is best—as in this commodious space, given the classic white brick/wood floors/bare windows treatment. This unassuming approach highlights all that makes loft living different from the "2 bdrm mod kitch" way of life—vast space, enormous windows, flow-through light and high-reaching ceilings.

The furnishings, kept spare and simple, show that you don't have to treat big space as an empty lot in need of immediate landfill.

A mattress and box spring, swathed in white, substitute for a conventional sofa, aided by stacks of trio'd cushions.

Horizontal surfaces take various forms: three-in-a-row Italian plastic tables, a slablike work/dining table made of birch plywood, and an antique oriental tea chest.

Ceiling-scraper bookcases scale the grand heights of the room. Indoor trees take advantage of the abundant natural light streaming in through warehouse-size windows.

The only art on the walls is homemade. This once-upon-a-mattress pad becomes faux patchwork with the help of wide seam binding and iron-on tape (available in many colors at fabric stores), plus a hot iron. Folk art in less time than it took your grandma to thread her quilting needle!

The Engineered Apartment

This room is organized into activity areas—bed/sofa, the alley office, and the round butcher block dining table—and each area sprawls into the other when necessary. This apartment is carefully engineered.

Behind the black folding doors (below) is a closet converted to a work area, complete with storage bins, desk, pegboard space and work light.

The white shelving system (right) is a working wall divider. One side is a stereo component/record storage shelf; the other side is a headboard with bedtime reading lamps. The divider sets up another office area as

seen on the following pages.

The big round table becomes even larger with a couple of leaves but it is also a worktable suitable for craft projects, paper work and food preparation too. The oversized black coffee table is an easily built plywood box covered with vinyl tile; inside are shelves and drawers for storage.

The simple hanging lamp is easy to connect: Run wire from an outlet up to the ceiling, drop it down through a screw-eye that's fastened into the ceiling. Run the wire through a brass-plated curtain rod so it will not sway.

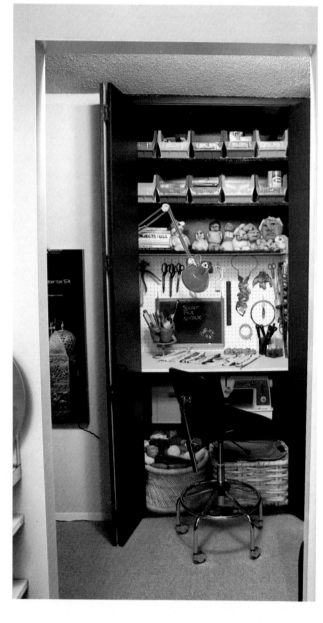

This sofa is actually a "floating" bed (supported by short, hidden legs) that doubles as a sofa. The office area is the other side of the wall of shelves. A file cabinet and desk-top, flexible reading/working lamp and storage shelves are ready to work. Corkboard covers walls.

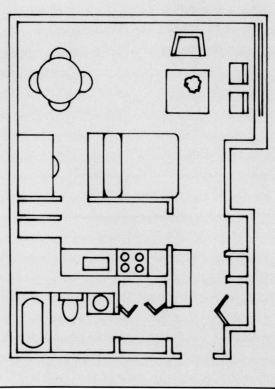

The simple hanging lamp is easy to connect: Run wire from outlet across ceiling, drop down through a screw-eye fastener into the ceiling. Run the wire through brass-plated curtain rod so it will not sway in the breeze.

HOW TO DO IT

Coffee Table: This mysterious black box is both a coffee table and a sophisticated storage system. Build it from plywood (see illustration) with a flip-out front door. Nail wood strips inside for loose shelves that slide out. Cover with self-adhesive floor tile.

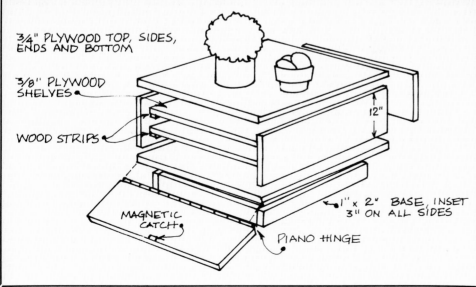

3/4" PLYWOOD TOP, SIDES, ENDS AND BOTTOM

3/8" PLYWOOD SHELVES

WOOD STRIPS

12"

MAGNETIC CATCH

1" x 2" BASE, INSET 3" ON ALL SIDES

PIANO HINGE

Shipshape Space

How does an ordinary 12-by-16-foot room become the most efficient space capsule this side of the NASA labs? Space planning, careful space planning.

Every built-in thing here is capable of playing several roles. The far-reaching plastic laminate peninsula serves sit-down at its swoopy circular end, buffet along its 12-foot length.

The extra-wide L-shaped platform sofa converts to a generous guest bed. Its thick, boxy cushions, covered in the soft melton cloth usually used for suits and coats, work warm wonders against the cool white surroundings. Storage is both high and low, with cabinets tucked in everywhere they'll fit. The one to the left of the fireplace rationalizes a quirky gap in the wall and provides deep shelves within for common clutter. A plug-in fluorescent tucked underneath brightens an otherwise dark, forgotten corner.

More storage is tucked under the extended counter and on the far right. Boxes conceal stereo speakers, with record cabinets just out of view.

All surfaces—tabletop, sofa back, cabinets—are exactly 28 inches high, creating a uniform horizontal plane that adds to the illusion of spaciousness by not forcing the eye to bounce up and down.

Telescoping floor lamps put together with components from a photographers' supply store ricochet light off the walls, painted a creamy vanilla to soften the shine of the white-white laminate furnishings. The custom table lamp, looking like a 1930s streamlined locomotive, is made of tiered frosted glass.

Uninterrupted blank walls echo the purity of the all-in-one design concept.

Walls: Creamy vanilla paint
Storage: Built-in cabinets

Lighting: Custom-made, home-made and plug-in fluorescents
Floor: Industrial carpet

Photo: Bradley Olman

Not Just Another Pretty Place

For all its high-gloss style, this one-room apartment in the thirties mode works strictly for the twenty-first century. Sleeping, dining and comfort are the true high points of this very efficient efficiency.

This studio apartment may look like a period piece—1920s or 1930s Art Deco—but in fact it is a *suggestion* of that design time. More a state of mind than a state of design, nothing in this room is actually authentic Deco. The mirrors, the geometric pattern on the floor, the shiny satin pillows, the molded plastic tables, the lighting—all recall the thirties but stop short of being a carbon copy.

Too often rooms end up formal and stodgy because some perfectionist has decided to be "true" to a period rather than to his own instincts. The point is not to get locked into exact imitations. Here are the details:

The elegantly quilted sofa becomes the bed for today, complete with built-in end tables.

Contemporary wicker chairs have the lines of our times with the texture of yesterday.

The high-styled coffee table is the rebirth of an idea born in the Deco era. The slick satin pillows can be pulled up for short-order dining.

Behind the sofa: desk and buffet service from one heavy-duty Parsons table.

One good, large painting deserves importance. Then you need no other.

At right, the Italian floor lamp is contemporary but its sharp, well-defined lines recall other eras. The exposed sound system in the corner and carefully selected accessories heighten the sense of machined detail.

Walls: Paint one wall a single striking color; a singular painting does the rest

Floor: Pattern in tile
Lighting: Sleek Italian Plexiglas

Not Just Another Pretty Place

This sleep sofa does more than aid your slumber. Like so many variations on themes evident in today's expanding furniture market, this sofa has adjustable arms that flop down—so it becomes an end table as well as a sleeper. The pillows become a comfortable backrest when the sofa is converted into a bed.

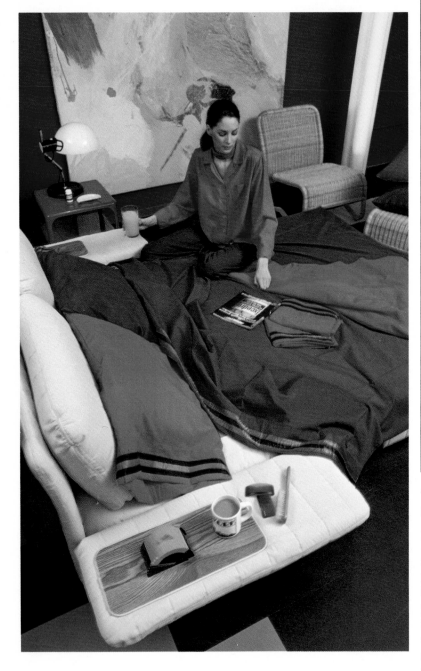

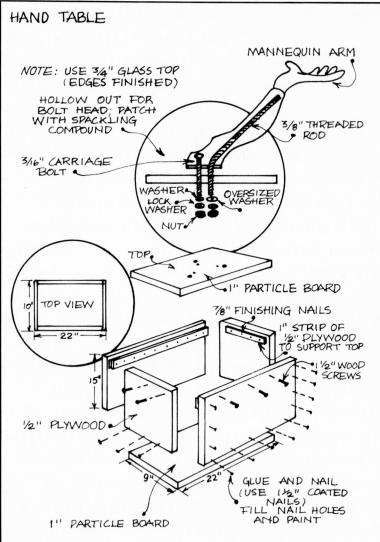

HAND TABLE

NOTE: USE 3/4" GLASS TOP (EDGES FINISHED)

HOLLOW OUT FOR BOLT HEAD; PATCH WITH SPACKLING COMPOUND

3/16" CARRIAGE BOLT

MANNEQUIN ARM

3/8" THREADED ROD

WASHER
LOCK WASHER
OVERSIZED WASHER
NUT

TOP

1" PARTICLE BOARD

TOP VIEW
10"
22"

7/8" FINISHING NAILS

1" STRIP OF 1/2" PLYWOOD TO SUPPORT TOP

1 1/2" WOOD SCREWS

15"

1/2" PLYWOOD

9"   22"

GLUE AND NAIL (USE 1 1/2" COATED NAILS)
FILL NAIL HOLES AND PAINT

1" PARTICLE BOARD

This Daliesque sculptured table (at right) fills a corner as well as a need. The mannequin arms literally hold up the glass top, reaching out from a simple plywood box. (For details, see illustration above.) This setting proves that the functional need not lack wit. Clear glass keeps the corner feeling uncrowded as do the readily available chrome and Plexiglas chairs.

On the table, more Deco designs: new teapot, silverware and inexpensive tinware; an old vase and embroidered hand towels from the forties used here as napkins. The old leaded-glass doors are freshly painted and hinged together to form a screen. Apricot-colored acetate gel (from an art store) taped to the back of the glass warms up the daylight. At night, a glowing spotlight sits on the floor behind the screen.

For more Deco dimension, one wall has been covered with mirrored tiles, palm trees cut from black self-adhesive paper. The tiles are also self-sticking and easy to install.

The floor shown on the previous page and reflected here in the mirror at right is made from an original arrangement of colored tiles that can be adapted to your room. First, plan out your pattern on paper (as shown in the illustration above). Then arrange the tiles on the floor in the same design. The tiles used here are made of glossy vinyl.

ALTERNATIVE SPACES

"The sweat ethic." It is what's needed to turn around an ungainly, unexpected space into a place you call home. It is taking old factory space and transforming it into a livable loft by lovingly carving an apartment out of it—a kitchen in that corner, a bedroom over there, the living and dining areas in the middle. In lofts and commercial spaces, once converted, there are no walls to fence you in. It is free-form living in which dictated spaces are out. You can even have a "backyard" in your living room if you want (and without rain). You can extend the kitchen as far as you want. You can build huge walk-in closets. And these alternative spaces are ways of assuring yourself built-in architectural detail: oversized windows, large open spaces, wood floors, high ceilings.

If you moved up to the top

loor of an old house and created rooms out of what used to be an attic—that would be a garret.

These alternatives are all part of the new urban frontier, where pavement pioneers are taking formerly useless space and making it livable.

The movement reflects a new commitment to the cities, a revival of the spirit of the settler days.

Lofts, garrets and commercial spaces have become the new big-city living locations that offer greater choices and opportunities for making your living space to your own specifications. On the following pages we show you a number of spaces that have had their faces lifted. It takes much muscle, some money, as well as rethinking old ideas and supplanting them with new concepts about new spaces.

Black-out Loft

Room to rattle around in: It sounds terrific in theory, but the reality can be terrifying. Like, what to *put* in all that wide-open space? What's needed to tame the acreage is a strategy that simplifies—an overall plan that relates the parts to the whole and reduces the infinite number of choices you have to make.

In this former toy warehouse, black is the tack: all-black furniture against all-white walls (albeit with a trail of air-brushed clouds). That fabulous black banquette, for example, with its thirty-four pillows—isn't that imposing presence some high-style number from Milan that costs as much as a new car? Not at all; in fact, it's a weekend project. The unit is simply a particle board platform topped with a four-inch foam pad, both resting on a 2 x 4 plywood box frame. Staple channel-quilted cotton fabric along the bottom edge of the frame; bring it up over the platform edge and staple again. Don't skimp on envelope-style pillows. They stitch up in a flash.

The no-nonsense coffee table—a rectangular box of black laminate—is surprisingly lightweight, visually speaking.

Slightly tired chrome-and-cane chairs take on the surreal character of a Magritte painting when popped into drapey, sew-up sacks.

New laminate tops and a fresh coat of black paint for their bases bring three mom 'n' pop luncheonette tables right into line.

Photo: Thomas Hooper

In the kitchen, the domino theory of all black and white finds fitting expression within the framework of the forties diner. The lower half of the room is largely black, from the plastic laminate on the counter to the metal-studded rubber elevator tile on the floor.

The stools were bought unfinished, painted black and equipped with white rubber feet, a little detail that sets them dancing off the floor.

Above, plastic-coated wire shelves provide open storage for dishes and shiny chrome accessories.

(Right) A bedroom is scooped out of the space with a wall curved into a quarter-circle. The platform bed, a standard item at unfinished-furniture stores, is incorporated into the overall scheme with a coat of black.

The effect of all this black and white is to make any shot of color really zing. Witness the red wicker chair, an English antique; and the plastic midsection of a former "Restaurant" sign over the kitchen counter.

The Upstairs Backyard

In the beginning, there were plants—and everything else in this loft followed. White walls reflect maximum sunlight from huge, bare windows. No partitions—that would block precious rays. Instead, the 1,300-square-foot space is rezoned into multi-function areas. The chief trick is the porch-like central enclosure, an illusion based on four made-to-order hollow-core pine columns, glued to floor and ceiling.

A loungeable bed/sofa floats within, made up of a queen-size bed and springs with bolted-on wooden head and footboards, all covered in quilted white duck. Two coats of tough gray deck enamel on the floor are spattered with red, white and pink confettilike dots, to downplay the dirt.

Wicker and rattan are the obvious choices for this indoor garden, along with some secondhand and unfinished pieces freshened up with white paint.

(Below) A view toward the kitchen. The plywood counter is 48 inches high—high enough to hide kitchen clutter, low enough not to compromise the open feeling. The healthy-looking plants are all in terra-cotta pots, best for breathing and for looks. Try displaying plants as sculpture on wooden pedestals of various heights. Another trick: Underplant ficus trees or other large plants with a bed of ivy or small ferns for extra lushness.

White Space

It is hard to believe that the sleek and modern living space at right was carved out of the old building below.

Yet, inside this floor-through former factory—smack in the center of an urban industrial area—is a very uptown-looking place.

More and more people are sculpting their own space within the caverns of old buildings. And with space that is impressive to start with, you can get away with less in furnishings.

The vast open space and high ceilings are reemphasized by low-scale, contemporary pieces. The light palette helps the feeling of space.

Foregoing draperies or curtains is part of the emphasis. A flood of white and natural light helps the room stay spacious and spare.

Use very few pieces—low, modular seating units and a rolling coffee table are comfortably flexible.

Track lighting and built-in spots throw illumination where you want it, while keeping the surfaces clear of lamps.

Careful use of plants softens starkness.

Dark wood floors, especially with light furnishings, look rich enough to get by without a carpet.

The industrial wire stacking unit can be moved at will.

The kitchen, presenting an organized view at the end of the living area, is uncluttered and functional. It was designed with the elegant dining area in mind.

The sleek lines and open counter space make this kitchen seem roomy and inviting. Helping out are a wide butcher block counter and open storage to display kitchenwares. Extending the kitchen is a birch veneer plywood table.

Photo: Bill Helms

Lofts: Elemental Breakdown

You can get the loft look in your own apartment—even if it is on the first floor of a five-story walk-up—by thinking of your space in big strokes. For instance, the room above has a skylight gracing it and built-in drawers, topped off with pillows for seating. But you can do the same thing by carving out a closet. Move in a chest of drawers, or build a simple plywood box (recess the top if you like), then top it with a 5"-thick foam slab for a mattress.

A giant-size Luxo lamp rules the area—minimally furnished with two director's chairs and a freshly painted metal trunk.

Photos: Bill Helms

Behind the mask of this dark, dated factory building is a surprise: a gracious cheery living space. This live-in loft is large and luxurious—a design dream.

The floor space, for example, is massive enough to accommodate duo-toned patterns (which are accomplished by painting with homemade stencils). Large trees make a pleasurable park atmosphere. The seating units are high Italian contemporary.

In another corner of the room is a work/play area—with space enough for both the office and the baby, thanks to a trellised-in recreation area.

The wonderful windows are best kept bare; the city outside beats draperies every time.

Return of the Century

No dentist's chair or drill can now be found in this room—but those were the main attractions here before this commercial building was renovated. The result is The Next Frontier—office buildings converted into housing. Rooms like this combine the architectural bonuses of older buildings with the advantages of modern interiors.

One grand feature of old buildings—the oversized windows—was emphasized with large, movable panels, pine frames with mosquito netting stretched tight. For energy conservation, the windows were fitted with double-paneled insulated glass.

The relaxed off-kilter furniture arrangement is a pleasant surprise and keeps your eyes roving until you discover other features—high ceilings and boxed beams. An upholstered sofa, fat, squashy pillows and muted, romantic colors soften and contrast the dark wood furnishings and white walls.

HOW TO DO IT

Window Panels: They swivel on a pivot system. The wooden frame is attached to the windowsill, top and bottom, with ½" stair bolts. Each bolt looks like a screw with two threaded ends. The tapered end goes into the frame; the straight end into the sill. So the frame swings freely, the bolts are screwed into T nuts that are a size larger (5/16") than the bolt. Washers separate the frame and the sill to keep things working smoothly.

The installation is similar to putting in a sliding door: The hole that the bolt slips into at top is deeper than the bottom one. The frame top slips in first, leaving room for the bottom to clear the sill.

The frame is made from pine 1 x 5s that are mitered, glued, then connected with ½" #5 corrugated fasteners. Staple mosquito netting to the frame's back. If you want, mask the staples with lattice.

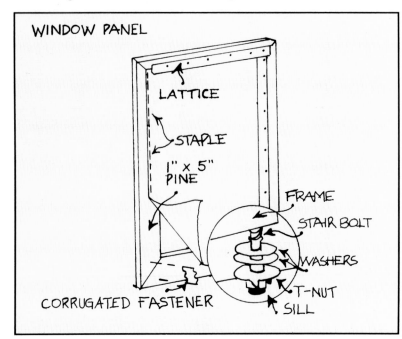

WINDOW PANEL

LATTICE

STAPLE

1" x 5" PINE

FRAME

STAIR BOLT

WASHERS

T-NUT

SILL

CORRUGATED FASTENER

Garrets

It may be hard at first glance to imagine that behind an unprepossessing facade and up steep, rickety steps, tucked high under a slanting roof, is a wonderful, unconventional living space. But it is true.

Garrets are found all over the country. They have all the characteristics that command huge sums when labeled "penthouse" but as attics they are the best bargains on the block. Garret spaces are pioneer penthouses, with charm and individuality already there before you even move in.

A garret doesn't have to be bursting with Old World furnishings. This one has all the clean, white airiness (yet none of the ordinariness) of a contemporary three-room apartment:

If you opt for modern charm, here is the angle:

Slanted ceilings are, of course, cozy and terrific. A garret given. But they do keep wall space to a minimum. The solution is to hang paintings on the ceiling itself—the highest form of the art.

Old-time imperfections in the walls and ceilings can be inexpensively covered by 4 x 8 sheets of paneling found at building supply stores.

The brick-bare chimney recalls the rustic origins—for contrast.

With the ceiling reaching for the floor at the sides of the room, you are best off with furnishings both few and low.

Neutral colors for the modular quilted sofa, plush chair and hassock are at ease with the

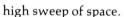

Apartment kitchens have enough space dilemmas without the added problem of missing half a ceiling, but that is exactly the joy (and the curse) of this garret kitchen. You can make it work *for* you by using imagination for some illuminating ideas—like this simple light fixture installed on the angle right into the ceiling.

Some other ways to combat the crunch in this kitchen:

Set everything out on open shelving—these are pine, mounted on ordinary standards and brackets. When staggered, the shelves give ample room for the tall and short of your wares.

Finesse the lack-of-drawers problem by hanging everything hangable. Baskets keep odd-shaped items at your fingertips.

A couple of stools are handy for sharing cooking chores or using at a quick-meal counter.

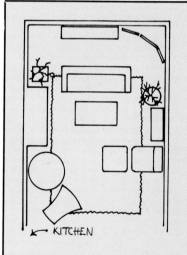

KITCHEN

high sweep of space.

The modern canvas chair holds its own beside a wicker table, found at a flea market.

An oriental carpet defines the living area and enriches the room's contemporary pieces.

In an awkward corner at right, a handsome screen is simply three glass-paned front doors hinged together. You can find the doors at antique shops.

Photo: Bradley Olman/Design: Richard Burford

Photo: Erik Arnesen

Garrets

There are as many different ways to transform a garret into liveable space as there are ways to live in them. The amount of remodeling varies. Some garrets are raw spaces—just exposed beams and rafters. Others need only cosmetic work. More often, though, a garret was left simple to store things. The floor and ceiling may be finished but you will probably find no plumbing, heating or cooling units and few electrical outlets.

This garret illustrates the transformation possible in an attic that once lacked proper insulation, electricity and flooring—but did have lumpy, bumpy walls along with its charm.

The Victorian atmosphere here makes thorough use of the garret's angles in order to keep the spirit of the room intact. Some angles were improved upon: The coffee table is made from an old theatre seat (simply remove the old seat and replace it with a marble top).

Through a curtained en-

trance—which allows privacy without having to build a door in the irregular space—is the bedroom (at right). The redwood wall is a rustic glory. Large pieces of furniture keep it simple: the carved oak bed and bird's-eye maple bureau. The comforter (new sheets sewn together to make a removable quilt cover) and the lace curtains graciously relax. Notice, for example, how the walls are accented by placing the oriental rugs at angles. The rich mix of textures and patterns results in a warm opulent atmosphere.

New wall paneling was the major change. Rough-cut redwood plywood boards were nailed to the original 2 x 8 rafters. Trim moldings and baseboards are lath and the painted portions of the wall are plasterboard (texturized to hide the irregularity of the old structure). Lengths of old oak flooring found at salvage yards were laid right over the old floor, then sanded and finished with two coats of polyurethane.

APT IDEAS

As the name suggests, this section is stocked with adaptable ideas, information and illustrations of the pieces that make up a whole room, the elements that give it personality.

You will see pretty pictures too, but, like so much else in this book, the furnishings in these pictures do not just sit around looking pretty—they *work*. And if you look closely, the photographs and drawings provide some simple solutions to some complex problems.

Some examples of what you will find:

Long, narrow hallways are often the unwelcome tag-alongs to charming, elderly apartments. What to do with them? Here are innovative ideas for two-toned painting and for art galleries that give corridors new personalities.

This section will answer the nagging question of how to find the space for an office at home: movable walls, for instance, make two spaces out of one—thanks to the use of lightweight screens. Other ideas show how to carve out work spaces that disappear when necessary.

Plants. You probably already know how to care for and feed

them—but where do you put them? We do not mean decorator-chic plant placement (a lone palm in a dark hallway for strictly aesthetic purposes), but places where plants can grow and glow, from bedroom greenhouses to roll-around planters.

Storage is always the big problem in any size apartment. These pages offer systems for housing books and records, crafts and collectibles, clothes and sound equipment.

And more—workable principles for how to make a lamp out of just about anything, how to make a desk or a table, how to tame the frame, and how to treat your windows.

All these ideas can work hard in your home without you having to work too hard or spend too much. You will not have to rush out and buy an expensive new breakfront or shelving system. No. Some of these ideas are projects, requiring some do-it-yourself time. Others are simply fast ideas that make the difference between an apartment with a half life and one that lives. And after looking through this section, we are sure you will come up with some apt ideas of your own.

STORAGE: Book Systems

Right: This unfinished floor-to-ceiling shelf system is surprisingly simple and versatile. Build it from four 2 x 4s cut to fit from floor to ceiling. Follow instructions on the diagram at left. Adjust the dimensions to fit your needs.

Once the 2 x 4s are on hand, use a saw and an electric drill with a 1½" spade bit to drill holes and cut slots as shown. From ¾" plywood, cut five shelves 15" x 36" and one shelf 18½" x 36". (The wider shelf toward the bottom is deep enough for a stereo system.) Notch this shelf to fit between the uprights. Use metal L brackets to fasten the uprights to the floor and ceiling. The distance between the uprights depends on the width of your shelves; allow for a 6" overhang on shelf ends.

Below: Build narrow shelves for those skinny paperback books that usually get lost on regulation bookshelves.

Build the shelves just deep enough to hold standard-sized paperbacks—6 to 8 inches. Then cut shorter sections to nail at the end of each shelf for built-on bookends.

These shelves fit standards and wall brackets found in hardware stores.

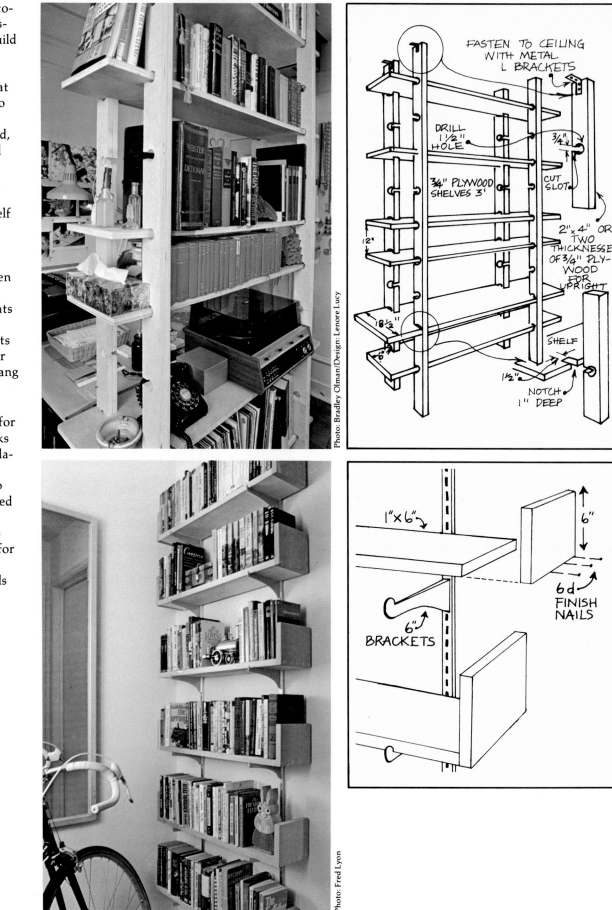

Photo: Bradley Olman/Design: Lenore Lucy

Photo: Fred Lyon

Photo: Armen Kachaturian

¼" × 3"
LAG SCREW

WASHER

1½" COUNTER-
SINK 3/8"
DEEP

16d NAILS

This shelving system is as simple as child's play—you can knock it together from a big pile of 2 x 4s.

The dimensions are up to you but if you are going to load the system with books and records, limit the horizontal pieces to a depth of three feet. And sketch your complete system before you truck off to the lumberyard; it is better than finding that you guessed wrong—after you are back home.

Leave the boards natural or stain them (light oak stain was used here). Seal with two coats of polyurethane (sand lightly between coats).

Start building by leaning the uprights in position along the wall. Nail them into the wall studs if you can (use 8d nails). Make sure these initial 2 x 4s are exactly vertical—use a carpenter's level to check. Then nail on the first layer of horizontal shelf pieces; check with the level as you go.

Continue stacking and nailing until the shelves are as deep as you need. For a professional touch, attach the last horizontals with countersunk lag screws.

STORAGE: Music Boxes

You do not have to hide your components away in dark places. If they are well designed, you can treat them like sculpture by putting them on pedestals or angle-iron units.

HOW TO DO IT
Pedestals: Measure the length and width of each component and use those dimensions for the top and bottom panels of its pedestal. Build them any height you like.

Have the lumberyard cut ¾" plywood to your specifications. Nail the pieces together, leaving the back of each box open for extra storage—albums, tapes and maintenance gear.

Fill any holes or hammer dents with wood putty and sand the entire surface smooth before painting or polyurethaning. You can also cover each pedestal with vinyl paper (self-adhesive or glued on with vinyl wallpaper paste); in this case, sanding and puttying are unnecessary.

If you put the pedestals on a rug or straw mat, you can even hide the wires under the floor covering (where you do not walk) and avoid the typical stereo system octopus.

HOW TO DO IT
Erector Set: Music Cart
Buy seven ten-foot lengths of slotted angle irons from an industrial supplier and have them cut to the following sizes (if you cut them yourself, use a hacksaw and wear goggles and gloves):

4 51" uprights
8 60" long rails
8 13" crosspieces

Bolt the two upright end frames first, using 5/16" and ¾" bolts throughout. Then join the long rails to the inside of the frame.

Cut three or four shelves out of particle board, each 12½" by 59½".

Finally, bolt 3" locking casters with corner brackets (from the hardware store) to the bottom of the frame.

Dimensions can be adjusted to any size; just remember to keep the width at 13" to accommodate record albums.

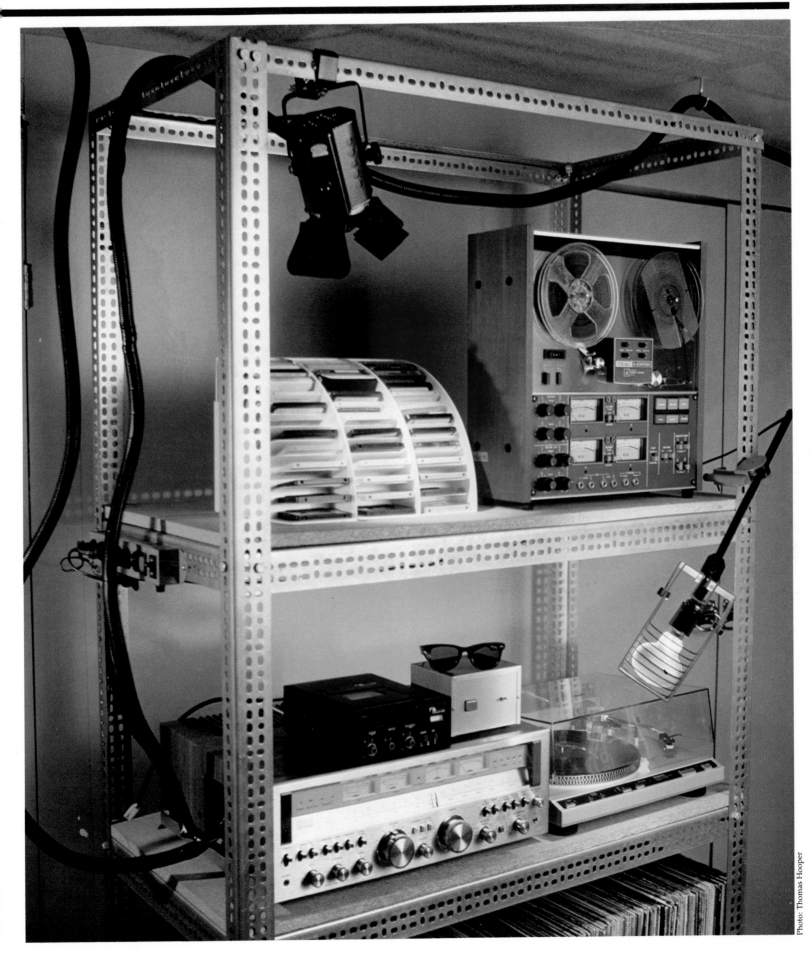

Photo: Thomas Hooper

STORAGE: Packing Cases

Right: Take the trunk table trick one step further—a piece of ¼" plate glass resting on top makes for see-through storage as well as offering a dandy display case. Cover the inside with paper or fabric.

Find old trunks at a Salvation Army store or antique shops. Get one that is in good condition since broken hinges and big dents are hard and costly to repair. Refinish the old wood, shine up the brass and metalwork and the unit is made.

Below Right: Let old suitcases travel out of the closet and be-

come a coffee table. Find the cases or trunks in thrift shops. Most clean up with soap and water. A coat of paste wax protects the finish. Or glue on a fabric covering (canvas or corduroy look good).

Below: These boxes seem to adhere to the wall by defying gravity but they are resting quite prosaically on shelf standards and brackets. The boxes were from department and discount stores—refurbished with spray paint (wallpaper or fabric work well too). The letters are art supply stick-ons.

tools
mats
sewing
sheets
towels
boots
tennis
ski gear

Photo: Bradley Olman

STORAGE: Wired for Wine

Within the heart of this monument to the medieval lurk some very entertaining trappings of the twentieth century.

The upper stories are craftily fitted out with felt-covered shelves to store a party's worth of glasses and liquor.

It's all done with shelving strips to make it adjustable. Below, another shelf takes all the stereo equipment—a cassette

deck, a tuner and an amp.

And below that, three wooden wine racks just happen to fit exactly, side by side.

WORKSPACE: Homework

Below: Design for designers: a studio filled with state-of-the-art equipment.

To start, a clear Plexiglas drafting table that can be rotated 360 degrees and tilt-adjusted 90 degrees, and a stool specially designed for people who work standing up.

The thin line of the chic Italian desk lamp slices the air like a pen stroke. The rolling wire rack with collapsible baskets is another Italian import.

Even the telephone, made in Denmark, is design-conscious—its prototype is in the Museum of Modern Art.

Opposite: This U-shaped home office is a consortium of odd pieces. The central desk is based on a kitchen counter unit and, as such, is full of down-under storage space. The top is a 30"-wide hollow-core door, covered with plastic laminate.

Against the wall, a set of drawers is topped with another door. A bought-unfinished bookcase stacks on top.

A drafting table and some plastic storage drawers complete the U. A fluorescent tube suspended by two lengths of chain and a clamp-on lamp shed light.

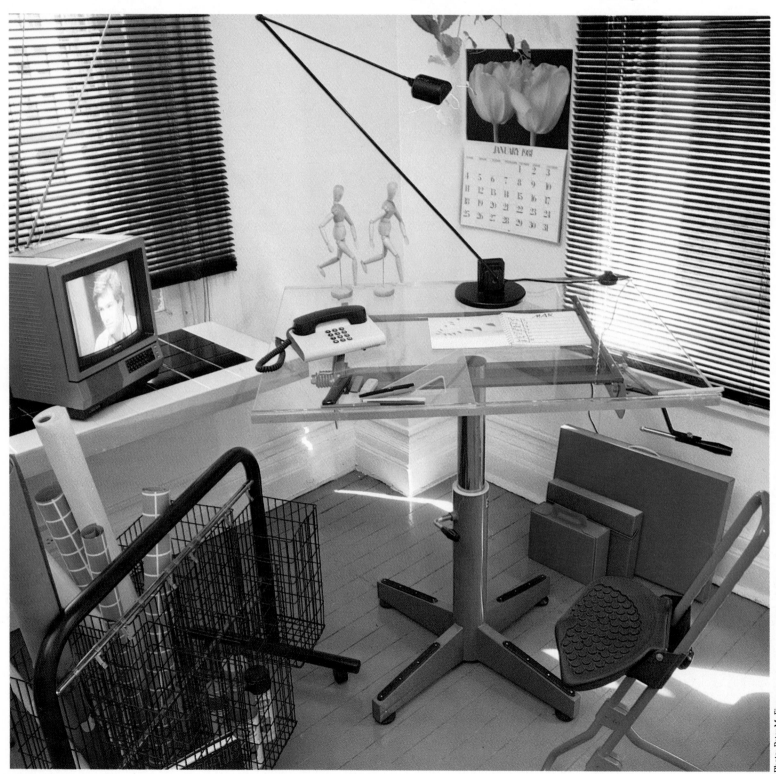

Photo: Thomas Hooper

WORKSPACE: Corner Offices

The office on the sly: a wall area turned into workspace.

Below: This hallway becomes an efficient work area with the artful addition of two clean-lined filing cabinets and a wooden slab slapped on top. The eye-level hanging plastic bins, a versatile clamp-on desk lamp and simple wicker baskets are functionally pretty.

Right: A bedroom Parsons night table can double for daytime duty when a set of sturdy plastic drawers is wheeled underneath. Once again, a useful clamp-on desk lamp can be extended over any desk-top area.

Below Right: A drop-down leaf exposes not only an efficient work spot but ample storage space.

Photos: Bradley Olman

WORKSPACE: Eating at Your Desk

One table can quickly change functions from dining to work if you plan a bit beforehand.

The room at right illustrates just how this is done. The table switches roles and becomes workspace with the simple addition of the tools of the trade. Everything can be stored away in a wooden trunk next to the bookcase.

The sawhorse table (below) doubles as both innovative workspace and dining place. Its design is obviously simple, it is easy to forget about. But when you need an inexpensive table, fast, there is nothing better

than a hollow-core door on two hardware store brackets and 2 x 4s. The kimono becomes clothing art with the addition of a dowel slid through the arms and supported on two nails.

HOW TO DO IT

Sawhorse Table: Four metal sawhorse brackets make this table easy to put together. Slip two 2 x 4 legs into each bracket, then clamp 2 x 4 crosspieces—cut to the width of the hollow-core door tabletop—between the two brackets. If you want permanence, nail the 2 x 4s in place.

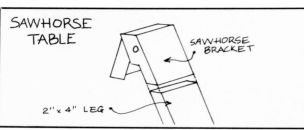

SAWHORSE TABLE

SAWHORSE BRACKET

2" x 4" LEG

Photo: Thomas Hooper

Photos: Bradley Olman

WORKSPACE: Closets with a Cause

If you are willing to sacrifice closet space, you can get yourself a whole extra room for working—with little work.

Below is the apartment shop, so economically planned and put together that there is plenty of room to do all your carpentering in one small space. A simple sawing system replaces sawhorses: Two 1 x 4s rest between the wood plank workbench and a dowel-studded 2 x 4 on the back wall. Holes (drilled into the ends of the 1 x 4s) slip over the dowels to position the boards.

The closet case at right is a neat transformation for that Fibber McGee storage space. A bunch of boards, some self-adhesive cork and a Formica counter turn it into a trim and tidy office.

Inexpensive, colorful plastic bins and accessories hold all kinds of office supplies and rest on shelves supported by L brackets, or the bins can also stack on top of one another. A roll-under-the-desk chair can be kept out of sight and out of the way. Bonus: You can close the door on your work.

WORKSPACE: A Clean Well-Lighted Place

All kinds of spaces in all kinds of rooms can be converted into efficient work areas.

Right: A standard drawing table with a comfortable swivel chair stands in a corner. Moved near a window, it gives you a room-within-a-room with a view. Walls become bulletin boards when work stuff is tacked up.

Use bright colors to ward off the feeling that you are working in a closet. Stack files and books on existing shelves, even add a few more, and put in filing cabinets to fit the floor space. Move in a small desk or drawing board for the work surface.

Below Left: Double take—even ordinary, everyday items can be put to use in the home office. Here a couple of bricks organize desk-top clutter.

Below Center: You can add a new room without knocking down or building walls. Simply turn a walk-in closet into much-needed office space.

Below Right: A tacking strip is a simple way to unclutter your desk while keeping oft-used supplies within reach.

Make one by nailing wood lath to the wall. Then pin or tack up your papers, work tools, pictures or whatnot.

Photo: Thomas Hooper

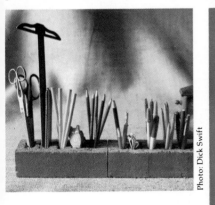
Photo: Dick Swift

Photo: Bradley Olman

Photo: Fred Lyon

MOVABLE WALLS: Staged Screens

Left: If your door opens straight into the room, you can build an instant entryway with movable walls.

Make the screen panels from ¾" x 6" birch veneer plywood boards, 7' long. Connect them with ¾" double-action hinges. Edge with birch wood tape, then sand the panels and leave the screen unfinished—bare is beautiful—or paint or cover with self-adhesive paper.

Right: Shoji screens—hinged together and freestanding—make a whole garden where there was once only a barren white wall. Shojis are available by mail order or from import stores.

Sticks and stones are the building blocks for this scene stealer. With the backlighting through the screens and a well-placed mirror, the effect is dramatic. Putting it together isn't.

The weathered branches and the plywood base they stand on come as a unit from a display store. If you have access to fallen timber, it is easy to hold scavenged branches erect with Christmas tree stands. Or brace them with pieces of lumber, notched to fit the trunks and nailed to a plywood base.

Camouflage the base with boulders—papier-mâché or real limestone—and white rocks (from a garden supply store).

Photos: Fred Lyon

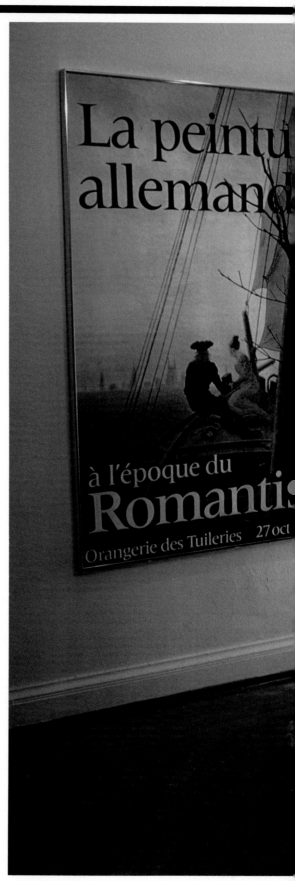

MOVABLE WALLS: Primal Screens

Left: Pop up—and then prop up—an instant wall and park it anywhere. Build the wall any height or width—but make sure it is not too big to carry out when you move. There are two ways.

HOW TO DO IT
Instant Wall #1: Nail together a framework from 1 x 2s (or use artists' canvas stretcher strips for walls up to 72" tall), then cover the frame with fabric. Hold the new wall upright with L-shaped brackets attached to an existing wall.

Instant Wall #2: Sandwich a lightweight panel (Gatorfoam, Fome-Cor, styrofoam or thick cardboard) between two pieces of furniture, or hang it from ceiling hooks. Paint the new walls or use adhesive paper or thin wood strips.

Right: This garden scene-turned-screen could nurture you through a long, cold winter. Unlike some potential blowup subjects, a bower of flowers effect doesn't have to begin with a professionally sharp image.

HOW TO DO IT
Blowup Screen: These blooms were captured with a 135 mm telephoto lens at a distance of 20 to 30 feet. Have your photo lab box-mount your custom blowup in three sections. Leave the backs unfinished or screw on plywood backing and paint.
   Screw bi-fold hinges to the sides (not the back) of the sections. Be sure to get hinges that work both ways, so you can fold the screen in either an S or a U shape.

TABLES: From Pillar to Post

Left: A little crash course in urban archaeology: Both tables started life a century ago as supporting members of a grand sweeping staircase somewhere.

The mahogany pedestal is a prime example of urban renewal. To make one, saw the ends off a newel post to form flat surfaces at top and bottom. Add an X-shaped base of 2 x 4s for stability and an X of 1 x 2s at top to support a ⅜"-thick glass circle.

In the foreground, angled balusters make a great splayed-leg base for a coffee table. They are first glued in place on a plywood square trimmed with quarter-round molding, then nailed in from the underside. A two-tone paint job and glass top complete the comeback.

Right: More photo magic here. This super-colossal flower is a 40-by-43-inch blowup of a 35 mm slide, mounted on hardboard.

Shooting ordinary things with a close-up lens—water, rock formations, dripping paint—often yields impressive results. For a floral subject like this one, shoot flowers on the stem rather than fast-wilting cut ones. A telephoto with close-up attachment brings you near enough to the subject without limiting your lighting options. Diffuse direct sunlight by holding a sheet between the light source and the subject. Set up around shadows so you have a dark background against which to position your flower.

Fill the frame, but leave enough margin to avoid losing part of the subject when you frame it. The table appears to float because of its glass-brick base—eight bricks epoxyed together in a square, with space left in the center for a bulb in a porcelain socket.

Photo labs can box-mount your blowup on hardboard to whatever depth you want; this one is six inches.

Photo: Bill Helms

TABLES: PVC Chic

This table lets you keep an eye on your favorite poster. Plastic piping and fine art may not seem like the most harmonious coupling but the result is high visibility when you put them together right.

HOW TO DO IT
Cut the PVC (polyvinyl chloride) pipe with a fine-toothed saw. Put all the pieces together, plumber style: Clean the ends with acetone and stick them together with pipe cement.

After painting with spray enamel, add tape stripes along the top edge (either art drafting tape or auto pinstriping tape).

Top with Plexiglas.

The illustration shows sizes used for this table.

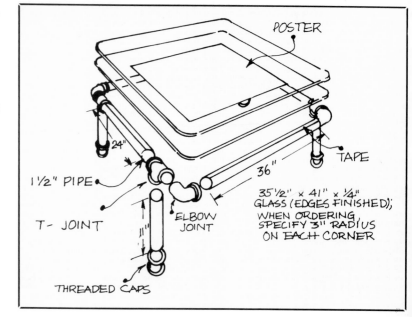

POSTER

24"

1½" PIPE

T- JOINT

ELBOW JOINT

11"

THREADED CAPS

TAPE

36"

35½" × 41" × ¼" GLASS (EDGES FINISHED); WHEN ORDERING SPECIFY 3" RADIUS ON EACH CORNER

TABLES: Slat of Hand

Cover a plain plywood box (rough edges and all) with thin cedar strips for a coffee table that floats on top of a lighted base.

HOW TO DO IT

Go to the lumberyard for ⅛" cedar strips—one package of random-length strips covers about 32 square feet. Cut the strips with a utility knife or scissors. Although manufacturers recommend contact cement, white glue also works.

To apply the strips: Spread glue or cement or both on a section of the box and the back of a strip with a 4" rubber roller. Wait a few seconds until the glue gets tacky and stick the strip in place. When the pattern is complete, protect the surface with a light oil finish.

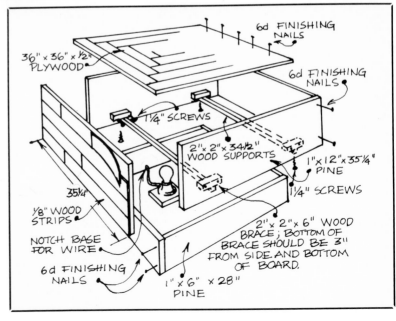

6d FINISHING NAILS

36" × 36" × ½" PLYWOOD

6d FINISHING NAILS

1¼" SCREWS

2" × 2" × 34½" WOOD SUPPORTS

1" × 12" × 35¼" PINE

1¼" SCREWS

35¼"

⅛" WOOD STRIPS

NOTCH BASE FOR WIRE

2" × 2" × 6" WOOD BRACE; BOTTOM OF BRACE SHOULD BE 3" FROM SIDE AND BOTTOM OF BOARD.

6d FINISHING NAILS

1" × 6" × 28" PINE

Photo: Thomas Hooper/Design: Chet Ross

TABLES: Freewheeling Function

Photos: Bradley Olman

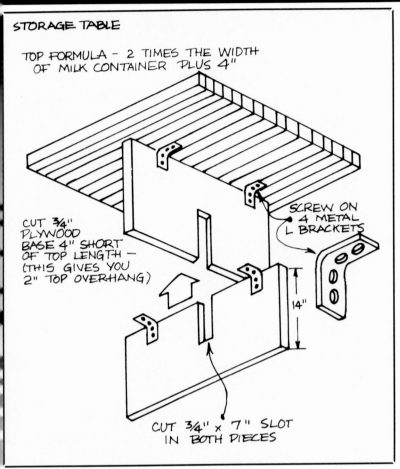

STORAGE TABLE

TOP FORMULA – 2 TIMES THE WIDTH OF MILK CONTAINER PLUS 4"

CUT ¾" PLYWOOD BASE 4" SHORT OF TOP LENGTH – (THIS GIVES YOU 2" TOP OVERHANG)

SCREW ON 4 METAL L BRACKETS

14"

CUT ¾" × 7" SLOT IN BOTH PIECES

There is a law somewhere that says the utility of a room increases geometrically by the number of working surfaces.

Left: The butcher block on the coffee table is natural looking and eminently serviceable. Underneath, plastic milk cartons with casters for rolling storage.

Right: Table tree, a table with a ficus growing right through it, rescues wasted space.

HOW TO DO IT
Coffee/Storage Table: This table can be a low buffet or a full dining table. Stash four plastic milk cartons on casters underneath the butcher block, for serving-cart-style meals.

The table is a butcher block top that sits on a big X base, made from two pieces of ¾" plywood. Cut slots in the middle of the base pieces with a saber saw. Glue wood edging tape to the plywood edges and paint the base pieces. Screw on the top as shown in diagram.

HOW TO DO IT
The Tree House: To draw the half circles for the top two pieces, use a yardstick with a nail in one end and a hole for a pencil point 24" from the nail. Cut out with a saber saw. Glue wood tape to exposed edges of plywood pieces. Assemble, as shown in diagram at right, then paint or stain.

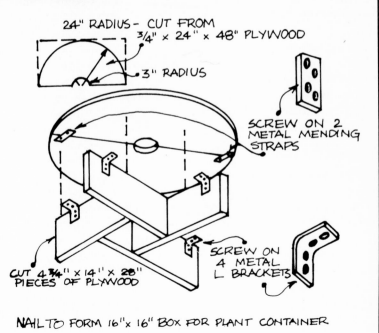

TREE HOUSE

24" RADIUS – CUT FROM ¾" × 24" × 48" PLYWOOD

3" RADIUS

SCREW ON 2 METAL MENDING STRAPS

CUT 4 ¾" × 14" × 28" PIECES OF PLYWOOD

SCREW ON 4 METAL L BRACKETS

NAIL TO FORM 16" × 16" BOX FOR PLANT CONTAINER

TABLES: Base Assumptions

Photo: Peter M. Fine

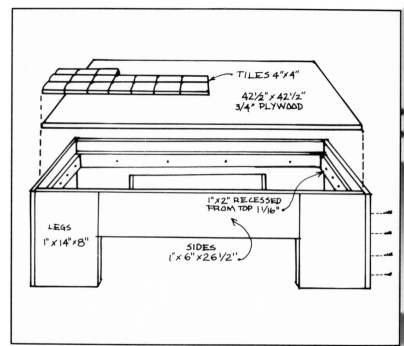

Above: Another way to put old house parts back into service is to rethink windows outside of their normally vertical context. Almost any window with sturdy panes and frame can make the transition to table.

Stained or leaded glass window sash from an antiques store or salvage yard make truly sensational tabletops, especially when lit from underneath. But even ordinary windows, like the two-over-two casements shown here, have a clear contribution to make.

HOW TO DO IT

Window Tables: Lumberyards sell table legs in a variety of straight and carved styles. The hefty legs shown here are simply 4 x 4s cut to 14″ lengths. Position them at each corner of the window and measure the

length of each side. With a hacksaw, cut four pieces of ⅛″ x ¾″ flat steel to these dimensions. Drill holes at each end of steel braces and attach near the top of each leg with one-inch-long #10 panhead screws. Mask the glass, spray-paint frame and legs, and place window sash on top.

Right: You want simple? We'll give you simple. Here's an unpretentious goodie you can toss off in an afternoon, though it won't look it. It combines a practical ceramic tile top with a plain pine frame. Simply recess a plywood top to a depth of 1¹⁄₁₆″ on 1 x 2 braces inside the frame. Spread on tile adhesive, position a few sheets of ceramic tile and spread on the grout. Stain or varnish the wooden base. You got it!

TILES 4″x4″

42½″ x 42½″
¾″ PLYWOOD

1″x2″ RECESSED
FROM TOP 1¹⁄₁₆″

LEGS
1″x 14″x 8″

SIDES
1″ x 6″ x 26½″

Above: Four wood-frame storm windows can also turn the tables. Find them at salvage yards. Get four storm windows of the same size and design, or try six narrower ones for a hexagonal base. Hinge together.

The tabletop is a piece of ¾" plywood, and the window base and tabletop were painted to match. Screw four small wood blocks into the underside of the tabletop (fitted to the base's inner corners) so the top will not slide.

Right: Another classic table design that will not cost the price of an antique: Build your own museum piece with modern materials and stain or paint it dark for a traditional look (or leave it natural).

HOW TO DO IT

X Table: Screw the wood frames together as shown in the drawing. Put the assembled sections on top of each other with the 2 x 6 uprights spaced 30″ apart. Then pencil mark the half lap joints (where the notches go). Cut these with a saw and chisel and assemble as shown. Furniture levelers will correct any small errors in measurements and will make the table steady.

Photo: Armen Kachaturian

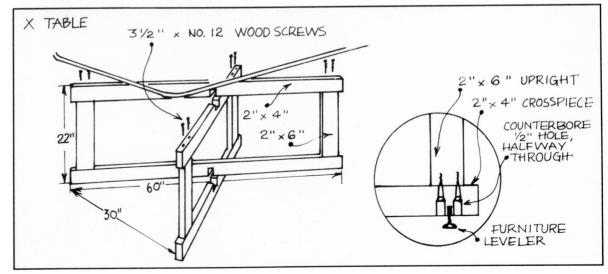

X TABLE

3½″ × NO. 12 WOOD SCREWS

2″ × 4″

2″ × 6″

22″

60″

30″

2″ × 6″ UPRIGHT

2″ × 4″ CROSSPIECE

COUNTERBORE ½″ HOLE, HALFWAY THROUGH

FURNITURE LEVELER

TABLES: Grand Illusions

Industrial chic goes tongue-in-cheek with this dustbin pedestal table. The sturdy Italian chairs, high-end Milanlike lamp and squares of different grades of sandpaper stapled on the wall all complete the picture.

HOW TO DO IT

Dustbin Table: Add wood 2 x 4 blocks to L brackets to make the tabletop high enough for eating. Put a concrete block in the can for stability. The table surface is a sheet of galvanized steel from a sheet metal shop, glued with contact cement to the plywood. Finish the tabletop with pine half-round edging strips.

Opposite: The bright, heavily lacquered coffee table has an inset electric hibachi in the middle (removable and replaceable by jade plants).

HOW TO DO IT

Lacquered Table:
Materials:
1 4' x 8' sheet of birch plywood
8 4' lengths of ¾" quarter round
2 50⅝" long 1" x 2" pine strips
12 3" L brackets
#4d and #6d finishing nails

This table comes out of one well-managed 4' x 8' sheet of birch plywood.

Build the top first by screwing the 1" x 2" strips to the underside edge of the plywood. Nail on the edge molding and cut the center hole with a saber saw (optional) to fit a hibachi or planter.

Nail the base sides together, add the shelf cleats and the shelf. Attach the base to the top with L brackets, and you are ready to finish. Fill cracks and gaps with putty. Sand thoroughly and paint with enamel, then add a final coat of polyurethane for luster and durability.

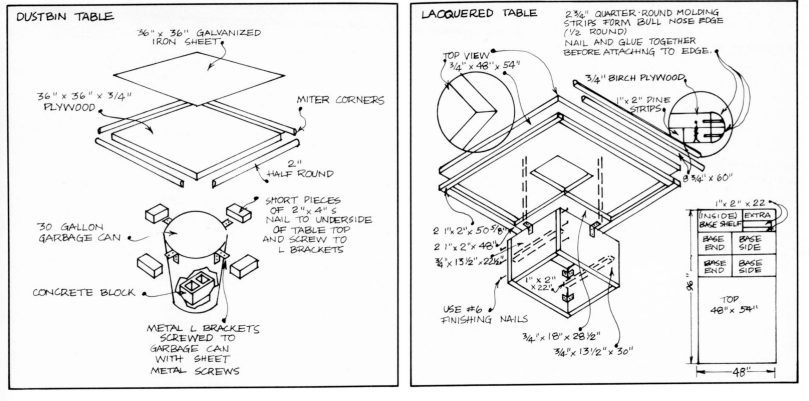

DUSTBIN TABLE

36" x 36" GALVANIZED IRON SHEET

36" x 36" x 3/4" PLYWOOD

MITER CORNERS

2" HALF ROUND

30 GALLON GARBAGE CAN

SHORT PIECES OF 2" x 4" 's NAIL TO UNDERSIDE OF TABLE TOP AND SCREW TO L BRACKETS

CONCRETE BLOCK

METAL L BRACKETS SCREWED TO GARBAGE CAN WITH SHEET METAL SCREWS

LACQUERED TABLE

2 3/4" QUARTER·ROUND MOLDING STRIPS FORM BULL NOSE EDGE (1/2 ROUND)
NAIL AND GLUE TOGETHER BEFORE ATTACHING TO EDGE.

TOP VIEW
3/4" x 48" x 54"

3/4" BIRCH PLYWOOD

1" x 2" PINE STRIPS

9 3/4" x 60"

2 1" x 2" x 50 5/8"
2 1" x 2" x 48"
3/4" x 13 1/2" x 22 1/2"

1" x 2" x 22"

USE #6 FINISHING NAILS

3/4" x 18" x 28 1/2"
3/4" x 13 1/2" x 30"

1" x 2" x 22	
(INSIDE) BASE SHELF	EXTRA
BASE END	BASE SIDE
BASE END	BASE SIDE
TOP 48" x 54"	

96"

48"

TABLES: Quick Assembly

HOW TO DO IT

Coffee Table: The coffee table above is just a pile of 1 x 4s, stacked Lincoln log style. Just dab white glue between each layer—no nailing necessary. The glass top is ¼″ thick and 3 inches wider than the base all around.

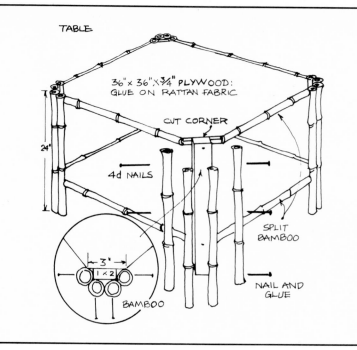

TABLE

36″ x 36″ x ¾″ PLYWOOD:
GLUE ON RATTAN FABRIC

CUT CORNER

24″

4d NAILS

SPLIT
BAMBOO

NAIL AND
GLUE

3″
1 x 2

BAMBOO

HOW TO DO IT

Bamboo Table: This is made of two pieces of plywood (cut from a single panel) with 1 x 2 legs. It is the covering that makes the difference. Put rattan-by-the-yard fabric on the plywood top and add lengths of bamboo edging to the 1 x 2s. Split bamboo finishes off the edges.

CARTS: Come Rolling Home

Below, left: Lightweight and tough, with a bonus of generous storage space down below, this industrial pipe dream on wheels is put together with aluminum tubing used for painters' scaffolding. T-joints, elbows and couplings are the fittings you need. Add a couple of plywood shelves covered with ceramic tiles, a set of casters, and you're ready to roll.

Above, right: Could this well-designed, richly colored, indestructible item that looks so handsome to our high-tech-accustomed eyes actually be a mechanic's tool chest . . . gas station furniture? It is—and it works as well in the kitchen as it does in the garage: a mobile work surface, with storage.

Below, right: Off the assembly line and into the living room— or the kitchen, or any room for that matter. This time, it's the factory that gets the credit for a traveling metal tool bin that rolls home to handle the bits and pieces of your life.

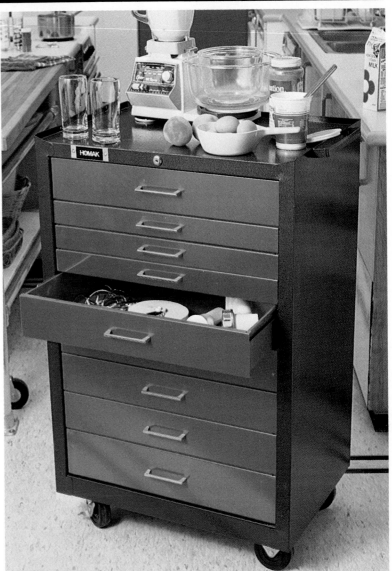

Photo: Raeanne Giovanni

Photo: Raeanne Giovanni

Photo: Thomas Hooper

FRAMING: Square Roots

Time was when framing meant spending dozens of dollars on a work of art worth considerably more than that. It meant packing up the work and taking it to a professional, who'd give you the mitered edges, the shining glass and the sealed back.

But now, posters are an essential part of the art of today—and it does seem silly to spend $75 on a frame for a $15 poster. More than that, we now hang photographs, treasured objects, collectibles and articles of clothing. That professional with the mitered experience can't help. So, once again, more options: How to tame the frame.

Right: Improve your outlook on life with this lace and plexiglas version of the old pressed-flowers-in-the-diary trick.

The poster behind the sofa only looks framed. Cut to size a ¼"-thick piece of Fome-Cor, heavy cardboard or hardboard with a mat knife or saber saw. Then mount the poster with spray adhesive.

HOW TO DO IT

Plexiglas frame: Sandwich old handiwork between two 1/8"-thick sheets of Plexiglas. Keep the pieces together with clear Plexiglas screws in the corners (see illustration below). You will need a special Plexiglas bit to drill the holes. To hang, use monofilament fishing line or a very fine chain.

Left: Framing does not need to mean mitered corners and matting. This 1904 sheet music cover is positioned on blue construction paper, then sandwiched between ⅛"-thick glass and ⅛"-thick Masonite. Swiss clips (from art stores) hold the whole thing together. The illustration below shows how the clips work.

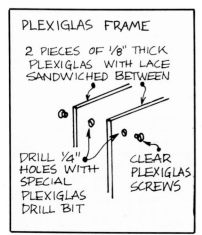

PLEXIGLAS FRAME

2 PIECES OF ⅛" THICK PLEXIGLAS WITH LACE SANDWICHED BETWEEN

DRILL ¼" HOLES WITH SPECIAL PLEXIGLAS DRILL BIT

CLEAR PLEXIGLAS SCREWS

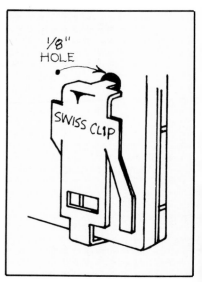

⅛" HOLE

SWISS CLIP

Photo: Thomas Hooper

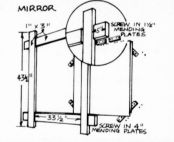

MIRROR

Above: You can frame a mirror just like a poster. Here's how:

Have the lumberyard cut 1 x 3s to length. Assemble and join with white glue and 1½" mending plates. Place mirror behind frame and allow 1¼" overlap all around to fit mirror. Screw in 4" mending plates at the corners (see illustration).

Photo: Bradley Olman

Photo: Bradley Olman/Design: John MacNamara

Above: You do not need eight little frames for eight small posters—one window frame can open up your point of view.

Hit the junkyards for an old window or door with lots of panes. Look for odd shapes, nicely aged wood or weathered paint. Cut out the posters from a poster book and tape one behind each pane. Use screw eyes and wire to hang it.

Right: A two-dimensional poster comes to life when floated a few inches from the wall.

HOW TO DO IT
Floating graphic: Hang the graphic from screw hooks in the ceiling and transparent monofilament fishing line (10 pounds test or heavier). Attach to the frame with two more screw hooks.

LAMPS: Make One Out of Anything

The unexpected—a wicker tray, a rattan mannequin, an ice sculpture—can become charming when light comes from imaginative sources. You really *can* make a lamp out of just about anything. The projects on these pages show you specific principles that can be applied to your own taste and ideas. For

example, any ceramic figure can become a lamp. And anything that covers a bare bulb can become a lampshade. Electrical supply stores provide any and all parts and hardware—and also offer useful advice. Do scout everything else—from a five-and-dime to display houses —for offbeat light sources.

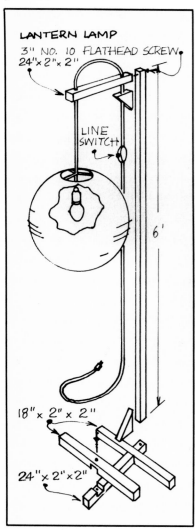

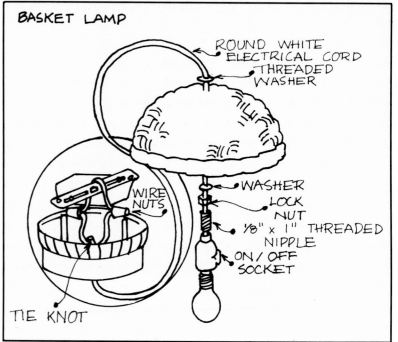

HOW TO DO IT

Lantern Lamp: A few lengths of 2 x 2s and cord transform a plain paper lantern into a standing fixture.

Cut the 2 x 2s to length as shown in the illustration. Notch

crosspieces with a saw and chisel. Drill two holes in the top board and corner brace for cord.

Assembling: Screw the 2 x 2s together. Glue on bracing triangles, top and bottom.

Wire it up as shown.

HOW TO DO IT

Basket Lamp: A big basket can hold lots of light. If the weave is loose enough, you won't need to cut a hole for the cord. Wire it as shown in the illustration above. Or hang it from an eyebolt held into the ceiling

with a Molly bolt anchor. Run the cord to the corner of the room, down to the baseboard and along to the nearest outlet. Add a plug and line switch. This method also works with a stainless steel bowl, a colander and other similarly shaped objects.

Photo: Thomas Hooper

Photo: Thomas Hooper

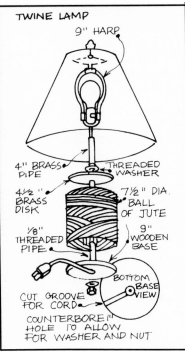

TWINE LAMP

9" HARP

4" BRASS PIPE

THREADED WASHER

4½" BRASS DISK

7½" DIA. BALL OF JUTE

⅛" THREADED PIPE

9" WOODEN BASE

CUT GROOVE FOR CORD

BOTTOM BASE VIEW

COUNTERBORE 1" HOLE TO ALLOW FOR WASHER AND NUT

HOW TO DO IT

Twine Lamp: Any large-scale spool—of wire, wool or twine—can become a lamp. This big ball of jute macramé cord came from a craft store. You will also need a wooden plaque for a base. Stack and screw together the pieces on a length of threaded pipe (see illustration at left). To make the base sit flat, use an electric drill with a 1" spade bit to counterbore a depression in the bottom of the wood plaque, then continue with a ⅜" bit to drill a hole on through. This way the nut and washer at the bottom of the rod nestle right into the base. The groove for the wire is easy to cut with a wood chisel or even a sharp knife.

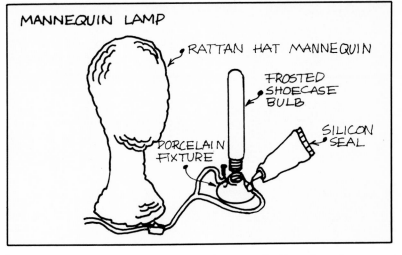

MANNEQUIN LAMP

RATTAN HAT MANNEQUIN

FROSTED SHOECASE BULB

PORCELAIN FIXTURE

SILICON SEAL

HOW TO DO IT

Mannequin Lamp: Any hollow form, open at the bottom, closed at top, can be lighted this way: Wire a porcelain ceiling socket, screw in a long, skinny showcase bulb and, in this case, plop a straw hat over the works. Hat stands are available at display stores. Cover the bare wires on the socket with silicon rubber sealer.

LAMPS: Make One Out of Anything

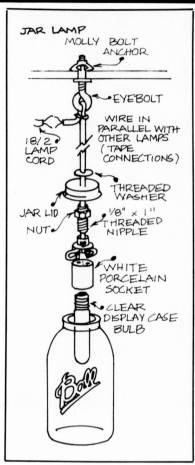

JAR LAMP

MOLLY BOLT
ANCHOR

EYEBOLT

WIRE IN
PARALLEL WITH
OTHER LAMPS
(TAPE
CONNECTIONS)

18/2
LAMP
CORD

THREADED
WASHER

JAR LID
NUT

⅛" × 1"
THREADED
NIPPLE

WHITE
PORCELAIN
SOCKET

CLEAR
DISPLAY CASE
BULB

Ball

Photo: Thomas Hooper

HOW TO DO IT

Jar Lamp: Here is a variation of
the kerosene lamp, using an
old-fashioned canning jar. Drill
a ⅜" hole in the jar lid for the
pipe nipple.

String all the parts together,
as above, on round white electrical cord, and attach the two
wires to the terminal screws of
the socket. Screw in the bulb,
screw on the jar and hang.

HOW TO DO IT

Swan Lamp: This plastic ice
mold is yet another example of
how just about anything can
become a lamp. You can buy a
hollow swan like this (or a
mermaid or many other molds)
at a restaurant supply store.
Wire it up as shown.

Photo: Bill Helms

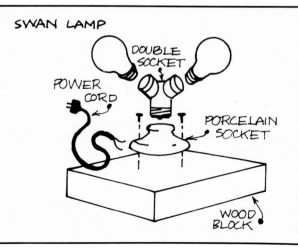

SWAN LAMP

DOUBLE
SOCKET

POWER
CORD

PORCELAIN
SOCKET

WOOD
BLOCK

Photo: Thomas Hooper

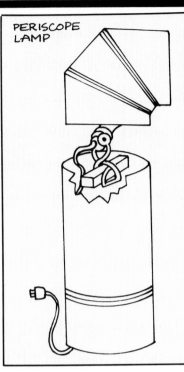

PERISCOPE LAMP

Photo: Bradley Olman

HOW TO DO IT

Periscope Lamp: No nuts, bolts, or skill are needed to make this lamp. It is made of stovepipe sections with a clamp-on light inside—an easy way to make sculptural lighting for little money.

Since builders' supply yards stock several sizes of stovepipe, you can make the lamps almost any scale. Before assembling, wedge a wooden crosspiece (the same length as the diameter of the pipe) into the pipe to hold the clamp-on light in the curve of the hood. Paint the inside of the hood to reflect more light.

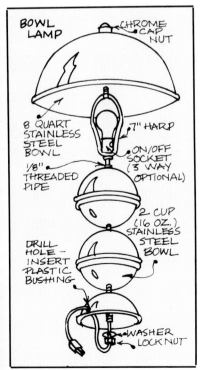

BOWL LAMP

CHROME CAP NUT

8 QUART STAINLESS STEEL BOWL

7" HARP

1/8" THREADED PIPE

ON/OFF SOCKET (3 WAY OPTIONAL)

2 CUP (16 OZ.) STAINLESS STEEL BOWL

DRILL HOLE - INSERT PLASTIC BUSHING

WASHER
LOCK NUT

HOW TO DO IT

Bowl Lamp: This sleek industrial design is actually a clever stack of stainless steel mixing bowls.

To drill holes in the bottom of each, set the bowl right side up on a piece of scrap wood. Use a center punch and a hammer to make a little dent in the bottom. (That will keep the drill point from scooting around.) Drill the holes with a ⅜" bit in an electric drill. Also drill a hole near the rim of the bottom bowl for the cord to exit.

Cut the threaded rod to length with a hacksaw, then screw all the parts tightly together and wire it up.

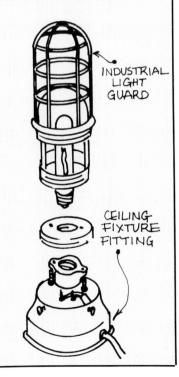

INDUSTRIAL LAMP

INDUSTRIAL LIGHT GUARD

CEILING FIXTURE FITTING

Photo: Thomas Hooper

HOW TO DO IT

Industrial Lamp: This lantern-like lamp practically makes itself. Its shell is an industrial light guard from a hardware store. For the base, match the guard to a porcelain ceiling fixture from a lamp shop. Wire as shown. A long showcase bulb fits inside the glass dome.

APT IDEAS 281

HALLWAYS: Cures for Tunnel Vision

If you have always taken a narrow view of hallways, take off the blinders: Think of them not as mere corridors to pass through but as extensions of other rooms. With space so scarce, spotlighting and adorning a hall is just one more chance to make a mark on your surroundings.

Have a private showing in your hallway. Ferret out gorgeous old frames and showcase antique portraits. Or, for up-to-date, but old-time-looking portraits, have sepia prints made.

Whether the collection is permanent or the show moves to another hall, you can have a versatile gallery by hanging portraits from picture rail molding. It will serve two purposes: The walls are left nail-free and the gallery takes on a Victorian air. The picture rail is attached near the ceiling and has a lip to hang hooks from.

For more turn-of-the-century design, try wainscoting one or more walls with sheet steel panels (formerly tin and used for ceilings). Paint or give them two coats of polyurethane so there is no chance of rust.

Time was, if you wanted fabric on the walls, it took hours of smoothing out tiny bubbles of glue or tacking it to clumsy frames. Now there is a simple solution, called Fabri-Trak, that eases the work and protects the fabric (available at wallpaper stores).

Frame a wall with long plastic strips that have "jaws" at the top to hide raw edges and an adhesive strip to hold the fabric tight. The fabric is stuck to the adhesive edge, then stuffed into the "jaws," using a special tool that looks like a fork without tines.

The hall works as a gallery here too. One grand romantic poster opens up the narrow space and makes the biggest impression—much more readily than many smaller ones would do. The made-yesterday (but of timeless design) clock deserves the throne position at the hall-way's end.

Dye-It Rite

Left: Artsy throw pillows start with canvas from an art supply store. Brush a solution of half dye, half water onto canvas that has been sponged down with hot water until it's evenly wet (*how* wet determines how much the dye will "bleed"). Apply dye solution with small brushes. When it's dry, take it to the dry cleaner to set.

Below, left and right: Revelation! Wicker and straw take dye, too. Dye soaks into the fibers so the color seems to emerge from within.

Tips: Wicker takes dye best if it has a dull surface; sand it lightly if the surface seems too slick. Small pieces—baskets, trays and such—can be immersed in a tub or sink for about 15 minutes, or until the desired color is reached. Rinse with cold water. If the items float, keep them pushed down and turning. Chairs and large pieces can be dyed too, but you'll need to sponge the solution onto those that won't fit in a tub. Wet the wicker first with water. Mix one bottle of dye to ½ cup hot water. Sponge it on until you get the shade you want. Let set ten minutes before rinsing.

Opposite: This candy-colored couch is a custom dye job. The plushness comes from fabric that's at least 50 percent cotton, like velour or terry, and polyester batting (the kind sold in packages for quilt-making) to plump out the mattress and box spring on all four sides. The covers are huge pieces of fabric measured to 12 inches wider all around, then elasticized around the edge like a fitted sheet.

The sausage-shaped pillows are rolls of batting. Make your own round and square ones, or use bed pillows.

Photos : Thomas Hooper

PLANTS: Indoor Bloomers

You do not need a backyard to enjoy a bed of flowering wonders. They can add living color to any room that has the right light. The following plants can be identified on the chart below:

1. Stephanotis Floribunda: Needs full to medium sun; keep soil fairly moist.

2. Clivia Miniata: Needs medium sun to partial shade; keep fairly moist.

3. Paphiopedilum Macrathon (Lady Slipper Orchid): Requires medium sun to partial shade; evenly moist soil.

4. Anthurium: Needs medium sun; keep evenly moist; keep leaves clean.

5 and **6. Agave:** Needs full to medium sun; keep soil dry to fairly moist.

7. Cymbidium (Orchid): Needs medium sun; soil fairly to evenly moist; blooms fall to spring.

8 and **9. Opuntia:** Needs full sun; dry soil.

10. Carnegiea Gigantea: Needs full sun; dry soil.

11. Echinocactus (Golden Barrel Cactus): Needs full sun; dry soil; cooler winter.

12 and **13. Sinningia Gloxinia:** Needs medium sun; fairly moist soil.

14. Gardenia: Needs full to medium sun; fairly moist soil.

15. Strelitzia Reginae (Bird-of-Paradise): Needs full to medium sun; evenly to fairly moist soil.

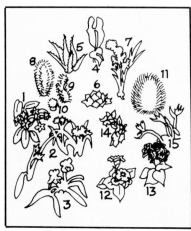

PLANTS: Balcony Garden

Here is the city version of that special truck-garden patch traditionally tucked in close to the farmhouse. In town, you cannot dig your toes into the soil but you can certainly harvest your crops, indoors or out, wherever there is space.

Here are a few things to know about growing vegetables and herbs:

Vegetables: Start tomatoes, peppers, cucumbers and onions from plants (not seeds) whenever you can. For tomatoes, the small varieties are best because they will not sprawl. Yield in 45 to 55 days. Most varieties of green bell peppers yield in about 60 days. Radishes grow from seeds in about 29 days.

Herbs: Buy plants, if possible, and start harvesting as soon as you bring them home. Pick the top leaves from most herbs to keep new growth coming. Keep sweet basil leaves pinched back or the plant will get tall and scraggly. Snip the tops off chives for mild onion flavor. Dill grows tall and wide so leave room. Keep oregano trimmed back. Parsley is a short, thick plant; pick the outer sprigs and leave the middle ones to grow.

HOW TO DO IT

Planters: A container can be practically anything so long as it holds dirt, has drainage holes or has a bottom layer of gravel. Or streamline things by making any of these quick-build boxes.

Each box is made from rough-sawn cedar 1 x 8s. The corners are butted together, then nailed with 8d galvanized casing nails. Decide your dimensions, cut the boards with a saw and assemble.

Photo: Thomas Hooper

Of Greenhouses and Sun Scoops

Greenhouse windows are one of the best gardening "tools" you can buy, and they are now available in kits that are reasonably priced ($300 and up) and relatively easy to install. Greenhouses don't guarantee runaway horticultural success, and they are not necessarily efficient solar collectors.

What *does* work is a passive solar collector called a sun scoop *(below, right)*, shown with its "beadwall"—an insulating layer of Styrofoam pellets sandwiched between two pieces of glass—to conserve accumulated heat.

APT INFORMATION

Putting together an apartment often means a lot more than buying and arranging furniture. In fact, putting together an apartment frequently means taking it apart first—fixing, stapling, drilling, hammering and dozens of other tasks. Sure, you can tip the building guy $15 to hang that lamp from the ceiling—but save your money: The following pages show you how to do it yourself and help to fill in the blanks about filling in the cracks of plasterboard, concrete and plywood ceilings. There's a special section that explains all about track lighting —how to choose it and how to install it yourself. And if you like your lighting sources a little lower than the ceiling, we also show you how to figure out the makings of a lamp.

In addition, there's a special self-protection manual all about your rights as a tenant. You may be surprised to learn how many you do have—and exercising them is not nearly as rigorous as most legal calisthenics. The key here is Protect Yourself, and we show you how to do just that—before, during and after your lease runs out.

Because living in an apartment is not just finding the right one (which this section also describes) or moving into one (ditto)—but also knowing what to do when something goes wrong.

Self Help: You as the Expert

A few decades ago, Doing-It-Yourself meant off-duty executives puttering around in their garages over the weekend in sprawling suburban homes, while their wives put in time at the potter's wheel at the local community college. It's all different now. After the back-to-nature and liberation movements of the sixties and the self-fulfillment and self-reliant movements of the seventies, we've been instilled with a new consciousness that, indeed, we can take pride in our own creations—whether they be a picture frame or a seating system.

This section tells you how to do many of the things that need to be done—yourself. You can be the expert when it comes to making a lamp or a coffee table or a desk—or even when you hang a lamp and then need to camouflage the hole you made in the ceiling.

The Handy Under-the-Sink Toolbox

THE BASIC KIT

1. Hammer: A 13-ounce curved-claw hammer is the handiest size. Buy a good one (not the $1.39 specials). Steel shanks are the strongest and Fiberglas the most flexible for good hammering action.

2. Screwdrivers: A set of three or four screwdrivers should meet most of your needs. Find a set with varying sizes, plus a small Phillips (often called cross-tip).

3. Pliers: Ordinary slip joint pliers work fine for most jobs, although parrot nose pliers open wider, squeeze harder and are especially good for plumbing work.

4. Adjustable wrench: Get a 6" wrench and a 9", for extra big jobs.

5. Mat knife: A handle for replaceable razor blades. You always have a sharp knife—great for opening packages.

6. Push drill: Start holes for screws and plastic anchors with this handy little tool; often handier to use than an electric drill. Bits store in the handle.

7. Cordless electric screwdriver: This works like a push drill and also drives screws. Keep it plugged in and charged up, then detach it when you need it.

8. Putty knife: Use it to fill holes in the wall with spackling compound and for scraping paint. Knives come in various widths and degrees of flexibility, but one medium-width, fairly stiff blade does most jobs.

9. Ice pick or **Awl:** Useful for various poking and chipping chores.

10. Combination square: Use to measure and mark exact right angles. Especially useful when cutting boards and assembling pieces for your projects. Also measures 45-degree angles, and the metal rule slips out to make a straight edge. Some even have little spirit levels in them.

11. Block plane: Use this to smooth the edges of wood pieces after sawing and to plane off mistakes in fitting.

12. Staple gun: If you plan to put up ceiling tile, reupholster furniture, or fasten fabric to a frame, this will come in handy. Keep a supply of ¼" and ½" staples.

13. Portable electric drill: For most people the quarter-inch drill is handiest. (Quarter-inch refers to the largest size drill-bit shank it will hold.) There are many different types of drills with many different options on the market but here are the important ones: Variable speed—so you can use the drill as an electric screwdriver and have better control when drilling holes; a reversing switch—so you can unscrew screws; and double insulation (a plastic or part plastic tool casing)—so it is almost impossible to get a shock.

Also, buy a good set of high-speed drill bits and a couple of screwdriver bits—flat blade and Phillips. Spade bits let you drill large diameter holes. Beyond that, there are all kinds of attachments to make your drill do everything from sanding to pumping water.

14. Portable electric saber saw (also called portable jigsaw): This saw is an inexpensive little workhorse that will do a number of different jobs well. Although designed to cut curves in relatively thin material, it will chew its way, with reasonable accuracy, through most materials that you are likely to use. It is a smaller version of the big circular saws carpenters use but it is a lot less noisy, more portable, and less expensive.

You can cut straight lines by clamping a straight stick to the wood, to guide the saw base, then use a block plane to smooth up the cut edge. You can also get special blades for plastic, metal, and other special materials. Two features to look for: double insulation and variable speed.

A SHOPPING TIP

When you buy any tool, choose one of good quality, one that will last a long time. Since a hand tool acts as an extension of your arm or hand, pick it up, hold it in your hand, and get the feel of it before you buy. This will tell you more about the quality and craftsmanship of the tool than anything else, and whether you will feel comfortable working with it.

IN THE BOTTOM OF THE BOX

Other items you will want in the under-the-sink toolbox: chalk, pencils, white glue, cup hooks, spackling compound, wood putty, a small G clamp and bar clamp, nails, screws, and drill bits. Anything else for more major projects can be rented from a tool shop.

A WORD ABOUT WOOD

All measurements for standard plywood are given as 1 x 2; however, in reality, the actual size is ¾" x 1¾" because wood shrinks at first. If you are using hardwood on any project, take note that the size will be different from the 1 x 2 plywood.

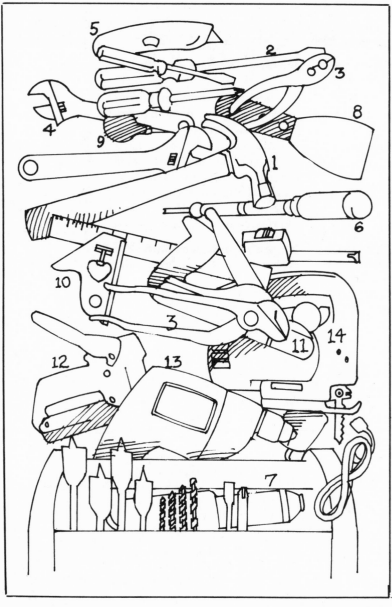

How to Hang Anything from the Ceiling

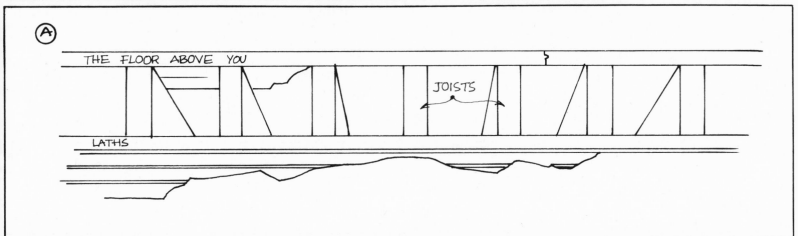

Once you get your bolts and tools together, you can hang anything—up to 200 pounds—in just a few minutes. What you hang and how you hang it depends on the kind of ceiling you have. Here are step-by-step instructions for whatever is over your head:

LATH AND PLASTER CEILINGS

Found mostly in older buildings, this type is probably the easiest to deal with. The only tricky part is locating the wooden joists when you want to hang something heavy.

Hanging heavy things: If you are going to put up something that takes a lot of weight (a hammock, for example), hang it from screw hooks in the joists, which are wooden beams spaced 16" to 24" apart that run the length or width of your ceiling. First you must find them.

How to do it: You will need an electric drill, a screw eye or a screw hook, and a coat hanger. The easiest way to find a joist is to drill a hole straight up. If you are lucky, you will hit one on the first try. If not, drill through the same hole again slantwise. Then straighten out the coat hanger and poke it through the hole. If you hit something solid, it is a joist. Measure how far away it is by keeping your thumb on the hanger, then lightly mark the

appropriate spot on the ceiling.

If you do not hit anything solid on your first try, it means the joists run in another direction. Drill slantwise again—in the same hole as before—but 90 degrees left or right. You should definitely hit a joist with another poke of the hanger.

Then drill a hole slightly smaller than the shank diameter of your screw eye or screw hook. Twist it in tight.

Hanging light things: You can hang plants (not trees) from the laths, which are little boards that run across the joists to

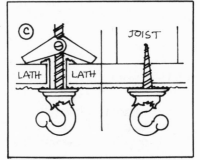

If you use a Molly bolt, drill a hole the same diameter as the bolt and insert it into the ceiling. As you tighten it, a split-sleeve will expand against the inside of the ceiling and hold it tight. Unscrew the bolt and the Molly will stay put.

support the plaster ceiling.

How to do it: You will need an electric drill with a spade bit and a toggle hook or Molly bolt. The only reason you might use a joist to hang something light in your lath and plaster ceiling is because you want it in a specific spot. So first, drill a tiny hole with a regular bit exactly where you want to hang it. If you hit a joist, just twist in a screw eye or screw hook and you are done.

If you do not hit a joist, switch to a toggle hook or Molly bolt. Drill a hole just big enough for the closed toggles to

fit through. (Instructions are usually on the toggle packages that come in a complete set.) Then push the toggles and bolt into the ceiling, making sure enough of the bolt sticks out to screw the swag hook on. Screwing the hook tight will lock the assembly in place.

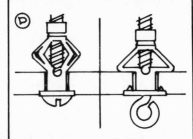

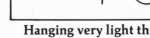

Hanging very light things: If you are hanging something that weighs under 25 pounds, just twist a little screw eye or screw hook right into one of those laths.

TOOLS

SCREW HOOK

SPADE BIT

SCREW EYE

MOLLY BOLT

TOGGLE BOLT

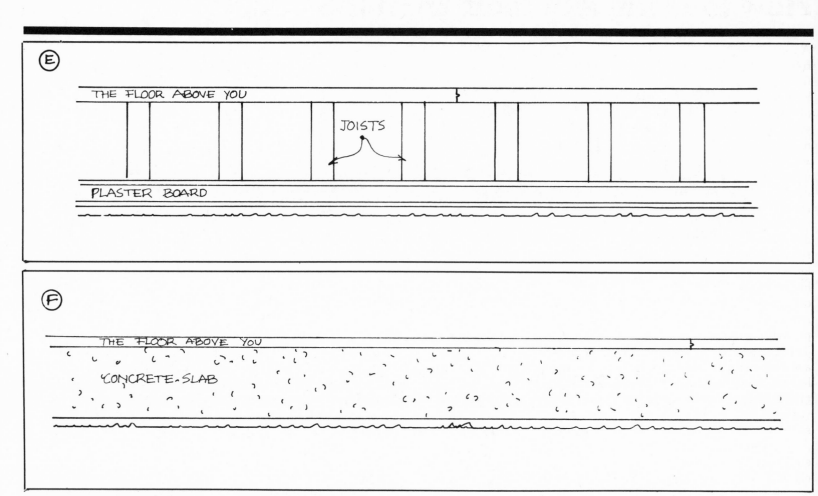

PLASTERBOARD CEILINGS

You will find these mostly in new low rises. For hanging purposes, plasterboard ceilings are almost the same as lath and plaster—minus the laths.

As before, hang heavy things from the joists. Lightweight items (under 50 pounds) can be hung from the plasterboard with a toggle hook. Follow the same instructions as for a lath and plaster ceiling.

CONCRETE CEILINGS

You will find concrete ceilings mostly in modern high rises. It is tough to drill a hole in concrete, but a carbide bit and an electric drill will do wonders. You will also need to get an "anchor" and a screw eye or screw hook. An anchor is made of soft material (lead, fiber, or nylon) that is threaded up the middle to receive the screw eye or screw hook.

How to do it: Be sure your carbide bit is the same diameter as the anchor, then drill a hole straight up—exactly where you want to hang something.

Insert the anchor into the hole. Make sure it is a tight fit. As you twist the screw eye or

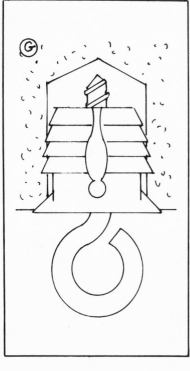

screw hook into the anchor, the soft material will actually expand into the concrete and hold the screw tight.

Important: The friction of the anchor against the concrete is all that is keeping things off the floor. Make sure the anchor fits tightly. If you are going to hang lots of things, you might want to put up a plywood ceiling (see below). Instructions are the same but use anchors instead of toggle bolts.

HOW TO MAKE A PLYWOOD CEILING

Measure the area you will use to hang things. Pick up a piece of ½" plywood from the lumberyard—cut to fit your measurements—and attach it with a toggle bolt in each corner. Paint it to match the ceiling.

Then, with screw eyes or screw hooks, you can hang anything. When you move, just pull the whole thing down and fill the four holes.

PATCHING UP

In most cases patching up simply means filling in the holes with spackling compound.

But if you use an anchor, part of it will still be visible after you remove the eyebolt. A few taps with a hammer will knock the offending anchor up into the ceiling so you can smooth over the surface.

If you have a textured ceiling, try dabbing the soft, wet spackling compound with a damp sponge to approximate the texture.

HOW MUCH WILL IT HOLD

In most cases the ceiling will fall before the hanging hardware will. Here is how much a sturdy ceiling will hold:

Plasterboard: Up to 50 pounds; anything heavier, find a joist.

Lath and Plaster: 75 to 100 pounds; anything heavier, start looking for a joist.

Concrete: Up to 200 pounds per lead anchor.

All About Track Lighting

A track system does it all. Affixed to the ceiling, it leaves floor space free, and it can also help change the look and mood of rooms with a mere flick of a switch. Track systems offer multicolored bulbs and filters, and are completely adjustable, moving as you move your furniture and objects within a room. Plus, track lighting can do a lot to visually alter the dimensions of space. Bathing the wall of a small room with light will make the space seem bigger. Large spaces on the other hand become more intimate with overhead spots complementing other lighting. Track fixtures, of course, can also help direct proper work light to desks, workshops, game tables, and kitchen counters without cluttering up work surfaces with table lamps.

Track lighting is easy to install, though you might need an electrician if you want the wiring recessed or if you put in more than one circuit with dimmer controls. To set up a system, the greatest effort goes into the preshopping decision. Before you buy ask yourself the following questions:

Where will the light be required?

What is the scale and size of the space?

Is the room or arrangement of the room apt to change, altering the lighting requirements?

Where will the track be mounted?

Will it plug into a wall outlet or be wired into a recessed power box in the ceiling?

Do the fixtures have proper tension or a locking device so they remain in position when aimed toward a particular area?

Does the mounting device on top of the fixture fit the track you are considering?

HOW TO CHOOSE A TRACK

There are two types of track: 1) a continuous open-channel track or 2) a track with outlets prespaced along a closed channel. Continuous channel track offers the most flexibility. Fixtures can be set in anywhere along its length and can be readily changed if the function or room arrangement changes.

Where lighting requirements are not apt to change, and flexibility is not the prime concern, you might choose closed channel tracks, which are protected from grease and steam. They can be painted along the bottom edge for a neater, finished look. Fixtures "stab" into outlets along the length of the track.

Both types of tracks are sold in various lengths and finishes. Most track sections are prewired and polarized to assure a safe, properly grounded electrical connection. They plug together as easily as model train tracks and, with flexible corner connectors, can be hooked together at any angle.

CHOOSING A POWER SOURCE FOR YOUR TRACK

There are two ways to supply power to a track system:

1. Connect the track to a recessed power box in the ceiling, which conceals the wiring. (A licensed electrician is needed for this job.)

2. Plug the track into a standard wall outlet with a cord-and-plug accessory. To minimize the cord, run it along the ceiling-wall line, down the corner of the room and along the baseboard to the outlet.

A word about circuits: The average 15- or 20-amp circuit in a normal room can safely supply about 1,200 watts of power. Add up the wattage of each bulb on your track to be sure you do not exceed your limit and blow a fuse.

A single circuit track system is sufficient for most apartments. However, more exciting effects are possible with a multicircuit system. You might have colored lights on one circuit, white light on another, all on the same track. In this case an electrician divides an ordinary electrical circuit into two, three, even four separate circuits, and replaces a wall switch with several switches or dimmers. Instead of the regular single-circuit track, you install a multicircuit track, which is deeper, and must be connected to a power box in the ceiling.

MOUNTING A TRACK

The easiest way to mount a track is directly on the ceiling by simply using the precut holes in the top of the track. Insert appropriate wood screws or toggle bolts through the holes. To attach a track to a concrete ceiling, drill holes with a special masonry bit, insert a lead or plastic anchor, then use a sheet-metal screw ½" longer than the plug to secure the track to the surface. (See How to Hang Anything from the Ceiling.)

To light objects on a wall or to wash a wall with light, the track should be mounted 2 to 3' from the wall when ceilings are 7½ to 9' high. Move the track one foot further from the wall for every two additional feet of ceiling height. If the track is mounted too close to the wall, any object hanging on the wall will be shadowed. If the track is too far from the wall, the light source may be reflected and cause glare.

CHOOSING THE TRACK FIXTURES

Cylinders, squares, and spheres are the most common fixture shapes. They are often used to provide work or accent lighting. Shovel-cut cylinders are especially made to wash a wall with light.

A WORD ABOUT LOW-VOLTAGE LIGHTING

Low-wattage bulbs and fixtures are more expensive than standard equipment but their cost is offset by their long life and savings in electricity. They use half the power of standard bulbs, and can be attached to any track. Low-voltage lighting is whiter, crisper, gives off less heat, and is more brilliant than standard lighting. When a low-voltage fixture is capped with a tinted filter, it improves the quality of colored light.

Anatomy of a Lamp

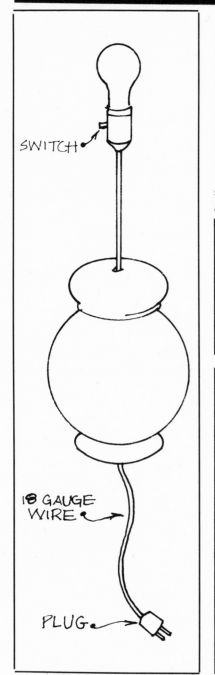

SWITCH

18 GAUGE WIRE

PLUG

Which wire: The wire you need for most lamps is 18-gauge, two-wire rubber, or plastic-covered lamp cord (called 18/2).

To connect wire: Split the insulation at the end of the wire with a knife, and cut off about ¾" of insulation from each wire. (Drawing A.)

Then unscrew the terminal screws on the plug or socket, and wrap one of the exposed wire ends around each of the screws. Retighten the screws and reassemble the socket or plug. (Drawing B.)

To splice lengths of wire: Twist the two pairs together as shown, and wrap with electrician's tape so one pair cannot touch the other and cause a short. (Drawing C.)

Line switch: A line switch installed at a convenient point on the lamp cord is especially effective with lamps that have no other on/off switch. Instructions come on the switch kits (from any lamp or hardware store) and they are assembled like this. (Drawing D.)

A safety note: To keep the wire from pulling off the terminal screws of a socket or plug (and to avoid shock), separate the two lamp cord wires and tie a knot like this. (Drawing E.)

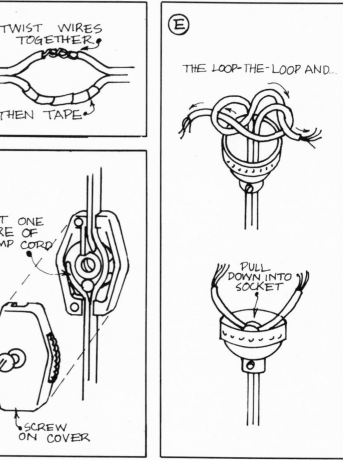

Ⓐ

Ⓑ TERMINAL SCREW

Ⓒ TWIST WIRES TOGETHER. THEN TAPE.

Ⓓ CUT ONE WIRE OF LAMP CORD SCREW ON COVER

Ⓔ THE LOOP-THE-LOOP AND... PULL DOWN INTO SOCKET

What You Should Know as a Tenant

When you own your own home, if you have an argument with the landlord, you are fighting with yourself. When you rent an apartment, you are usually arguing with an anonymous voice on the other end of the line, or writing monthly checks to a phantom address. But what happens when that post office box does not fix the lock on the outer door? What if you get no heat, and you want to know how to give your landlord heat about it? What happens if you need to sue your landlord? Do you know the difference between arbitration and negotiation? And what about finding a new apartment? How can you make sure you are getting a good one? And after you have secured an apartment, how can you make it secure? All this is explored on the following pages, which offer some basic tenets about tenancy.

Finding the Right Apartment

With some places you will want to sign a lease after your first walk-through. But even when the apartment has that can't-live-without oak floor or enormous bay window, you still need to pay attention to some of the everyday things: the way the place is laid out, what kind of neighborhood it is in, how the fixtures work. Here is a step-by-step guide for inspecting your apartment:

Neighborhood: Where you live can turn sour if things like transportation, shopping, and recreational facilities are not all they should be. A convenient location, for instance, would be at the end of a more-or-less straight line from work. Conversely, a commute that requires complicated changes from one highway to another—or bus transfers—might be rated "far out," even though the distance is not far. And you can be too close to wheezing buses, noisy (and nosy) neighbors, busy highways, and the local fire engine route. Nearby schools are important if you have children.

It is a good idea to psyche out the kind of people who are living in the building or complex—singles, families with young children, older people. Many places have become very specialized according to life situations.

Do not just look on the block. Travel a few miles to get a clear idea about shops and services and places to play. If these are missing or remote, the area hardly qualifies as a neighborhood.

Parking: Will you park your car on the street, in a lot, or in a garage? Are parking fees as much as the rent? Will parking be available to your guests?

Entrance: The way a landlord maintains the front door and lobby areas of the building is a good indication of what his attitude will be when you want

more heat in the winter. Check for security: a good intercom system, adequate locks, and/or a doorman to fend off offenders. Well-lit entries make it easier for people with keys and harder for those without.

On the way up, check out things like the size of elevators and the width of stairways to see if you can get what you already own into the apartment. If there are stairs, how many will you have to climb everyday?

Floor plans: There are certain human factors to consider about how an apartment is laid out: Is the bathroom within stumbling distance of the bedroom? The dining area near the kitchen? Is there a place near the door where you can pull off boots? Can the kitchen be closed off from the living room if you need to do it?

Mentally move in your furniture and try to arrange it, estimating whether there is adequate wall space for the sofa and enough height for your bookcases. If you have an odd piece of furniture or if the apartment has a lot of nooks and crannies, it is a good idea to take along a tape measure.

General condition: Here is where you have to have a clear idea of what you are able and willing to do yourself. If things look a little shoddy and you do not mind doing a little work, you should expect a break on the rent. Try bargaining. You may at the very least get the management to supply materials.

Windows should operate smoothly, with no gaps for air or noise to leak through. To check out just how sound resistant a window or sliding glass door is, open it, wait for a large truck or other noisemaker to pass, then close the window. The din should substantially dim.

Peace and quiet: The more

solid a wall, the quieter the apartment will be. So take time to thump on common partitions. Old-fashioned plaster and lath walls do a fairly good job of blocking noise if they are not badly cracked and pierced with holes. Middle-age buildings—built in the fifties and early sixties—frequently have nothing but flimsy dry-wall construction, which is notoriously noisy. Many newer buildings use double walls, staggered-stud construction, and a variety of other techniques to protect your ears from noise.

Kitchen: Investigate the stove, refrigerator, fans, dishwasher, and garbage disposal to see how well they work.

Make sure there is enough space in the kitchen and that it is well organized.

Bathroom: Make sure everything here works. Extra storage space is a bonus.

Storage: You will never have enough space to store everything but can this apartment at least neatly file away most of your belongings? Is a big closet or a locker in the basement available for bicycles, skis, barbecue grill, etc.?

Can you control heating and cooling precisely? Find out who pays for the heat and cool—you or the landlord. If the building is not air conditioned, does it at least have wiring adequate for window units? Check to be sure each room has at least one electrical outlet per wall (although you can add more with surface wiring). Is there an antenna on the roof for television?

Extras: Swimming pools, saunas, health clubs, and putting greens are nice but do not forget about the less flashy amenities. Do check out laundry facilities. (You can often tell how well run a building is by looking at the laundry room.) Is there a doorman or someone in the building who can accept

packages and messages when you are out?

Apartment guides: Apartment hunting in a strange city is not necessarily the chore it used to be. Over the past years apartment guides—publications giving detailed information about available rental housing —have been started in most major cities.

The guides do not list every apartment in town, and they are not objective about the places they mention. (The cost of printing the booklets is paid by the complexes and a few other companies who want your business. It is a form of advertising usually dominated by the middle and upper income places.) But they give you more to go on than the classified ads. Complimentary copies are available through most chambers of commerce.

Who are you renting? If the manager is brusque or long-winded when you ask about the apartment, you can multiply that by fifty the day the furnace breaks down. When you arrive on the premises, size up the manager's own quarters. If he has been relegated to a former coal bin on the dark side of the furnace, you can be certain the owner does not care who is minding the building. If you are visiting a big complex, expect an office, not a corner of the manager's own apartment.

If the person who shows you the apartment is not the manager, ask for an introduction. Find out about the chain of command, who will give you answers and action after you have moved in, especially if you are being shown around by a real estate agent.

Flexibility is another mark of a manager who is in command of the job. If you suggest something out of the ordinary, he or she should be able to give you an answer within a reasonable time, or pose an alternative.

What to Look for in a Lease

Contracts between landlords and tenants are rooted in a tradition that has total regard for the owner of land, with little thought given for the well-being of tenants who lived on that land. Just the words landlord and tenant are indicative of that historically unequal relationship.

But in the last ten or so years, great strides forward have been made. Enlightened lawmakers, jurists, and fair-minded apartment owners are making the management of apartments more businesslike: Money is paid and services are rendered in return. But there are still landlords who offer you an apartment on a take-it-or-leave-it basis, complete with an archaic lease they bought at the corner stationery store. These leases are usually margin to margin with small type and contain clauses that discriminate against you as a consumer: They may severely restrict how you use your apartment, ignore the need for maintenance of your apartment, and even try to bluff you out of rights that you are given under the Constitution.

So the first step, after sizing up the management and property, is to examine the lease or rental agreement you are asked to sign.

HOW TO READ A LEASE

Read every word. It is good advice in any contract but especially in apartment leases—and for a very good reason: More often than not it is the sentence buried in the middle of a paragraph that tells you what you really need to know.

Most leases are divided by section titles that are supposed to make reading it easier; they are often no help. The sections seem to be thrown in at random. Read the lease with an eye for how the different sections relate to each other.

Be wary of a sentence that begins: "It shall be deemed a substantial violation..." A substantial violation is the legal term for something that could get you evicted. Although some judges have said that these rules are unreasonable in the context of the entire agreement, others stick to the letter of the lease. Beware of phrases and words in all capital letters, heavier print, and italics; some judges would consider them "substantial" also.

Before you sign, read over all apartment "Rules and Regulations." Most leases state that these rules are part of the lease agreement. Plus, they are the day-to-day rules you will have to live with.

A few states have regulations that leases must be written in plain English. But, until yours does, here are some of the most used "legalese" words demystified.

Lessee: The renter.

Lessor: That is the owner or one of his employees, such as a manager or rental agent.

Demised premises: It sounds foreboding, but it is the legal jargon for the property you are renting.

Term of the lease: Just the length of time the lease is in effect.

Ejectment: The "nice" word for eviction.

Notice to quit: This is a written order for you to get off the landlord's property.

Notice to vacate: That is your written statement that you are getting off the landlord's property.

Assign or sublet: You will see these words together but they have a little different meaning. Subletting is when you lease out your place for only part of the time you have signed for (for instance, just for the summer). Assigning is when you lease out your apartment for the remainder of the time your lease runs.

Indemnify and render the lessor harmless: This means to make the landlord free of any responsibility even to the point of your not suing him.

Arrears: Money not paid when it is due, such as overdue rent.

Distraint proceeding (or proceed by distress): If you owe the landlord money and do not pay up, he can "proceed by distress" against you—that is, take your personal property to force you to pay or eventually sell it to get his money.

Goods and chattels: That is your personal property—both animate and inanimate. It is usually what the landlord will threaten to take if you do not pay.

Replevin: That is the legal action you can take to get property back that was unlawfully seized (taken through "unlawful distress"). Watch out though—many leases say you agree not to take this action.

Inure (or enure): It simply means to "take effect." Most leases inure when you sign them.

Special lease sections to double-check:

Sublet or assign clauses: If you cannot sublet your place, find out if the lease stipulates that there is no penalty (loss of your deposit or the demand for entire lease's rent immediately due and payable) if your employer transfers you.

Security deposits: Make sure you will get your entire deposit back by a reasonable date if you fulfill your lease duties. Although the matter is still up in the air legally, many tenants are fighting landlords who automatically—no matter if the place is spotless—deduct cleaning fees from security deposits. Also, in some states, you will be able to get interest on your deposit.

What happens when you move: See how long in advance you will need to notify your landlord that you are moving. (The contract will most likely say "in writing"; even better, send the letter by certified mail.)

When the lease is up: See if the lease automatically renews if you take no action (like writing the landlord that you are leaving) or if it turns into a month-to-month tenancy.

Privacy: Is there a clause restricting your landlord from entering your place at will?

Repairs: Does the lease mention anything about your landlord keeping the place in shape?

It's a bluff: Some lease clauses are unconstitutional, and many landlords ask you to sign away your constitutional rights. There are lease clauses hidden in tiny type that would take away:

Your right to free speech
Your right to assembly and petition
Your right to a jury trial

These clauses are designed to intimidate you and make you believe you have no rights. For years, landlords—who either accepted the old form lease without question or who planned to use it against you—have perpetuated the myth that they have all the rights and you have all the obligations. The lawyers who wrote leases and judges who upheld them did their share to keep the myth going.

Your best way to fight these oppressive clauses is to strike them out of the lease before you sign. But that is not always possible, especially if you are faced with a take-it-or-leave-it situation.

If you have already signed a bad lease, there is hope. Today you will be hard pressed to find a judge who would uphold so flagrant a denial of your rights. These intimidating clauses are no more than that—a bluff that will not hold up in court.

Your rights to trial by jury: Your right to a jury trial is one of the most basic of your constitutional rights. Yet some leases state that both you and the landlord will waive your right to trial by jury. On the surface it may sound reasonable since *both* of you give up that right. But most landlords know that you are more likely to receive sympathy from a jury than he or she is—that is the *real* reason it is written into the lease.

Even if you have signed a waiver of jury trial in your lease, there are still some protections through state laws and court decisions. A number of state legislatures have passed laws that make any waiver of jury trial in residential leases completely void. Even where there is no protection by state laws, more and more judges are interpreting the lease waivers in a way that will give the tenant every possible opportunity for a trial by jury.

Your rights to free speech and assembly: It is hard to believe but some landlords will try to squash your rights to free speech and peaceful assembly. A typical lease clause might say that you will be evicted if you "approach other tenants for the purpose of organizing a group to take concerted action relative to the operation of the complex."

The First Amendment guarantees your right to free speech and assembly; the Fourteenth Amendment guarantees that no state will take away that right. That is big protection.

A number of states have laws that protect you from landlords who would evict you for griping. Even without those laws, a few courts are recognizing that sort of eviction denies your right to free speech.

In addition, you are protected by what is technically called "public policy." For instance, housing codes are written to protect people from substandard housing; and, after all, how will housing authorities know where problems exist if they do not hear from tenants? So, trying to shut you up is against "public policy" and would thwart the codes that are designed to protect you.

Your rights to sue a negligent landlord: In many leases you are asked to sign away your right to sue the landlord or hold him liable in any way, even if you are injured or your property is damaged and it is his fault. Recently, because of a number of new laws and court cases, it has been hard for landlords to enforce this type of clause.

One of the strongest (and most recent) protections given to tenants is a court decision that says a landlord (like any other business person selling or renting goods) must guarantee that the apartment he rents is fit to live in. On the surface that does not sound so earth shattering, but it reverses all the years of common law that said if you rent an apartment, you must accept it as is.

In a number of states, where there are not implied habitability rulings, courts have protected tenants in three ways: (1) by ruling that "no-sue" clauses are void because the landlord has a duty (under housing codes and state statutes) to perform certain services. So, it is against "public policy" to relieve him of those duties—and your right to sue if he does not perform them. (2) by ruling that the tenant was forced to sign away his right not to sue because he was given a take-it-or-leave-it lease—and, so cannot be held to the waiver. Or (3) by interpreting the waiver not to sue *strictly* against the landlord. This last example does not make the waiver void but just allows a judge (who is enlightened on the subject of civil rights) to look out for the tenant.

Your rights to fix up your apartment: You are probably all too familiar with the clause in your lease that says you cannot make any "additions or alterations" in your apartment. Many landlords will tell you that means you cannot change anything—not even make nail holes for pictures. Do not buy that oppressive explanation. Of course, you cannot tear down a wall, take out the plumbing fixtures or lower the ceiling, but impermanent decorations or changes that do not alter the structure of the property are certainly within your rights.

There is another catchy little clause that says any changes you make stay with the land-lord when you move. Taken to the extreme (the way some landlords want it), this means that the towel rack you put up stays behind when you move. It is still a gray area in the courts but more and more judges are interpreting the clause to mean only changes that are permanent. Also, judges interpret the clause by its "intent" in relation to the rest of the lease. For instance, if the landlord says you must leave behind all improvements and at the same time says you must restore the apartment to its original condition, a judge might rule that the intent was not for you to leave something behind, because the clauses are contradictory.

If your lease itemizes the "alterations" that are to become the landlord's property such as curtains, window shades, lighting fixtures, or wall decorations, do not meekly fill the landlord's hope chest. Get a lawyer and fight it. No reasonable judge would enforce such an oppressive clause.

Talk the landlord into a change? If you and the landlord agree to add or subtract anything from the lease or to make any special repairs before you move in, do not rely on verbal agreement. If you disagree later, it will be your word against the landlord's. To make it legal, both of you should initial the paragraph you change, delete, or add on all copies of the lease.

Moving

HOW TO MANAGE A DO-IT-YOURSELF MOVE

You can save a lot of money by moving yourself and, if you get your act together beforehand, you will not take all of that savings out of your own hide. Here's help:

1. Picking the right truck size is not as difficult as it sounds. Start by estimating the total cubic feet of your belongings because that is how truck capacity is measured.

First measure each piece of furniture. Multiply the length times the width times the depth to get the cubic measurement of each item. Then estimate the number of cartons you will need for other items such as dishes and clothing.

Wardrobe cartons, which will hold up to ten suits and are available from most moving companies, simplify things by allowing you to take clothes directly from the closet to the carton. Normally a small closet's worth of clothes requires only one such carton.

A wardrobe carton takes up to 19 cubic feet, and a medium-size carton fills four cubic feet of space. Add your furniture's total cubic feet to the estimated total carton cubic feet. Pick the truck that matches the resulting figure. You can find out about van sizes and capacities by asking any rental agency.

2. Smart packing means tight packing with lots of cushioning. Save newspapers and other materials in advance. If you use supermarket cartons, be sure to tape the bottoms.

Pack cartons tightly. Use towels and paper to fill all gaps and cushion breakable items. Since most cartons will be handled a number of times, do not pack in more than 50 pounds for your back's sake. Also, cartons are likely to break with anything heavier.

Mark each carton with its contents and which room you want it delivered to.

Folded clothing can be left in dresser drawers and moved that way. Pack books in small cartons—they are heavy.

Mirrors and picture frames demand special attention. Make your own cartons for them from large flattened cardboard boxes.

Lampshades damage easily and are difficult to repair. Box each separately and cushion with paper.

Rent at least two to three dozen furniture pads to wrap around your furniture and secure these with ropes.

3. Loading the truck is important. Pack the truck in four sections. Fill every section tightly from top to bottom by putting light cartons on top of heavy items. Use furniture pads to fill odd-shaped spaces.

There are metal rings along the interior sides of a moving truck. As each quarter of the truck is filled in, tie the load to these rings so the furniture will not shift in transit.

Place the heaviest items in the front quarter of the truck. Long pieces of furniture, like sofas and mattresses, should go along the sides of the van. Place dresser drawers facing the mattress so they will not tip during the trip. Do not load flammable items such as paints, turpentine, or gasoline.

When you get to your new apartment, unloading should be easier than loading. The worst is over—and you are home.

HIRING A MOVING COMPANY

Big van lines that handle interstate business are regulated by the government. So when it is time for a major move, figure that their charges are based on similar rates and they all do about the same job.

There is not much price competition, but just because the moving companies offer similar services does not mean they will all perform with equal finesse. The differences show up in scratched furniture, stained upholstery—little things that are hard to claim damages for—and in time-wasting aggravation. Whether you or your employer is picking up the tab, taking time to audition several carriers can pay off in a smoother move.

Start the screening process by picking at least three of the most reliable movers in your area; ask your friends for recommendations and check the Better Business Bureau for complaint records. Once you have picked the most likely candidates and scheduled their visits to your apartment, it helps to lead the movers' representatives through your questions instead of waiting for them to volunteer bits and pieces of information. You will want to know: 1) how much they estimate your move will cost, 2) what packing materials and procedures they will use, 3) insurance and contractor details, and 4) who you will be dealing with at the other end of the line.

Get detailed written estimates. The estimates for a long-distance move are based on the approximate weight of your shipment, the miles it will cover, the size and number of packing cartons, and other materials and services you will need. (For a local move, they will charge an hourly rate.)

Be picky about packing. Make sure the movers provide enough of the packing cartons. Let them know how you want things packed, and how much you will do yourself—and how the difference will be reflected in the cost.

No mover will assume liability for plants, pets, food, or aerosol cans. Also: Carry your documents, securities, jewelry with you. Insurance is pretty standardized but you might want to get special coverage on antiques and unusual pieces.

Discuss the terms of the contract. Get the name and address of each mover's agent nearest your new home. They are the people who may be unloading your belongings and will handle all problems or damage claims. Make sure you are getting experienced hands at both ends of the move.

MOVING PLANTS

It is not impossible to take them along—it is just extra work. Some things to know:

1. Just before you wrap the plants, water them thoroughly. Most will be okay for up to five days if they are well insulated with newspaper or plastic wrapping and sealed in a box. Do not worry about the lack of sunlight, but trim off any buds or blooms that might strain the plant while it is in limbo.

2. Smaller plants are easier to handle if you wrap them individually and box several together. Each pot can be tucked into a grocery sack or slipped into a funnel of newspaper that gently pushes the foliage up.

3. Plants should be the last thing on the truck and the first thing off. If your plants must spend several days on the road, untended, in either very hot or very cold weather, the risk of loss is high. For shorter hauls, you can ease the dangers of freezing or baking. In summer, use only paper for wrapping. A block of dry ice in the plants' vicinity (not on them or up against their wrapping) is an effective way to cool part of the truck, and it gives off carbon dioxide, which is good for plants. In extreme cold, extra newspaper will help, but if the truck makes an overnight stop and cools off to below 50 degrees, your plants will suffer. A straight-through trip would be better.

Securing Your Apartment

IS YOUR LANDLORD RESPONSIBLE?

No landlord can absolutely ensure your safety—a professional thief can get in no matter what. But it is reasonable to expect your landlord to maintain the security system that was installed. A landlord's negligence should not make you the victim of a crime.

What to do? If you see security in your building deteriorating, notify your landlord in writing. Give details—front door lock is broken, doorman takes three-hour coffee breaks. The object is to put the landlord on notice. If he is diligent, he will act. If not, and you sue him for negligence, he will have a hard time claiming that a crime was unforeseeable.

WHAT TO DO FOR YOURSELF:

Burglars who hit apartments are usually amateurs. Lacking talent, they rely on a high-volume approach; they try lots of doors and windows until they find an easy entry.

Here are some ways to thwart those beginners whose skills are often limited to "card jobs" (using a credit card to spring a lock), jumping sliding doors and windows out of their tracks, and occasionally using a wire on a window latch. Securing your place takes only about two hours of work. Here's how: Your first step is thinking like a burglar as you survey your apartment. Pay special attention to openings that cannot be seen from the hall or street and have flimsy latches that should be replaced. And do not underestimate a crook's agility and motivation to reach an unguarded balcony or window.

The door: If you do not have a dead bolt and cannot get the landlord to put one on, here is how to do it yourself.

With a plain, hollow-core door (no steel edging), the sim-

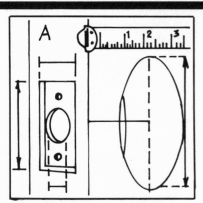

plest answer is to add a rim-type dead bolt (sometimes called the drop dead bolt, vertical dead bolt, or jimmy-proof lock) that is usually installed above the existing lock. You have to drill a hole in the door for the key mechanism and do a little wood gouging on the jamb for the strike (see drawing A).

Usually, it is easier to just replace the unsophisticated lock that came with your place. A lot of them are the vulnerable key-in-knob types with either no dead bolt or a short, ineffective one. You can substitute a tough cylindrical lock with a dead bolt ¾" to 1" long, and do little or no cutting on your door. There are no standardized sizes for locks; to avoid unnecessary wood gouging, get the measurements of your old lock before you buy a replacement.

Sliding glass door: There are three ways to secure sliding glass openings: 1) You can drop a piece of sawed-off wooden broomstick into the track so the door cannot slide (it can still be jumped). 2) Screw two metal (not wood) screws into the top center of the upper track (see

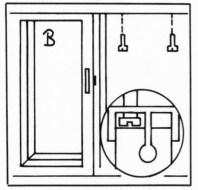

drawing B) and adjust their height so the door will barely slide under them. That way there is no extra space to lift the sliding section up into. Use a nail to start the screw holes; the job takes about ten minutes, and you cannot even see the screws when the door is closed. 3) This alternative leaves some visible holes but it is even easier than the screw-in-track method. Drill a hole in the top of the fixed part of the doorframe at the upper inside corner (see drawing C), and a second hole immediately behind the first, into the sliding frame while it is closed. Slide a three-penny nail into the lined-up holes and the door cannot be slid or lifted. (Tie a piece of monofilament line from the hole in the frame to the nail so it will not get lost.)

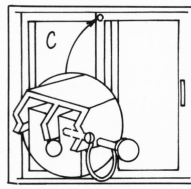

If you want to secure the door in a partially open position, get one of the friction-type track stops sold in hardware stores. A track stop will not keep the door from being lifted out of its track but the door cannot be opened wide.

Windows: The wooden sash, double-hung windows found in older apartments are the least challenging for a burglar and the easiest to burglar-proof. If they are even slightly warped, with a gap between the top and bottom sections, they are ideal for the crook who knows enough to force the latch with a knife blade or a piece of steel.

At the outside edge where the frames meet (see drawing

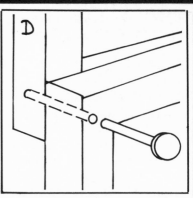

D), drill a hole in the bottom frame, then partway into the top frame. Slip a big nail or carriage bolt into the holes and the window cannot be moved. Another hole a few inches higher on the top frame, and the window is secure while open.

Take another look at any reachable casement window. Is it big enough for someone to climb through when it is open? Is there even the slightest gap where a thin flexible instrument could be used to dislodge the latch? If there is a crank, is it so freewheeling that the unlatched window could be pushed open? You don't trust it? Replace the simple pull latch with a locking-lever latch that has to be moved in two directions to open, or that has a lock button you hold down with one hand while you unlatch with the other. There are plenty of suitable latches around so look for one with screw holes to match the existing latch. The replacement is as simple as two-screws-out . . . two-screws-in, and you can even put the old hardware back when you leave.

HARDWARE TALK FOR LOCK BUYERS

1. Lock mechanism: the part that fits through the door; knobs, keyhole, sometimes a decorative plate.

2. Latch: the part that comes through the edge of the door.

3. Strike: the metal plate that is screwed into the doorframe. The latch and/or dead bolt slip into it.

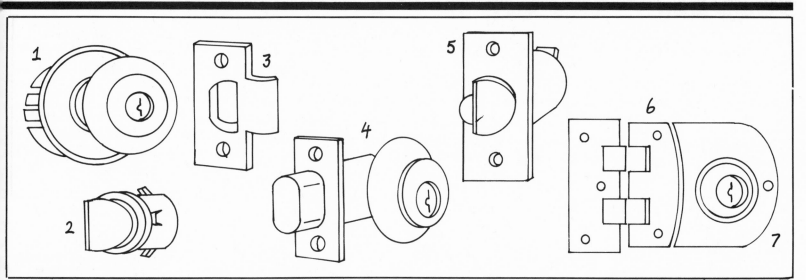

4. Dead bolt: a flat ended, steel plunger that is held locked into the doorframe and cannot be pushed back into the latch.

5. Deadlocking latch: a latch with an adjoining small plunger that deadlocks and makes the latch immune to card jobs.

6. Rim-type dead bolt: extra lock; puts bolt across surface of door and jamb.

7. Template: a paper pattern that comes with some locks. Shows what size holes are need ed to put the lock in the door.

BURGLAR ALARM SYSTEMS

No matter what the burglar alarm salespeople say, no alarm system can give you foolproof protection against a cool, professional burglar. You still need good locks, solid doors and jambs to attach them to, and security-conscious people around you.

The burglar alarm's real value is that it can scare off a nervous, amateur crook, and the majority of burglars are those flappable types.

No matter what alarm you get, these generalities apply:

1. Simpler is better. The complicated systems usually have more breakdowns and cost more.

2. If you are getting a monitoring service with your system, check out the company with the Better Business Bureau or a consumer protection group. And make sure you get a warranty on the equipment as well as quick maintenance and service commitments.

3. Any alarm that uses electricity should have the UL tag for safety's sake.

4. Check to make sure the siren, bell, or other noisemaker is legal in your community.

You may not want to spend the time, money, and effort to wire up a complicated alarm system. But less expensive, portable, plug-in models are available. One of them is made up to look like a dictionary with a cord that plugs into any electrical outlet. Left on a shelf or table, it goes off if anyone comes within 10 feet and doesn't deactivate it within 10 seconds. The fact that they last for years and may be taken from one apartment to another with no fuss makes their cost just that much more reasonable.

Also, there is an inexpensive model that may be left against your door to topple and go off if someone forces it. Some people get one for their apartment and take another along on vacation to be propped against the motel door for the night.

PROPERTY INSURANCE FOR RENTERS:

Liability protection, under the usual tenant package, covers mishaps in your apartment, accidents you could be blamed for outside the apartment, and your legal fees if you are sued.

Most policies also cover loss of goods and damage in the event of fire, lightning, explosion, vandalism, and a number of other perils—17 in all. Any coverage on the building is up to the landlord.

Here are some things to know about apartment insurance:

Premiums for basic coverages will not vary much within your part of town but most companies offer extras at various prices. There are qualifications to most policies too. And since some of them run to ten or more pages, you might do better shopping the "disclaimers" and the extras instead of the basic price.

The basic renter's package is sold by most of the country's property and casualty insurance companies—directly, through licensed agents, or through brokers who sell for many companies.

An agent signs contracts with one or several insurance companies and represents only them. A broker, on the other hand, works independently, with no insurance company contract. He can offer whatever insurance he feels is best for you, right up to signing you with Lloyd's of London. Some people prefer the licensed agent's small, personal office; others, the broker's versatility or a company agent's direct line to his firm.

If you live in an inner city neighborhood that does not have a good crime record, there is still hope that you will be able to get coverage. One way is through what is called the FAIR (Fair Access to Insurance Requirements) Plan, a voluntary program by the insurance industry. A number of insurance companies in a state get together and agree that they will insure what would ordinarily be poor risks. You can find out if there is a FAIR Plan in your state and what its requirements are by writing the National Committee on Property Insurance, 800 Valley Forge Plaza, King of Prussia, Pennsylvania 19406.

Another route is to get coverage from the Federal Crime Insurance Program; it is set up in states where there is no FAIR Plan or where the government decides there is an inadequate one. For more information about Federal Crime Insurance and eligibility requirements, call (800) 638–8780 or write Federal Crime Insurance, P.O. Box 41033, Washington, D.C.20014.

Your Rights as a Tenant

Tenant/landlord laws have evolved very quickly over the past decade. Many states are in the process of enacting legislation that is designed to treat the tenant in a more equitable way. Most of these laws are based on the same principles, but the specifics vary. For example: Most states put a maximum amount on the security deposit you pay to your landlord; it can range—depending on where you are—from one month's rent to two month's rent.

Laws vary greatly. Some states may provide for a slap on the landlord's hand while others make him pay off in triple damages, with attorney's fees and court costs included. One state's law may cover only security deposits while another covers every facet of tenant/landlord agreement from painting requirements to unlawful eviction. So it is smart to know exactly what your own city and state laws say. It is not as difficult to find the laws as you might think. The answer is as close as your nearest law library (at government offices and law schools).

Then when your landlord swears that fixing a leaky pipe is not his job, call his bluff. The point: The informed consumer is the most effective one. Tell your landlord about a few laws and court cases. He will usually see your side of the story—fast. If not, you have got the information you need for Small Claims court.

THE LAWS THAT PROTECT YOU

Security deposit laws: Getting a security deposit back from your landlord used to be about as easy as walking out of Fort Knox with a load of gold. In the past, landlords have often stalled endlessly about refunds, or deducted large amounts for undocumented damages.

Now, thanks to security deposit laws in most states, you will have an easier time getting your money back. The laws are not identical but they do have some common safeguards:

Maximum security deposit: A ceiling is set on how much money the landlord can demand.

Interest: Many states require the landlord to pay you interest on your security deposit, although they allow him to keep some portion for bookkeeping services.

Use of the deposit: A deposit can be used only for legitimate purposes such as covering unpaid rent, cleaning expenses and repairs caused by negligence or abuse—but never the cost of ordinary wear and tear.

No more waiting for refund: All laws set a deadline for returning the deposit.

Itemized bill: If the landlord deducts any expenses, he must send you an itemized statement, usually by the same deadline that is set for refunds.

Penalties: You can sue your landlord for wrongfully withholding part or all of your deposit beyond the deadline. Under some laws you can get up to three times the deposit plus attorney's fees and court costs.

Some tips: Before moving in, inspect every inch of the apartment and make a list of the defects; get the landlord to sign the list. Then when you leave, you should not be charged for the leftover sins of former tenants. On moving day, send your landlord a certified letter, including the list of defects, and request a prompt refund on your deposit. (Be sure to include your new mailing address.)

If the landlord does not refund your money on time, or if you think his deductions are wrong, tell him—in writing—that you plan to sue him for the penalty, as provided for under

your state's law—unless, of course, the matter can be straightened out to your satisfaction. If you sue, your best bet is to take the case to a judge in your local Small Claims or Housing Court. It is an inexpensive, fast way to sue, and you do not need to hire a lawyer.

Under repair-and-deduct laws, you can have repairs made yourself and take the money out of your rent. The rent check is great leverage but you will have to follow some rules to make it work:

You must warn your landlord before you act—it is best by certified letter. After notification, the landlord is entitled to adequate time to make the repairs. Some states set a deadline such as 20 days while others say the landlord must have "reasonable time." If water is flooding through your ceiling, reasonable could mean 24 or less hours; on the other hand, for nonemergencies, it could mean a few weeks. A judge would make that interpretation.

There is a limit on how much you can deduct out of one month's rent. In your state it might be as little as $50, an entire month's rent, or "a just and reasonable amount" (the judge decides here).

Of course, it is unlikely that your landlord will stand idly by when you are not paying full rent. He may try to evict you on the grounds of nonpayment of rent. But if you can prove that you properly followed the law, you should have a good defense. You might have to prove that you did not negligently cause the defects, that you gave adequate notice and time for repairs to be made, and that the repairs were both appropriate in cost and necessary to the apartment's habitability.

Rent-withholding laws have the same purpose as repair statutes: They direct your rent

money into repairs, not the landlord's pocket. But instead of making the repairs yourself, you let a court do it. First you have to petition a court to let you withhold your rent money and put it into the hands of the court. Then the judge will usually appoint an administrator to use the money to make repairs.

Privacy laws: In many states there are renters' privacy laws that say your landlord cannot enter your apartment without good reason. There are variations in how strict the state laws are, but there are instances under most laws when you can ask your landlord to return another time.

In most states, the landlord must announce a visit at least 24 hours in advance (in some states it is 48 hours) unless there is an emergency.

Laws on apartment upkeep: In an apartment you want more than just a good buy; you want a buy that stays good. In a growing number of states a landlord can no longer say that there is no guarantee on repairs. These laws recognize that if rent is paid, services must be rendered; often, that rent is the leverage to get a landlord to make needed repairs.

There are three different laws—implied warranty of habitability, repair-and-deduct and rent withholding. Some are not formally in the statute books, although they have the effect of law because they come from court cases that have set precedents.

Essentially, the basis of the implied warranty of habitability is that the landlord must guarantee that your apartment is fit to live in. And he must keep it that way—the warranty never expires. In essence, your landlord warrants to keep your apartment and the common areas (such as halls, stairways, lobby) in "habitable" condition.

In most places it is up to a judge to decide what is habitable or uninhabitable. Some have strictly ruled that it means the bare essentials and nothing else —such as heat, water, unbroken windowpanes. Others, however, have broadened the warranty to include things that the tenant could "reasonably expect" when the lease was signed—such as elevator service.

The repair-and-deduct and rent-withholding laws are based on a similar principle: You ought to get what you are paying for; namely, a fit place to live. These two laws are simply different means for arriving at the same goal—to force your landlord to make repairs.

Implied warranties of habitability provide for varying remedies, depending on what the precedent or law in your state allows. Some say you can repair and deduct from your rent; others allow you to hold out on your rent.

Discrimination laws: Despite recent laws and guidelines, housing discrimination still exists across the country in the form of jacked-up rents, extra charges, and choosing one prospective tenant over another. But the 1968 Civil Rights Act and city and state fair housing laws are on your side. Title VIII of the 1968 Civil Rights Act prohibits discrimination on the basis of race, color, religion, sex, and national origin. Some state and city fair housing codes are even tougher, also including marital status, age, or the fact that you have children.

If you believe you have been discriminated against, you will need evidence. Proving that the landlord would rent to someone else is the best way to support your claims. And such tests stand up in court. The evidence also gives you the bargaining power to settle out of court.

To set it up find someone to apply for the same apartment as soon as possible after you have been turned down. This substitute must be someone who will not be rejected for the same reason you think you were. Your friend should offer the same information you did—income, marital status, and so on—and make sure he gets a commitment from the person showing the apartment, saying that the apartment is still available. Then your friend should stall and promise to call back later. Be sure that each of you immediately writes down what happened. Include the name of the person you spoke to, apartment number, address, and every detail you can remember.

If you are being discriminated against, you can also call the U.S. Department of Housing and Urban Development. The local office will be listed under "U.S. Government" in the phone book or call HUD's toll-free number, (800) 424–8590.

HOW TO FIGHT BACK

Form a Tenant's Union: There is power in numbers. More and more, landlords are recognizing the power and consumer clout tenant organizations wield—and are correcting the problems they point out.

If you think you need a tenant group in your building, here is how to get one organized:

You and other organizers need to tell fellow tenants that you are having a meeting to take action on a particular problem. Door-to-door and personal contact is the best way, followed up with reminder notices. At the first meeting spend some time getting acquainted, then select leaders. Form two committees: one for publicity, the other for finances. Ask for volunteers to canvas the building again to get more tenants involved.

Draw up a list of grievances from the tenants and set priorities on those complaints. Keep the list at a moderate length. One that is too long will make you sound unreasonable and put the landlord on the defensive. A short list with only major points leaves you with nothing negotiable—and your landlord with no "victories" at the bargaining table. Then decide strategy. Negotiation is the first step. Write the landlord a letter that 1) informs him that you have organized, 2) explains your purpose in general terms and in specific complaints, 3) invites him to set up a meeting, and 4) asks him to answer your invitation within a certain number of days.

Some general rules: 1) Meet on a neutral ground. 2) Make it clear that you want to meet with the landlord or his representative—not the building manager. 3) Have only a small negotiating committee represent the entire group. 4) Clearly define your complaints and what you want done about them. 5) Get the landlord to put all agreements in writing; add penalties if he does not carry out his promise (rent strike, legal action, etc.).

If negotiations fail: Get a lawyer. 1) You can sue if the conditions in the building are bad enough. 2) You can harass the landlord (picket lines). 3) Make the necessary repairs and deduct the cost from your rent but only if your state law recognizes this remedy. 4) Go on a rent strike.

Arbitration: Half the battle in arbitration is getting the other party to arbitrate once a dispute starts. You can save yourself a lot of grief by putting a clause right in your lease that says you and your landlord will use arbitration. It is less expensive than a long court battle and less time consuming. When and if you need arbitration, you and your landlord can contact Community Dispute Services of the American Arbitration Association, 140 West 51st Street, New York, N.Y. 10020, or one of its regional offices. There is no problem getting an impartial arbitrator to hear the case in your area. Usually both parties split the fee (often several hundred dollars).

Either you or the landlord submits a written statement outlining the basic dispute and calling for arbitration. When the case is heard, it usually takes about 18 days for settlement.

Hire a lawyer, coop style: Your tenant group raises money to put a lawyer, law firm, or panel of lawyers with experience on a partial retainer. The annual fee gets each member a chunk of the lawyer's time, plus a big discount if you need serious help. Of course, the range of services and fees will vary according to the number of people in your group and the program you work out with your lawyer(s). There is no "model plan" that works for all groups because each group has special needs. The best way is to find a sympathetic lawyer and make your own deal.

Take it to court: There are two types of courts that cover most landlord/tenant problems: Small Claims and Housing courts.

Small Claims Court: All states have Small Claims courts. The rules governing them vary from state to state so your best source of accurate information is the court clerk. Look up "Small Claims Court" in the Yellow Pages under the heading for your city or county. Talk with the court clerk, briefly explain whom you want to sue and for how much, and ask what steps you must take to file suit. Here are some things to know:

The court clerk will usually tell you the day your case will be heard, not a specific hour.

Keep the entire day open.

You have to pay a small amount to cover the expenses of the court. You will also have to pay to have the summons delivered.

You can only sue for so-called money damages, the value of what you have lost.

The maximum amount of damages you can sue for as "small claims" varies, most often between $500 and $1,000.

There are some tricky rules about where you must file your lawsuit. You have to sue in the court that has what lawyers call the "proper venue," frequently the court located in the district where the defendant lives, works, or maintains a place of business.

Make sure you have the correct legal name of any business you are suing. Ask the court clerk how you can locate the true name of the business.

Lawyers are not required. You can do it yourself.

Bring to the trial any documents—warranties, bills, leases, letters—that support your side of the story. Make arrangements with the clerk if you want to subpoena witnesses or documents.

The defendant will be notified by the court of any judgment you win. If he does not pay up, remind him of his obligation by certified mail. You may even have to return to the court and enlist the services of a sheriff or marshal. The court clerk can best explain the alternatives.

Housing Court: This is a relatively new type of court that operates much like a cross between arbitration and Small Claims court. Few cities have them yet.

Call in your complaint to the city's Housing Violation Bureau. If the matter is not settled in 30 days, go down to Housing Court, deposit $10, and you will be assigned a trial date not more than ten days away. You will also be given a summons for delivery to your landlord by anyone but you. On the trial date the judge will assign you to a small hearing room, presided over by special housing judges. Then—sometimes in just two sessions only a few weeks apart—the housing dispute is settled.

An alternative that has been growing in numbers and usefulness is the Neighborhood Court, which deals in conflict resolution. Trained mediators help people learn techniques to work out their differences.

For more information about mediation centers, write to Community Mediation Center, 356 Middle Country Road, Coram, New York 11727. By sending $4 to the Superintendent of Documents, U.S. Government Printing Office, Washington, D.C. 20402, you can receive a copy of *Neighborhood Justice Center: An Analysis of Potential models* (#027-000-0598-5).

THE APT SOURCE GUIDE

Having moved in and out of dozens of apartments every year over the years, we have learned some shortcuts for finding furnishings, accessories, and wares that make life easier and make rooms better looking. These sources come in two varieties—the retail store where you can walk in and buy what you need and the others which include wholesalers, manufacturers, importers and to-the-trade-only showrooms. The wholesale sources will usually answer all written queries so that you can find out where in your area the products are available. Occasionally, you will be able to buy direct from wholesale sources. Do not count on it but it does not hurt to try. This source guide is broken down into categories that will make it faster for you to find exactly what you are looking for.

CONTEMPORARY FURNISHINGS

Retail

The Chair Store
1694 Union St.
San Francisco, CA 94123

Conran's
145 Huguenot St.
New Rochelle, NY 10801
One of the largest selections of furnishings and accessories under one roof.

Cost Plus Imports
2552 Taylor St.
San Francisco, CA 94133

The Door Store
One Park Ave.
New York, NY 10016
A classic mix of finished and unfinished furnishings.

H.U.D.D.L.E.
9373 Wilshire Blvd.
Beverly Hills, CA 90210
Innovative furniture, fabrics and sono tube kids' systems.

Storehouse
2737 Apple Valley Rd., N.E.
Atlanta, GA 30319
High quality furnishings.

The Workbench
470 Park Ave. So.
New York, NY 10016
Good solid furniture at good prices.

Other

Boling Chair Co.
Box 409
Siler City, NC 27344
Manufacturers of light-wood windsor chairs.

Domani
A Division of Burris Industries
Lincolntown, NC 28092
Good-looking European styles.

Gold Medal Inc.
1700 Packard Ave.
Racine, WI 53403
The new director's chair.

Kartell-USA
225 Fifth Ave.
New York, NY 10010
High-style Italian design furnishings.

Kinnovations, Inc.
2828 Virgo Lane
Dallas, TX 75229
Simple canvas and steel furniture.

Otto Gerdau Co.
82 Wall St.
New York, NY 10005
Chairs and desks in chrome, glass and butcher block.

Overman U.S.A., Inc.
200 Lexington Ave.
New York, NY 10016
European-style seating.

Scandinavian Design, Inc.
127 East 59th St.
New York, NY 10022
Interesting imports.

Telescope Folding Furniture Co., Inc.
Granville, NY 12832
The classic director's chair.

Thonet Industries
305 East 63rd St.
New York, NY 10021
The original bentwood chair.

Trend Pacific
507 Towne Ave.
Los Angeles, CA 90013
Light wood and canvas furniture.

TRADITIONAL FURNISHINGS
These furnishings are widely available at retail stores across the country. If you write to the main offices, you can find the outlet in your area.

Baker, Knapp & Tubbs
200 Lexington Ave.
New York, NY 10016

Basset Furniture Industries, Inc.
Basset, WV 24055
Good prices, availability and a range of styles.

Burlington House Furniture
1345 Avenue of the Americas
New York, NY 10019
A broad selection of many styles.

Chapman Manufacturing Co.
21 East 26th St.
New York, NY 10010
Lamps, furniture and accessories.

Davis Cabinet Co.
901 South Fifth
Nashville, TN 37206
Good range of styles and finishes.

Drexel Heritage Furnishings, Inc.
Drexel, NC 28619
Selection of styles and pieces.

Ethan Allen, Inc.
Danbury, CT 06910
Good early American as well as other periods.

Henredon Furniture Industries, Inc.
Box 70
Morganton, NC 28655
Tasteful reproductions.

Riverside Furniture Corp.
Drawer 1427
Fort Smith, AR 72901
Oak reproductions.

Sarreid, Ltd.
Box 3545
Wilson, NC 27893
Accessories, lots of brass.

White Furniture Co.
Mebane, NC 27302
Quality reproductions.

WICKER AND RATTAN FURNITURE

Retail

Cost Plus Imports
2552 Taylor St.
San Francisco, CA 94133

Fran's Basket House
Route 10
Succasunna, NJ 07876

Kreiss Ports of Call
8445 Santa Monica Blvd.
Los Angeles, CA 90069

The Patio
1325 Columbus
San Francisco, CA 94133

Other

Brown Jordan Co.
9860 Gidley St.
El Monte, CA 91734

Ficks Reed Co.
4900 Charlemar Dr.
Cincinnati, OH 45227

The McGuire Co.
38 Hotaling Place at Jackson Sq.
San Francisco, CA 94111

Tropi-Cal
5716 Alba
Los Angeles, CA 90058

Walter's Wicker Wonderland
991 Second Ave.
New York, NY 10022

DESIGNER SOURCES

Other

Atelier International
595 Madison Ave.
New York, NY 10022
Modern Italian furnishings and some accessories.

Castelli Furniture, Inc.
950 Third Ave.
New York, NY 10022
Modern Italian furnishings.

Herman Miller
600 Madison Ave.
New York, NY 10022
Modern classics.

ICF, Inc.
305 E. 63rd St.
New York, NY 10021
Slick imports, great storage systems.

Knoll International
655 Madison Ave.
New York, NY 10021
Good selection of modern pieces.

Stendig
410 East 62nd St.
New York, NY 10021
Lush leather and innovative seating.

UNFINISHED FURNITURE

Retail and Mail Order

Country Workshop
95 Rome St.
Newark, NJ 07105

Mondrian Custom Cabinetry
1021 Second Ave.
New York, NY 10022

The Unpainted Place
1601 Hennepin Ave.
Minneapolis, MN 55403

BEDS

Retail

Isabel Brass Furniture
120 E. 32nd St.
New York, NY 10016
Brass beds. Mail order catalog available.

Murphy Bed & Kitchen Co.
40 East 34th St.
New York, NY 10016
Old standard.

Other

Simmons U.S.A.
Box 105032
Atlanta, GA 30348
Sleep sofa specialists.

RECLINERS

Other

Barca-Lounger Company
Box 20104
Raleigh, NC 27619

The Berkline Corp.
One Berkline Dr.
Morristown, TN 37814

La-Z-Boy Co.
1284 N. Telegraph Rd.
Monroe, MI 48161

OUTDOOR INDOOR
Other

Cottage Shops, Inc.
8008 West Third
Los Angeles, CA 90048

Gentle Swing
156 Calle Cresto
San Juan, Puerto Rico 00901
Beautiful hammocks.

The Hammock Shop
Box 308
Pawleys Island, SC 29585
The classic rope hammocks.

Meadowcraft, Div. of Birmingham
Ornamental Iron Co.
Box 1357
Birmingham, AL 35201
Contemporary and traditional indoor-outdoor furniture.

Medallion Industries, Inc.
2900 NW 77th Ct.
Miami, FL 33122
Very contemporary and stylish pieces in a great range of colors.

Tropitone Furniture
Box 3197
Sarasota, FL 33578

Lee L. Woodard Furniture
317 Elm St.
Owosso, MI 48867

GIANTS

Retail and Mail Order
A surprisingly good variety for all the basics. Time-saving sources found in every city.

J.C. Penney Co., Inc.
1301 Avenue of the Americas
New York, NY 10019

Montgomery Ward
535 W. Chicago Ave.
Chicago, IL 60607

Sears, Roebuck and Company
Sears Tower
Chicago, IL 60684

Spiegel
1040 W. 35th St.
Chicago, IL 60609

FABRIC

Retail

Black Sheep
The Cannery
2801 Leavenworth
San Francisco, CA 94133
Bright contemporary cottons.

Calico Corners
681 E. Main St.
Mt. Kisco, NY 10549
Barn full of choices at good prices.

Fabric Barn
2717 N. Clark
Chicago, IL 60614
Big retail outlet with many contemporary fabrics.

Fabrications
146 East 56th St.
New York, NY 10022
Wide selection of many styles.

Far Eastern Fabrics
171 Madison Ave.
New York, NY 10016
Thai silk, scarves, batik and authentic antique oriental fabric.

Jensen-Lewis Co., Inc.
89 Seventh Ave.
New York, NY 10011
Canvas by the yard.

Laura Ashley, Inc.
714 Madison Ave.
New York, NY 10021
English prints in a variety of colors.

Liberty of London
229 E. 60th St.
New York, NY 10022
Famous for the Liberty Lawn and William Morris cotton prints.

Pierre Deux
381 Bleecker St.
New York, NY 10014
The spirit of the south of France in fabrics.

Other

Bloomcraft
295 Fifth Ave.
New York, NY 10016
Fabrics for everything at good prices.

Central Shippee
Box 135
Bloomingdale, NJ 07403
The source for felt.

Cohama/Riverdale
200 Madison Ave.
New York, NY 10016
Well-priced, widely distributed range of styles.

Covington Fabrics
267 Fifth Ave.
New York, NY 10016
Traditional prints, checks and Kanvastex.

Cyrus Clark Co., Inc.
267 Fifth Ave.
New York, NY 10016
Traditional prints.

F & F Tergal Importers
252 W. 40th St.
New York, NY 10018
Laces for every purpose.

International Printworks, Inc.
100 Wells Ave.
Newton, MA 02159
Post Marimekko and European cotton prints.

Quaker Lace
24 West 40th St.
New York, NY 10018
Laces of every description.

Schumacher
939 Third Ave.
New York, NY 10022
Huge collection of traditional textures and prints.

Waverly Fabrics, div. of
Schumacher
58 West 40th St.
New York, NY 10018
Traditional prints and contemporary fabrics.

LIGHTING

Retail

George Kovacs
831 Madison Ave.
New York, NY 10021
Home of the best contemporary lighting.

Light, Inc.
1162 Second Ave.
New York, NY 10021
Designer lighting in many styles.

Thunder 'N Light, Inc.
171 Bowery
New York, NY 10002
Industrial lighting.

Other

Basic Concepts, Ltd.
141 Lanza Ave.
Garfield, NJ 07026
Inexpensive contemporary lighting.

Halo Lighting
Div. of McGraw-Edison Co.
400 Busse Rd.
Elk Grove Village, IL 60007
Good track lighting systems.

Koch and Lowy
940 Third Ave.
New York, NY 10022
Contemporary fixtures.

Laurel Lamp Manufacturing
   Inc.
111 Rome St.
Newark, NJ 07105
Brass pharmacy lamps, green glass cone lamps and many favorites at realistic prices.

Lighting Associates
305 E. 63rd
New York, NY 10021
Selection of contemporary designs.

Lightolier
346 Claremont Ave.
Jersey City, NJ 07305
Makers of the track lighting system.

Luxo Lamp Corp.
Box 951, Monument Park
Port Chester, NY 10573
The classic work lamp.

Stiffel Co.
700 N. Kingsbury St.
Chicago, IL 60610
Wide range of traditional styles.

FLOORING

Retail

Central Carpet Co., Inc.
426 Columbus Ave.
New York, NY 10024
Good used orientals and other styles.

La Chambre Perse
347 Bleecker St.
New York, NY 10014
Beautiful orientals.

Other

American Olean Tile Co.
1000 Cannon Ave.
Lansdale, PA 19446
Classic ceramic tiles.

Armstrong World Industries,
   Inc.
Box 3001
Lancaster, PA 17604
Large selections of good, practical floor coverings in many materials.

Bigelow-Sanford, Inc.
Box 3089
Greenville, SC 29602
Good choice of carpetings in many colors.

Concepts International
919 Third Ave.
New York, NY 10022
Designer area rugs at good prices.

Congoleum Corp.
195 Belgrove Dr.
Kearny, NJ 07032
Hard surface flooring.

Country Floors
300 East 61st St.
New York, NY 10021
Beautiful ceramic tiles in all shapes and colors.

Couristan
The Carpet Center
919 Third Ave.
New York, NY 10022
Good selection of quality reproduction Indian and oriental rugs.

Jenstar-Flintkote
580 Decker Dr.
Irving, TX 75062
Vinyl tiles.

Hoboken Wood Flooring Corp.
100 Willow St.
East Rutherford, NJ 07073
Wide selection of wood strip flooring.

Import Specialists
230 Fifth Ave.
New York, NY 10001
Sisal and the sisal look.

Karastan, a division of
   Fieldcrest Mills
919 Third Ave.
New York, NY 10022
Good variety and great quality.

Lee Carpets, div. of Burlington
   Industries
1000 Adams
Valley Forge Corporate Center
King of Prussia, PA 19406
Good selection in various colors.

Regal Rugs, Inc.
295 5th Ave.
New York, NY 10001
Designer area rugs at good prices.

INDUSTRIAL SUPPLY SOURCES

Retail

Abstracta Structures, Inc.
38 W. 39th St.
New York, NY 10018
Flexible chrome tube display and storage system.

Manhattan Ad Hoc
   Housewares
842 Lexington Ave.
New York, NY 10021
The source for the slickest industrial look.

Other

Able Steel Equipment Co., Inc.
50-02 23rd St.
Long Island City, NY 11101
Industrial shelving and storage.

Albert Cayne Equipment Co.
421 Bruckner Blvd.
Bronx, NY 10455
Industrial lockers and shelving.

Garland Commercial
   Industries, Inc.
Freeland, PA 18224
Professional ranges.

ANTIQUES AND COLLECTIBLES

Retail

Added Oomph
P.O. Box 6135
High Point, NC 27262
Good selection of old things,

advertising and store artifacts, hardware, rustic furniture.

C.I.T.Y.
213 W. Institute
Chicago, IL 60610
Funky and interesting things.

The Florentine Craftsman, Inc.
654 First Ave.
New York, NY 10016
Classic wrought-iron and ceramic furniture, urns, pedestals.

Fly-By-Night Gallery
714 N. Wells
Chicago, IL 60610
Museum quality twentieth-century art pieces, tabletops and sculpture.

Howard Kaplan's French
   Country Antiques
35 East Tenth St.
New York, NY 10003
French provincial furnishings.

Merchant of Venice
2260 N. Lincoln
Chicago, IL 60614
Excellent crafts and accessories.

Pierre Deux Antiques, Inc.
369 Bleecker St.
New York, NY 10014
Exquisite country French antiques and fabrics.

Second Hand Rose
573 Hudson St.
New York, NY 10014
Specializes in late thirties to fifties pieces.

Steve Starr
2654 N. Clark St.
Chicago, IL 60614
Classic Deco.

ACCESSORIES

Retail

Adventures in Crafts
51 E. 93rd St.
New York, NY 10028
Ready-to-finish lightwood and ceramic accessories.

Crate and Barrel
850 N. Michigan Ave.
Chicago, IL 60611
Sophisticated contemporary household furnishings.

Dean & DeLuca
121 Prince St.
New York, NY 10012
Dazzling display of food and kitchen equipment.

The Gazebo
660 Madison Ave.
New York, NY 10021
Expensive old wicker, quilts and baskets.

Jadis
2701 Main St.
Santa Monica, CA 90405

Jenny B. Goode
1194 Lexington Ave.
New York, NY 10028
Beautiful accessories.

Joia Interiors
149 E. 60th St.
New York, NY 10022
Deco accessories.

Let There Be Neon
451 West Broadway
New York, NY 10013

Limited Editions
253 E. 72nd St.
New York, NY 10021

Matt McGhee
18 Christopher St.
New York, NY 10014

The Pillow Salon
238 E. 60th St.
New York, NY 10022

The Pottery Barn
231 Tenth Ave.
New York, NY 10011
Housewares, glassware and kitchenware.

Propinquity
8915 Santa Monica Blvd.
West Hollywood, CA 90069

Turpan Sanders
386 West Broadway
New York, NY 10012

Wolfman, Gold-Good Co.
484 Broome St.
New York, NY 10013
Large selection of tableware.

Other

Anchor Hocking Corporation
109 N. Broad St.
Lancaster, OH 43130
Smart-looking glass.

Ball Corporation
345 S. High St.
Muncie, IN 47302
Canning jars that store everything.

Blair Rubel Ltd.
225 Fifth Ave.
New York, NY 10010
Lacquer trays and boxes.

Corning Glass Works
80 Houghton Park
Corning, NY 14830
Functional glass for every need.

Cosco
2525 State St.
Columbus, IN 47201
Contemporary chrome pieces.

Dax Manufacturers, Inc.
955 Midland Ave.
Yonkers, NY 10704
Plastic box frames.

Fallani & Cohn, Inc.
14 E. 38th St.
New York, NY 10016
Table linens.

Faroy Sales
Room 533
225 Fifth Ave.
New York, NY 10010
A mix of accessories—baskets, boxes, candles, etc.

Heller Designs, Inc.
41 Madison Ave.
New York, NY 10010
Bright-colored plastic dinnerware and tableware.

IDG Marketing Ltd.
1100 Slocum Ave.
Ridgefield, NJ 07657
Functional plastic accessories.

Import Outlet, Inc.
801 Broadway
New York, NY 10003
Copper and hand-painted ceramics.

John Ritzenthaler Company
40 Portland Rd.
West Conshohocken, PA 19428
Dish towels.

Leacock & Company, Inc.
1040 Avenue of the Americas
New York, NY 10018
Table linens.

Libbey Glass
Div. of Owens-Illinois
Box 919
Toledo, OH 43639
Glassware at reasonable prices.

Marilyn Barnett, Inc.
225 Fifth Ave.
New York, NY 10010
Soft sculpture.

Nancy Peterson, Inc.
225 Fifth Ave.
New York, NY 10010
Country-style accessories.

Pot Covers, Inc.
101 W. 28th St.
New York, NY 10001
Baskets and accessories.

Primitive Artisans
Room 711
225 Fifth Ave.
New York, NY 10010
Baskets of all kinds.

Purofied Down Products Corp.
319 Fifth Ave.
New York, NY 10016
Classic comforters.

Sigma
225 Fifth Ave.
New York, NY 10010
Imaginative, functional accessories.

Terraillon Corporation
95 Q South Hoffman La.
Central Islip, NY 11722
Good-looking scales.

The Ulster Weaving Co., Ltd.
148 Madison Ave.
New York, NY 10016
Dish towels and linens.

Van Dow-Fenton, Inc.
225 Fifth Ave.
New York, NY 10010
Accessories in a mixture of styles.

Vandor Imports
690 Fourth St.
San Francisco, CA 94107
Eclectic selection.

GRAPHICS

Retail

A Clean Well Lighted Place
363 Bleecker St.
New York, NY 10014

Corwith Gallery
1833 Union St.
San Francisco, CA 94123

Dean Gallery, Inc.
2815 S. Hennepin
Minneapolis, MN 55408

The Metropolitan Museum of
  Art
P.O. Box 224, Gracie Station
New York, NY 10028

Museum of Modern Art
Publications Sales
11 W. 53rd St.
New York, NY 10019

New York Graphic Society Ltd.
140 Greenwich Ave.
Greenwich, CT 06830

Pace Editions
32 E. 57th St.
New York, NY 10022

Poster Originals, Ltd.
924 Madison Ave.
New York, NY 10021

Poster Portfolio Ltd.
438 Avenue of the Americas
New York, NY 10011

Thackrey & Robertson
2266 Union St.
San Francisco, CA 94123

Union Street Graphics
1690 Union St.
San Francisco, CA 94123

Walker Art Center
Center Book Shop
Vineland Pl.
Minneapolis, MN 55403

KITCHENWARE

Retail

Bazaar de la Cuisine
1003 Second Ave.
New York, NY 10022
Everything for the kitchen.

Bridge Kitchenware Corp.
214 E. 52nd St.
New York, NY 10022
Professional quality kitchenware.

Williams-Sonoma
Box 3792
San Francisco, CA 94119
Choice selection of tabletop and kitchen equipment.

KITCHENWARE

Other

Boston Warehouse Trading
   Corp., Inc.
39 Rumford Ave.
Waltham, MA 02154

Copco Inc.
50 Enterprise Ave.
Secaucus, NJ 07094
Enamel cast-iron cookware.

Hoan Products, Ltd.
615 E. Crescent Ave.
Ramsey, NJ 07446
Cooking accessories.

Le Creuset America
Div. of Schiller & Asmus, Inc.
1525 Merchandise Mart
Chicago, IL 60654
Cast-iron cookware.

Rubbermaid, Inc.
1147 Akron Rd.
Wooster, OH 44691

Schiller & Asmus, Inc.
1525 Merchandise Mart
Chicago, IL 60654
French white ware and wood bowls.

Taylor & Ng
2400 Maxwell
Fairfield, CA 94533
Well-designed kitchenware.

PROJECT MATERIALS

Retail

Charette Corp.
215 Lexington Ave.
New York, NY 10016
Supplies and furnishings for artists.

Harry Zarin Company
292 Grand St.
New York, NY 10002
Curtain rods and hardware.

Hoboken Wood Flooring Corp.
100 Willow St.
East Rutherford, NJ 07073

J. & D. Brauner, Inc.
298 Bowery
New York, NY 10012
The source for butcher block.

Rosetta Electric Co., Inc.
79 Chambers St.
New York, NY 10007
Hard-to-find lighting equipment.

Sam Flax
55 E. 55th St.
New York, NY 10022
Art supplies.

Veterans Caning Shop
550 W. 35th St.
New York, NY 10001
Cane chairs.

PROJECT MATERIALS

Other

American Olean Tile Co.
Consumer Service Dept.
1000 Cannon Ave.
Lansdale, PA 19446
Quarry and ceramic tiles.

Certain Teed Corp.
750 E. Swedesford
Valley Forge, PA 19482
Fiberglas (sound and heat) insulation.

Equipto
2205 S. Highland Ave.
Aurora, IL 60507
Dexion slotted angle iron.

Gascoigne Industrial Products
   Inc.
Box 207
Buffalo, NY 14225
Key clamp pipe rail system.

Kirsch Company
309 N. Prospect
Sturgis, MI 49091
Curtain and drapery hardware.

Ozite Corporation
1755 Butterfield Rd.
Libertyville, IL 60048

Rennert Mfg. Co., Inc.
93 Greene St.
New York, NY 10012
Quilted movers' mats.

Stanley Tools
Div. of Stanley Works
195 Lake St.
New Britain, CT 06050
Electrical and hand tools.

United States Gypsum Co.
101 S. Wacker Dr.
Chicago, IL 60606
Drywall, tape insulations and ceilings.

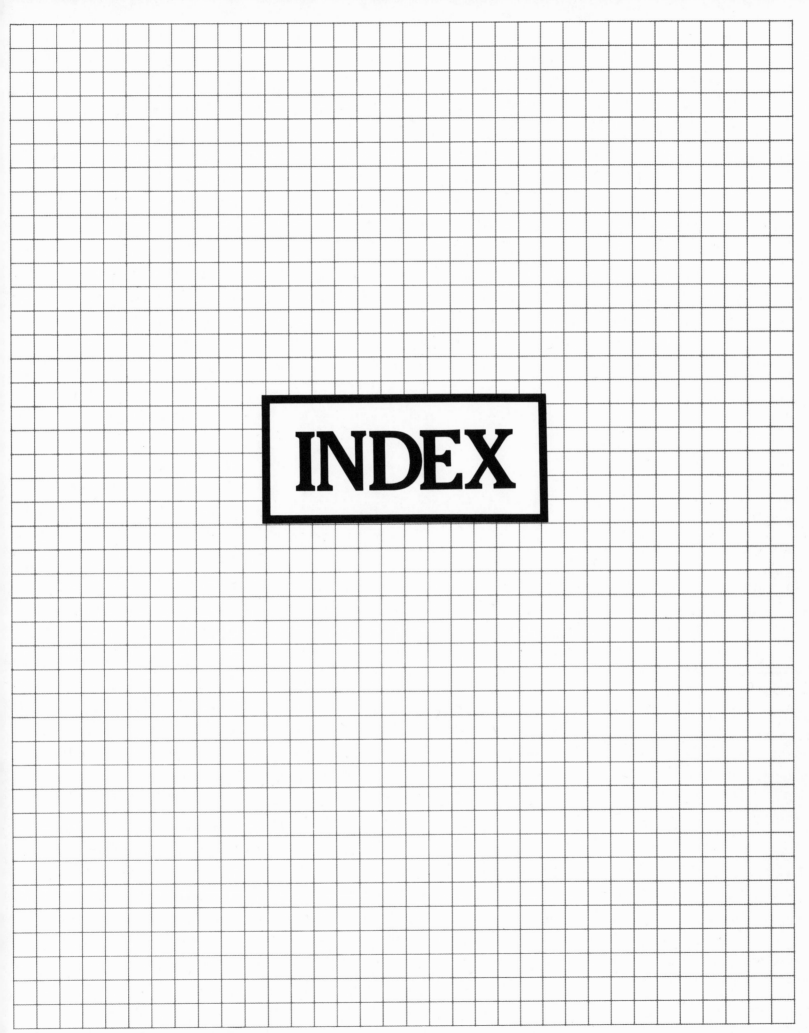

INDEX

Murphy beds, 168–69
music cart, erector set, 250–51

N

neighborhood, 298
neon letters, 167
new antiques, 93–107
    in bedroom, 162–63
Newport News style, 13
new traditional style, 49–66
    drawing room, 52–55
    living room, 56–66
    salon, 50–51

O

offices, 254–59. *See also*
        workspaces
one-room living, 214–27

P

palm trees, dried, 132
paneling
    redwood plywood, 245
    tongue-and-groove, 84
Pattern-on-Pattern, 16–17
pedestals
    newel post, 264
    for stereo components, 250
pegboard, 142–43
periscope lamp, 281
photographers' umbrella, as
        light fixture, 70–71
photographs, *see* blowup
pillows
    covered with floral pillow
        covers, 104–5
    dyed, 284
    floor, 102–3
    Indian cotton, 84–85
planters, 287
plants, 83–92
    in bathroom, 213
    in bedroom, 178–79
    flowering, 286
    greenhouse windows for,
        288
    herbs and vegetables, 287
    in kitchen, 152
    in lofts, 216–17, 234–37
    moving, 301
    in multilevel room, 76
platforms
    how to make, 68, 76–77, 82
    in split-level bedroom,
        172–73

pliers, 292
porch swing, 178, 179
post-modern style, 12
privacy laws, 304
property insurance, 303
Provence style, 10–11
putty knife, 292

Q

quarry tiles, 138–39
quilt
    hanky, 188
    linen, 180–81
    no-sew, 160
    old, 189

R

rag rug, 98–99
rattan
    chairs, 102–3, 132, 234–35
    furniture, 87
    headboards, 176–77
    sofa, 26–27
    table, 132
rockers
    painted, 178
    wicker, 106
rolling cart, 140, 154, 275
    how to make, 150
rolling work counter, 144
rug
    American Indian print, 131
    braided, 59
    chenille, 102, 105
    Flokati wool, 190
    kilim, 35, 40–41, 66
    oriental, 244, 245
    rag, 98–99
    Saltillo, 66
    sisal, 42–43, 132

S

saber saw, portable electric,
        292
sawhorse table, 257
screens, 62, 260–63
    blowup, 262–63
    how to make, 63
    Shoji, 38–39, 260–61
    three glass-paned front
        doors as, 243
    wicker, 48
screwdrivers, 292
seating, *see* chairs; modular
        seating

seating/storage unit, 74–75
seats, low-slung basket-weave
        folding, 84–85
secretary, English, 174, 175
security deposit laws, 304
shades, *see* window shades
shelves
    from barn boards, 58
    for books, 248–49
    in children's rooms, 197–99
    glass, 64–65
    headboard/wall with, 172–73
    kitchen, 136–37, 141–43,
        152–53, 157, 243
    plastic-coated wire, 232
    for stereo equipment and
        wine, 253
    wicker, 132
Shoji screens, 38–39, 260–61
shutters
    with dish towel inserts,
        180–81
    latticework, 116
    natural wood, 139, 182–83
    unfinished wood, 147
sink enclosure, 205, 207
sisal matting, 70–71
sisal rug, 42–43, 132
skylight, 238
sleeping places, 158–90. *See
        also* bedrooms
Small Claims Court, 305–6
sofa
    afghan as cover for, 106
    Art Deco, 102
    bed as, 216–17, 220, 234–35
    camelback, 52–53, 56–57
    Chesterfield, 26
    convertible, 26–27, 50–51
    dyed, 284–85
    futons as alternatives to,
        38–39
    lace tablecloths as cover for,
        88–89
    L-shaped platform, 222–23
    modular (sectional), 34–37,
        42, 44, 46–47, 62–63. *See
        also* modular seating
    overstuffed, 60–61, 94
    quilted, 224–25
    rattan, 26–27
sofa beds, 26–27, 42–43, 48,
        185, 194, 222, 224–26
spool cabinet, 106
stacking drawer units, 140
staple gun, 292
stencil, Mexicali border, 92
stereo equipment, 253

pedestals for, 250
storage, 298
    bathroom, 203, 206–9,
        212–13
    book systems, 248–49
    for children, 192–99
    in coffee tables, 80, 218–21,
        268–69
    grids for, 140, 144, 155
    in home office, 254–56
    in one-room apartments,
        215
    under sofa cushions, 80–81
    in trunks, suitcases, and
        boxes, 252
    see also bins; cabinets;
        étagères; shelves
storage cubes, 40–41
storage/seating unit, 74–75
storage unit
    erector set, 145
    industrial, 40–41
    as wall divider, 218–20
suitcases, as coffee tables, 252
super graphic, 70–71
swan lamp, 280
swing, porch, 178, 179

T

tablecloths, forties style,
        122–23
table-shelf, 125
tables
    bamboo, 274
    bamboo and glass, 87
    card, fabric-covered, 113
    coffee, *see* coffee tables
    dining, *see* dining tables
    drafting, 254, 255
    dustbin, 272–73
    end, *see* end tables
    galvanized steel top, 272
    garden, 24
    glass, 110
    grid pattern laminate, 70–72
    luncheonette, 231
    multi-use, 76–77
    oak, 114
    Parsons, 74, 256
    plastic laminate, 24–25, 74
    Queen Anne, 62–63, 114
    sawhorse, 257
    storm windows as base for,
        271
    tile, 72–73
    tree house, 269
    trestle base, 42–43